I0795636

IMAGES of America

CONNECTICUT WHISTLE STOPS

GREENWICH TO NEW HAVEN

IMAGES
of America

CONNECTICUT WHISTLE STOPS

GREENWICH TO NEW HAVEN

Lennie Grimaldi

ARCADIA PUBLISHING

ISBN 978-0-7385-1003-3

Published by Arcadia Publishing
Charleston, South Carolina

Printed in the United States of America

Library of Congress Catalog Card Number: 2002100865

For all general information contact Arcadia Publishing at:
Telephone 843-853-2070
Fax 843-853-0044
E-mail sales@arcadiapublishing.com
For customer service and orders:
Toll-Free 1-888-313-2665

Visit us on the Internet at www.arcadiapublishing.com

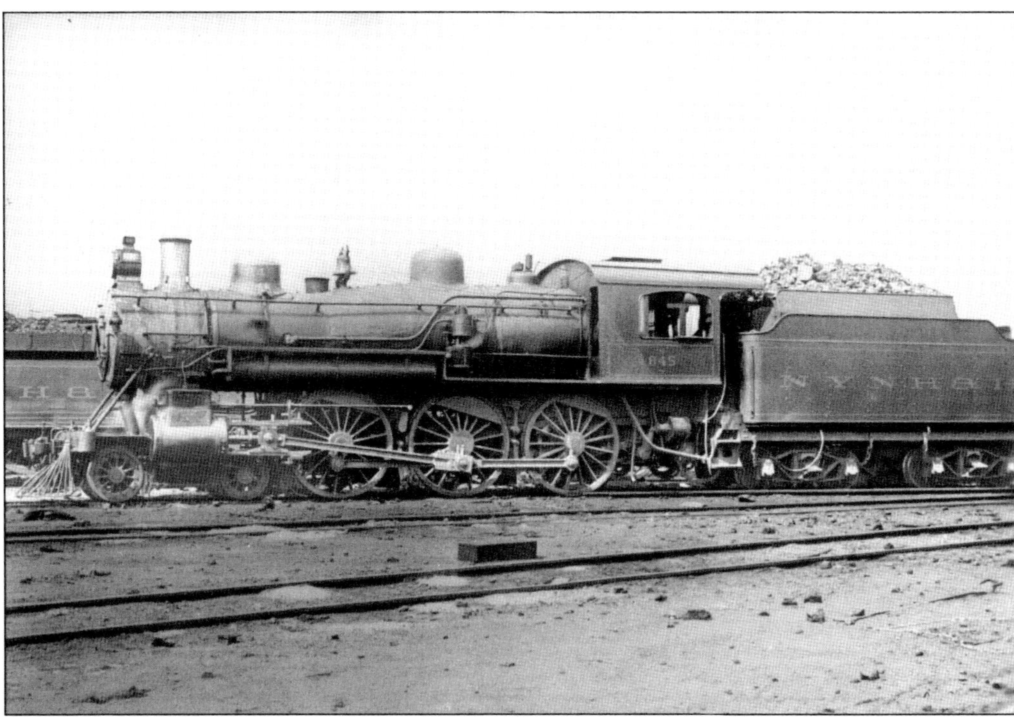

This 1912 view shows a New York, New Haven & Hartford engine with a tender capacity of 10 tons of coal and 6,000 gallons of water. This was an era in which maintenance of the New Haven took a backseat to J.P. Morgan's profits. Morgan, who was born in Hartford, turned the line into one of the most powerful corporations in the country. (Courtesy J.W. Swanberg collection.)

Contents

Acknowledgments

It sounds so trite, but in this case it is so true: *Connecticut Whistle Stops* would not be in your hands were it not for the benevolence of two key historians.

The first is Jack Swanberg, a globetrotting train traveler and rail historian. Swanberg donated nearly half the photographs, many of which he snapped himself, and countless hours fact-checking my work. He has dedicated his life to the rails, first as a New Haven Railroad locomotive fireman and then on to supervisory positions with Penn Central, Conrail, and Metro-North. He is a world traveler now, and in between trips he allowed me into his home in Branford to sift through photographs, pick his brain, and pose corny questions. Swanberg is the author of *New Haven Power 1838–1968*, a 600-page work about New Haven Railroad equipment.

The second historian is Laura Katz Smith, who oversees the archives and special collections for the Thomas J. Dodd Research Center at the University of Connecticut. She provided painstaking assistance from the Connecticut History Online collection, a digitized project by the university.

Many generous members of the New Haven Railroad Historical and Technical Association, including Marc Frattasio, Robert Johnson, and Chris Adams, shared and provided leads for information.

Historical society directors, curators, and archivists, such as Kirsten Jenkins in Greenwich, Barbara Raymond in Westport, Dennis Barrow in Fairfield, Mary Witkowski in Bridgeport, and Carol Lovell and Louis Knapp in Stratford, combed their respective rail collections. The Coastal Fairfield County Convention and Visitors Bureau provided community profile information.

Finally, a note of thanks to Arcadia Publishing and my editor on this project, Pam O'Neil, for her gentle encouragement. Deadlines are like trains. We must be on time.

INTRODUCTION

The genesis of this book goes back many years. The finest things emerging from my newspaper background at the Bridgeport Post-Telegram, the predecessor of the Connecticut Post, include relationships, friendships, and a love of history. I was 18 years old in 1977 when I walked into the boiler-hot newsroom at 410 State Street for the 6:00 p.m. to 2:00 a.m. shift. The place housed an eclectic group of eccentrics, writers, reporters, and copy editors. It was full of Underwood typewriters, noisy wire rooms, carbon paper for copies, field reporters calling in dictation, editors screaming for copy, and still other editors, no doubt confounded by the pressures of their jobs, screaming at water coolers.

I checked in with the city editor, a gentle, laconic, red-faced man named Tom Micks, who told me to go to the "obit desk." In those days obituaries were free of charge, and funeral home directors called in the information to Extensions 241 and 242. There, you answered each call by saying "Newsroom, obits," jammed the telephone between your ear and shoulder, and pecked away at the typewriter keys. The Post-Telegram had a particular style for obit writing. Unfortunately, I had no clue: I could not write, type, or figure out the style because no one told me there was a style. Any old-time obit writer will tell you that you ask the funeral home for the basic information in the newspaper style and then fill in the biographical stuff.

Well, apparently the first obit I handed in was good enough for Micks to use for practicing his one-handed set shot into the trash can. Information sharing among guarded reporters was not a big thing in the newsroom. The reporters wanted to meet their deadlines and head out for their evening refreshments. My obit writing was so awful that Micks had to send someone over to bail me out. That is when I met James G. Clark, a silver-maned, bespectacled veteran of the newspaper industry. "Grimaldi," he warned, "let me show you how to do this before they throw you out of the newsroom."

Clark guided me through the cookie-cutter style of obit writing: name, age, address, occupation, and so on. Then, he explained I could open up and capture the personality of the deceased during the biographical portion of the obituary. "Grimaldi," he said, "obituaries are important because they provide the deceased the last chance to express themselves." Clark was showing the teacher within him.

So, what does this have to do with the New Haven Railroad? Everything. Mr. Clark, as I always called him because of his professorial looks, wicked wit, and bon vivant lifestyle, loathed cars. He did not own one, nor a television for that matter. He believed cars were for clogged highways and trains were for travelers. He knew how to negotiate public transportation better than anyone on the planet. Interstate 95 was nothing more to him than a human sardine can poised to explode. So, riding the rails was his primary choice of travel, whether heading to Stamford for a martini at the Landmark Club or to New Haven for a pizza on Wooster Street.

Several years ago I approached Clark about collaborating on a book that would chronicle the history and happenings of the rails along Connecticut's Gold Coast, a magnet for New York commuters and day-trippers. Clark was a masterful wordsmith and yet, after stringing sentences together for 30 years, a published book had always escaped him. He loved the idea so much that he began writing a guide for the "leisurely tourist who may want to go someplace on the spur of the moment without making a strong commitment in time and planning." It did not matter that we had no publisher for the project.

James G. Clark died after a long and difficult illness in the summer of 2000. A few months earlier, feeling his mortality, he wrote me a note of thanks for mentioning his name in a history book I wrote about the city of Bridgeport. "It's probably the only piece of immortality I'll ever get."

Not so fast, Mr. Clark. The good people at Arcadia Publishing decided to take on a variation of our book idea, a pictorial history of the rails from Greenwich to New Haven. Watch along the way for some of Clark's community quips, which are preserved in the chapter introductions.

When Clark talked about obituaries as the last bastion for expression, it was much more wisdom than an 18-year-old could ever know. Now, I know better. So, please join us as we hop aboard the *Mr. Clark Express*.

One

All Aboard

For residents as well as visitors, Connecticut is a wonderful state to see, savor, and get to know. It is compact enough to visit from any part, find what you are looking for, step into shopping districts, see the sights, enjoy lunch or dinner, and be back home long before midnight. It is the place for a perfect day trip. Connecticut's coastal communities, from Greenwich to New Haven in particular, are exceptional places to visit, loaded with specialty shops, tourist attractions, fabulous restaurants, intriguing inns, and engaging history. Getting there is easy, especially by rail; yes, by train. Connecticut rail service offers much more than the romance of its history. Seven days a week, multiple times a day, it swings through a buzzing life of activity within easy accessible reach.

The motto of the state of Connecticut is *Qui Transtulit Sustenet,* which translates loosely from the Latin as "He who commutes thrives." And Connecticut's rail line, from Greenwich to New Haven, is a thriving transportation network for Manhattan-bound commuters. Each workday, roughly 84,000 commuters ride the rails of the New Haven Line into Grand Central Station in New York.

Connecticut was founded by commuters of a sort: itinerant preachers looking for congregations. When the railroads finally came along, the state took off. The history of the New Haven Railroad has all the elements of an award-winning movie: laborers building the road, America's best-known tycoons financing a monopoly and then running it into the ground, bankruptcy, and rebirth.

The Hartford & New Haven Railroad was chartered in 1833 and, after some trouble raising money, finished the line between New Haven and Hartford in 1839. The charter for the New York & New Haven Railroad was issued in 1844, and the railroad was finished in 1848. The two railroads merged as the New York, New Haven & Hartford in 1872. It was known as the Consolidated. Eventually, it incorporated other chartered lines, such as the Housatonic, which initially included Bridgeport.

Train travelers suffered many inconveniences in the early days of the railroad. Sometimes the weight of a passing train would force track spikes to pop up and poke through the train floor. Sledgehammer-wielding employees would watch the track for stray spikes and drive them back into the rail. The wood- and coal-burning steamer engines sprayed sparks over the passengers, causing frequent fires. Traveling coaches were hard and uncomfortable, and springs were scarce. Stopping the trains with the use of a hand or foot brake was a nightmare. When the trains reached the station, several powerful porters were poised to seize the end of the train while the station agent thrust sticks of wood through the wheel spokes.

Laborers working on the railroad did not just pass the time away. The average wage for an immigrant laborer making rail improvements in 1891 was $1.35 per day. For instance, the padrone (boss) or barracks system for housing laborers heaped indignities on Italian colony workers. On the promise of work, they were forced into cramped, unventilated housing in old carriage shops, with provisions forced upon them at exorbitant rates. For the privilege of work and residence in the colony, subscription collections often amounted to the sum of their weekly paychecks. The general store sold dairy and poultry products of poor quality at inflated rates. Meats that went for 12¢ per pound in other stores went for 20¢ there, and postage stamps were often double the regular cost.

Italian immigrant Luigi Ricciardi, who learned about the power of law as a clerk in a New Haven law firm, lobbied the Connecticut legislature to pass a bill for the abolishment of the shanty system for housing rail workers. Ricciardi described the rail workers as "human beings with no rights, men with no souls, who cannot live normally with their families, who have little or no money at the end of the week to support their wives and children . . . and who are powerless to change their lot." On May 21, 1901, the state legislature passed the bill that shattered the exploitative shanty system and strengthened state employment laws.

John Pierpoint Morgan, the feared and revered financier, catapulted the Consolidated into one of the most powerful corporations in America. Technological advancement also shaped the future of the Consolidated. Tracks began electrification in 1905, and the process took some years to complete. By the time of J.P. Morgan's death in 1913, the line had achieved a total monopoly of practically all of the transportation in New England: the railroads, steamship lines, and trolley lines. The railroad reached the pinnacle of its success in 1912, when its stock was selling for $200 a share. That was the same year the railroad suffered 12 major accidents and its president, Charles Mellen, was kicked out because of the carnage. The public rebelled against the monopoly control, and the motor industry capitalized on it: carmakers, road contractors, and real estate developers aligned with the federal government, which had attempted to regulate the railroad.

In 1913, Louis Brandeis, a future member of the U.S. Supreme Court, pressed Congress and the Interstate Commerce Commission to look into the maze of companies, payoffs, and missing money that were all part of running a successful railroad. Witnesses called before congressional hearings suffered memory retrieval problems: one could not remember giving $3 million to a 20-year-old messenger boy, others came down with mysterious diseases that forced them to seek cures overseas, and documents magically disappeared.

J.P. Morgan, the only one who knew where all the money was, had the good sense to die before the federal government could discredit him. John Pierpoint Morgan Jr., who assumed control, just did not have his father's steam. World War I kept the railroad from going under but, by 1935, with $364 million in debts, the railroad filed for bankruptcy. World War II infused economic life. Then, in 1948, the legendary twosome of Frederick Dumaine and Patrick McGinnis picked up the New Haven for a meager $4.5 million, less than one percent of its capitalization.

Dumaine sold off real estate, laid off 2,000 employees, fired anyone making more than $10,000 a year, and lost interest in railroad maintenance. McGinnis seized control after a proxy fight against Dumaine's son. Poor equipment, unkept schedules, and a rider-be-damned attitude threw commuters into a fit. In 1955, McGinnis wanted to charge $5.50 a day for parking, when parking at railroad stations had been free. "Because I want to charge a lousy five bucks, people act as though I've torn up the tracks," McGinnis said after one stormy session with irate commuters.

In 1956, the New Haven's Board of Directors forced McGinnis out. It was back to bankruptcy and reorganization in 1961. When the New York Central and the Pennsylvania Railroads merged, they were told they had to take the New Haven. Penn-Central failed a few years later, and then Conrail took it over. Today, Metro-North keeps the trains running on time, multiple times a day, seven days a week, for commuters, casual travelers, and day-trippers experiencing the history and happenings of southern Connecticut's coastline.

So, pick a stop. At each one, you will find the essence that makes up the New Haven Line's West End.

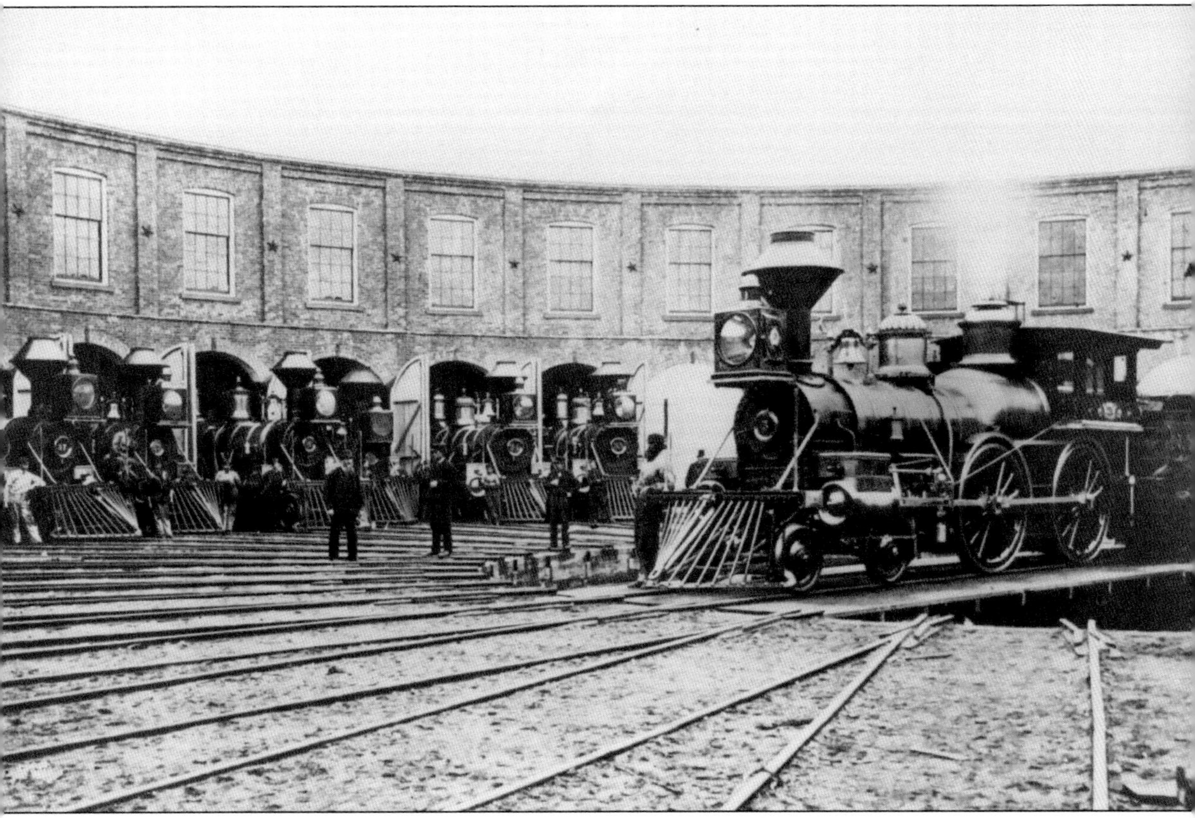

Shown here is the Spring Street roundhouse maintenance facility in New Haven *c.* 1870. A half dozen engines of the New York & New Haven Railroad Company are lined up at the left, with a steamer, built in 1861, up front. This photograph was taken just before the consolidation of the two major rail lines into the New York, New Haven & Hartford Railroad. (Courtesy J.W. Swanberg collection.)

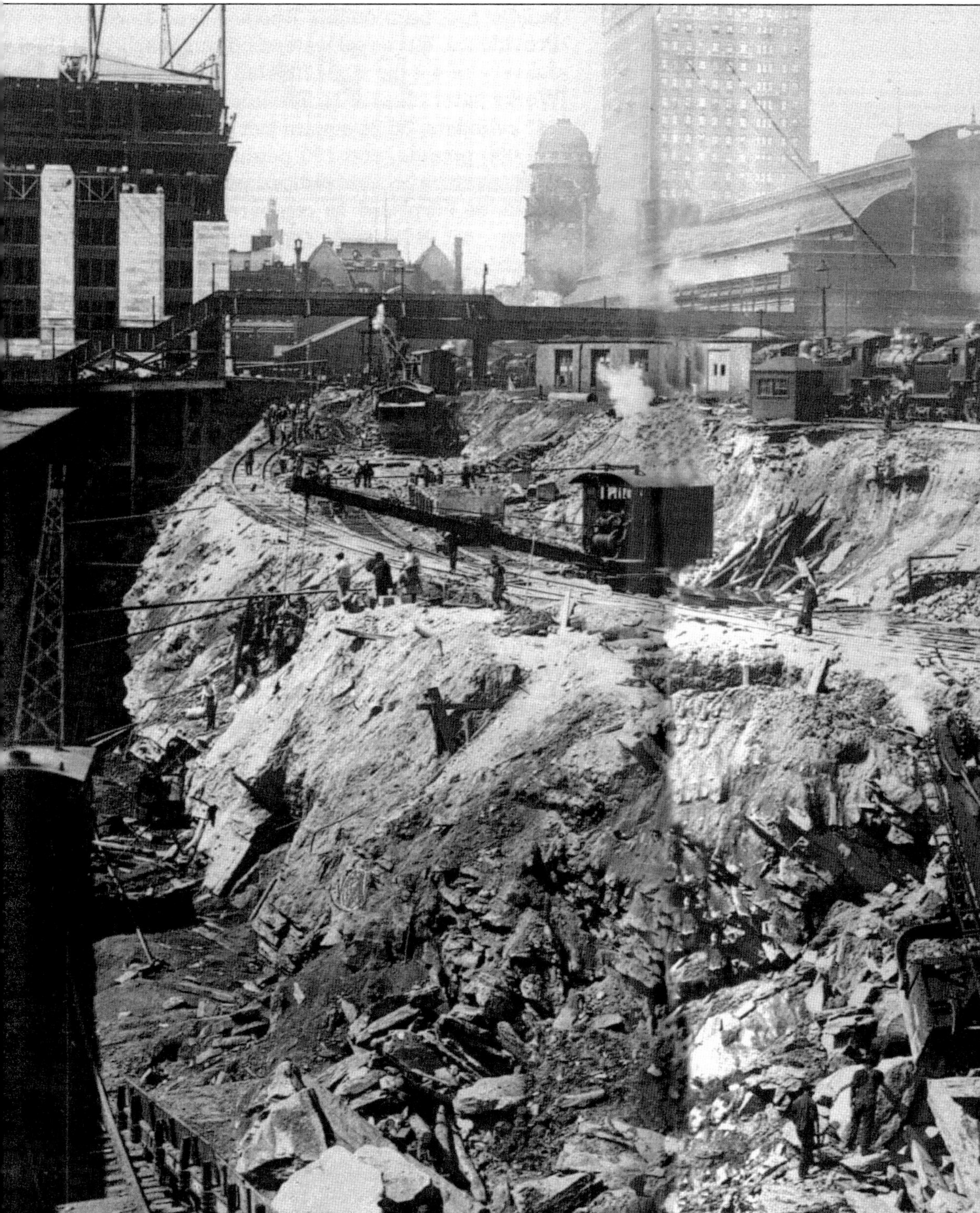

For passengers who have wondered about the spooky blackness of the commuter train ride into Grand Central Station in Manhattan, this photograph captures the excavation that placed

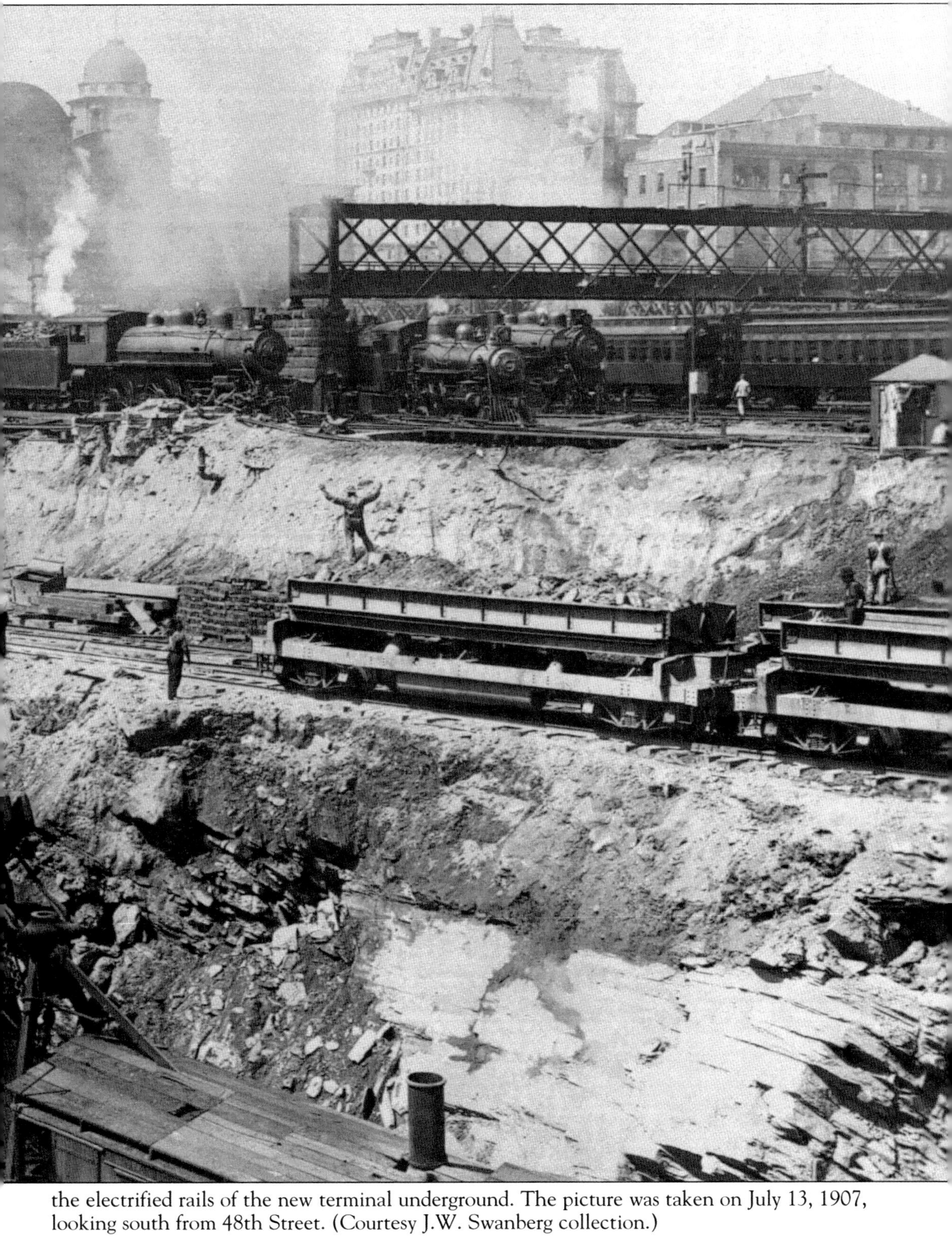

the electrified rails of the new terminal underground. The picture was taken on July 13, 1907, looking south from 48th Street. (Courtesy J.W. Swanberg collection.)

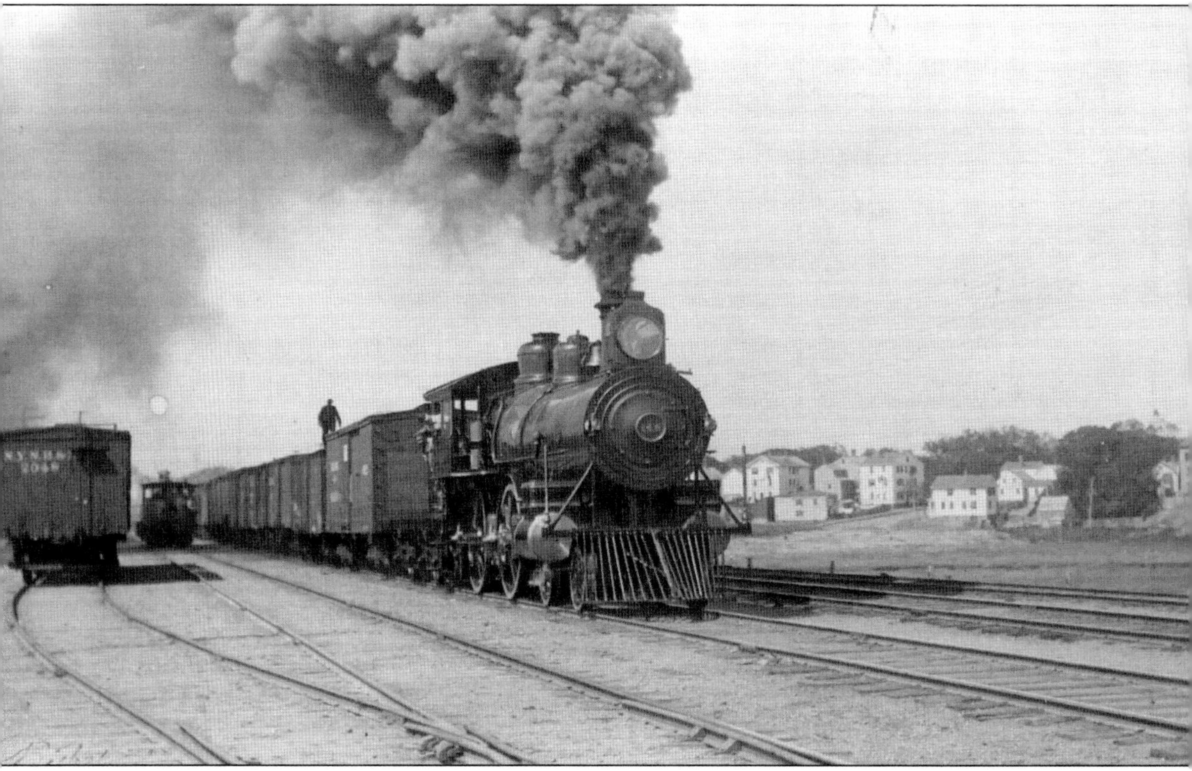

A steamer in New Haven in 1888 belches in front of freight trains as the brakeman walks on top. Rail buffs refer to this freighter as 4-4-0 No. 148. It stayed in use until 1925. This era is nearly 20 years before the start of electrification. (Courtesy J.W. Swanberg collection.)

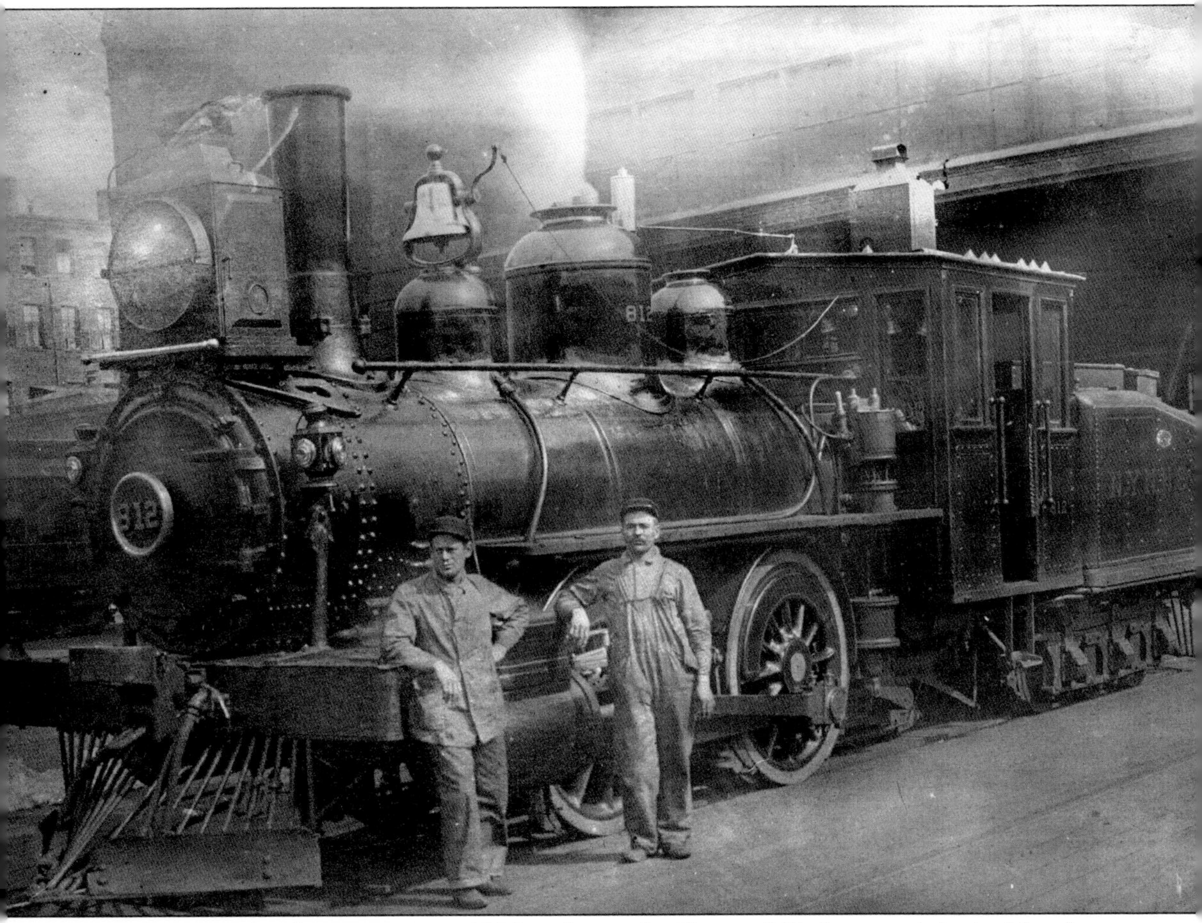

An engineer and a fireman pose *c.* 1890 in front of a Forney 812 that was inherited by the New Haven from the Boston & Providence Railroad. This engine was built to operate in either direction. (Courtesy J.W. Swanberg collection.)

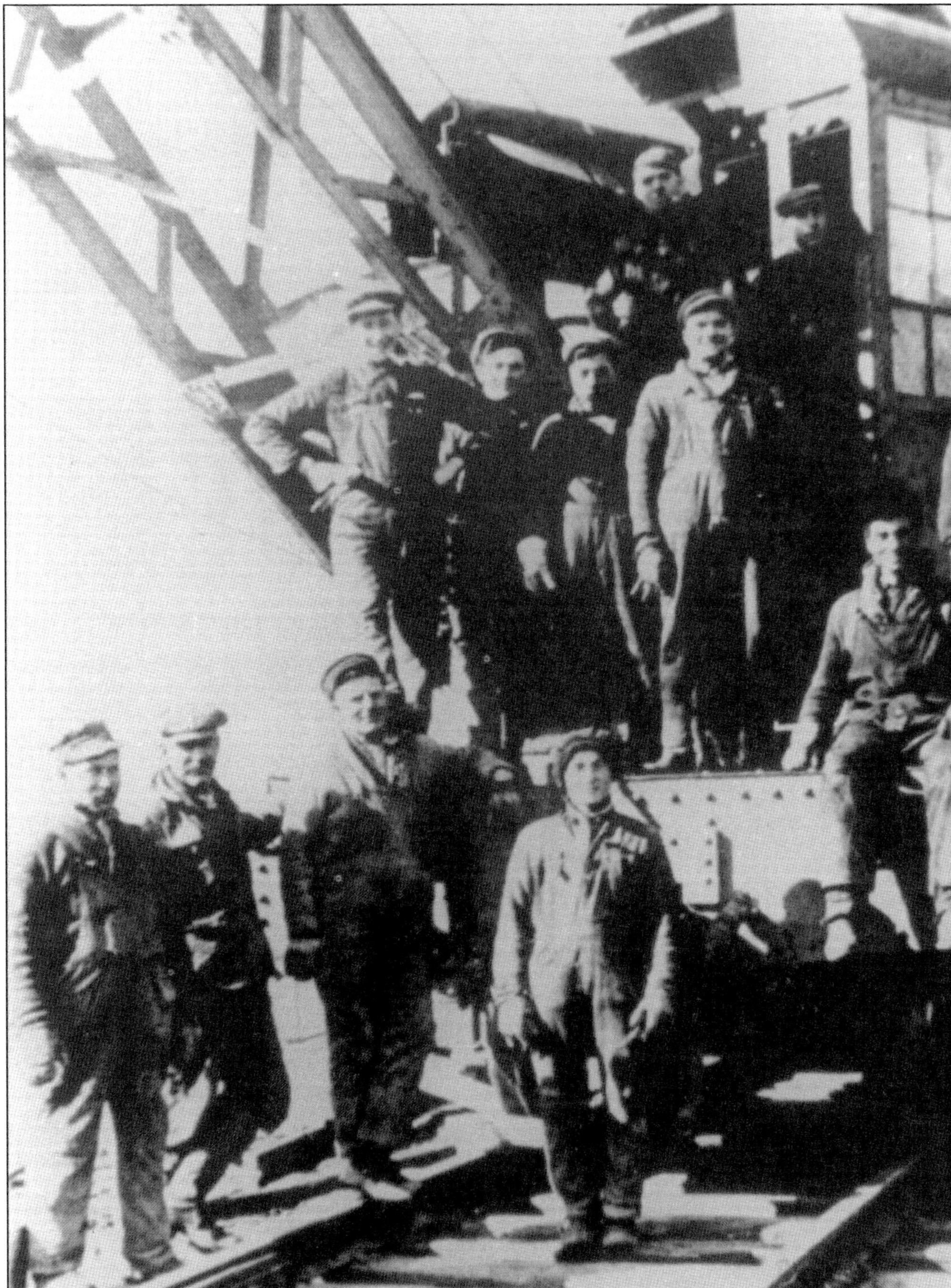

The muscle of European immigrants helped to expand the New Haven Railroad. Many rail workers, such as those shown here *c.* 1900, lived on a rail compound in chicken-coop shanties with little ventilation, earning $1.50 per day. Still, the dream of a new way of life and the determination to provide for their families fired their passion to achieve. These laborers take time out during the rail expansion in the Saugatuck section of Westport. (Courtesy Westport Historical Society.)

These two men were key figures in the development of the New Haven Railroad. Charles Peter Clark (right), "New Haven's greatest president," according to rail historian Jack Swanberg, served from 1887 to 1899. During this period, the road grew from 450 miles to more than 2,000 and the number of locomotives increased from 133 to 900. Clark four-tracked the New York Division and began the foundation for the 1907 main line electrification. Charles S. Mellen (below), J.P. Morgan's close associate, served as the New Haven Railroad's president from 1903 to 1913. The "M & M boys," Morgan and Mellen, seized control of practically all transportation in New England, including trolley and steamship lines. Unfortunately, respect for customers and equipment did not keep pace with the bottom line. Wrecks abounded, including the legendary *Federal Express*. After Morgan's death in 1913, Mellen was blamed for the carnage and mismanagement and he got the boot. (Courtesy J.W. Swanberg collection.)

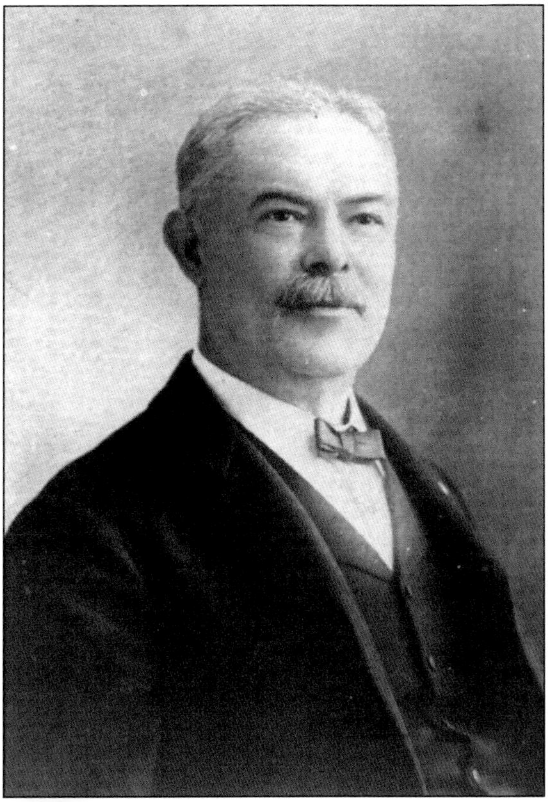

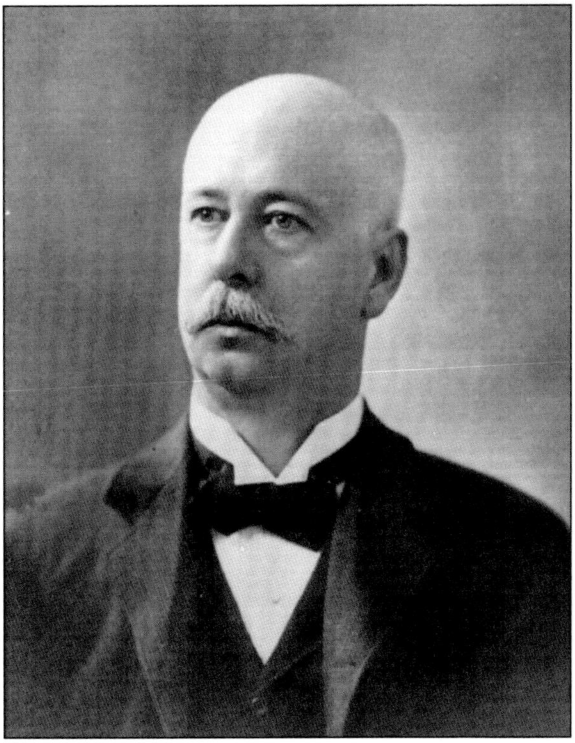

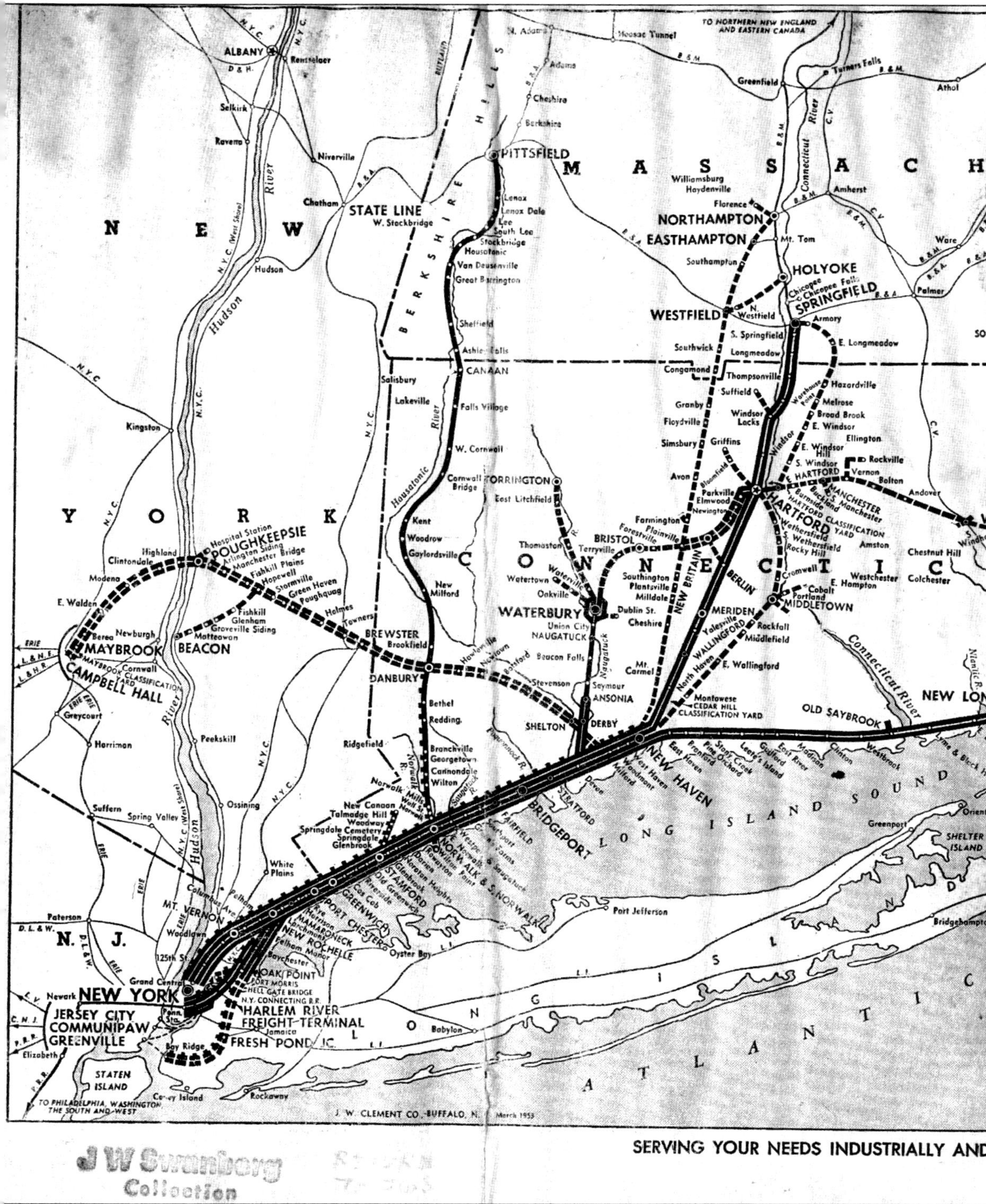

A 1968 map of the New Haven Line shows the variety of branches and fingers of the railroad in New York and New England leading south into Grand Central and Penn Stations. The

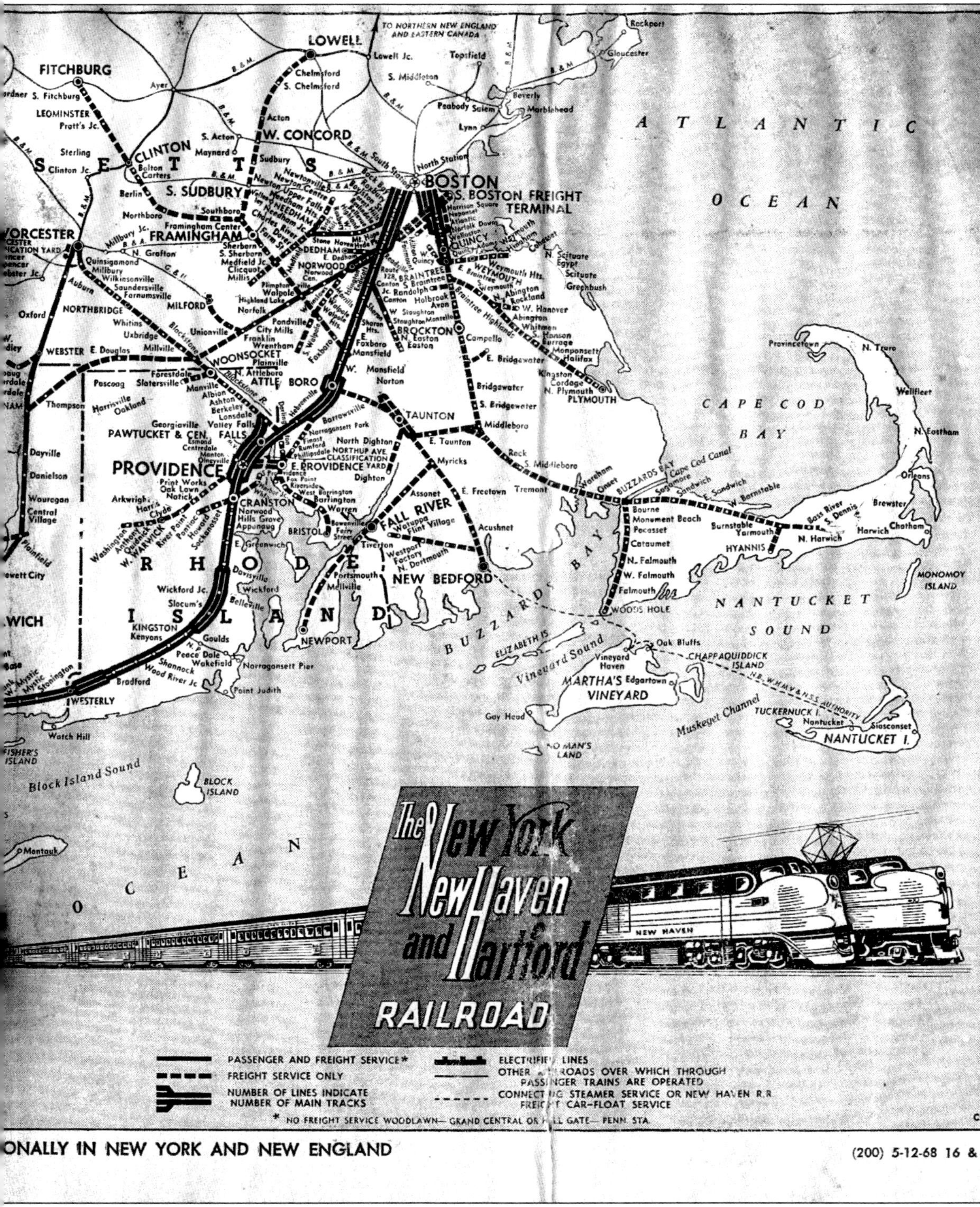

heaviest commuter activity in Connecticut, then and now, covers those stops from New Haven down to Greenwich. (Courtesy J.W. Swanberg collection.)

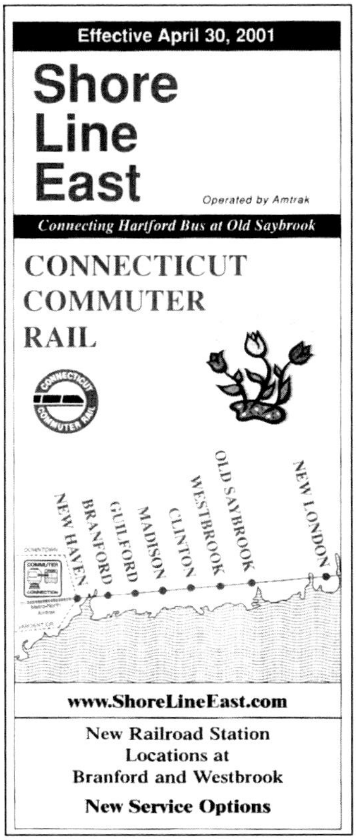

Shown here are two sections of a pocket brochure for the Shore Line East, a commuter rail that covers several towns east of New Haven with connections to mainline stops in New Haven and Bridgeport. Late in 2001, the state of Connecticut announced increased travel options for residents of these communities seeking western commuter destination points. (Courtesy J.W. Swanberg collection.)

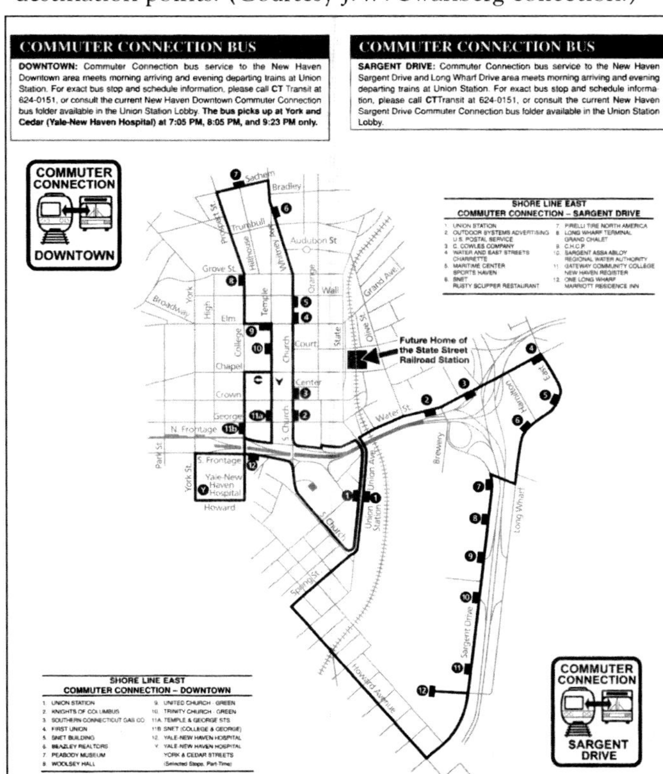

Two

Greenwich Station

The Byram River is an unassuming little tributary that separates Port Chester, New York, from Greenwich. For when crossing that stream on Metro-North, you enter Connecticut and, more specifically, the rarified air of the state's most exclusive stop on the train line.

Greenwich, as a community, offers a quality of life that is arguably unmatched anywhere in the country. Waterfront treasures, community theater, art galleries, trendy restaurants, public recreation, and shopping . . . lots of it. The genesis of its exclusivity dates back to the emergence of the railroad in the late 1840s and the Industrial Revolution. The back country of Greenwich became a magnet for wealthy industrialists who commuted to New York, thus igniting a community romance with the rails. Rich business families such as the Gimbels, owners of the department store chain, built summer mansions that have become symbolic of the traditional lifestyle of this town of 60,000.

Once out of the station and up Greenwich Avenue, you begin to get a feel for the town. Most of the buildings along Greenwich Avenue are two and, at the most, three stories high, which gives the town a nice human scale. The personal touch comes in the form of police officers who direct traffic, stopping all the cars to let you cross the street.

There is no crass commercialism here, just shop after shop of upscale stores, antiques dealers, boutiques, bakeries, and dress shops that let you know this is a shopper's shopping district, the closest thing Connecticut has to Rodeo Drive.

The town boasts some of the best restaurants in the state. When the Greenwichites are not going out to dinner, many can be found playing with their horses. Polo here comes in shirts, jackets, and ponies. It is not uncommon to be dining next to someone in an expensive tweed coat and his riding boots. Having the riding whip along seems to get better service, public transportation traveler James G. Clark noted.

What the local citizenry lovingly call the back country is replete with horse trails, polo fields, and other necessities of the good life. Most of the big estates are located in the back country, which is generally that part north of the Merritt Parkway. Of course, the other big estates are down near the water. You can see some of the estates from the road, but the really big ones are discreetly hidden away from common view.

A good trip is to go up North Avenue one fine weekend afternoon and take in the views while on the way to Conyers Farm, where there usually is a polo match. Polo is taken seriously here, and it is fun to watch all those breathy horses run up and down the field while you sip a refreshment.

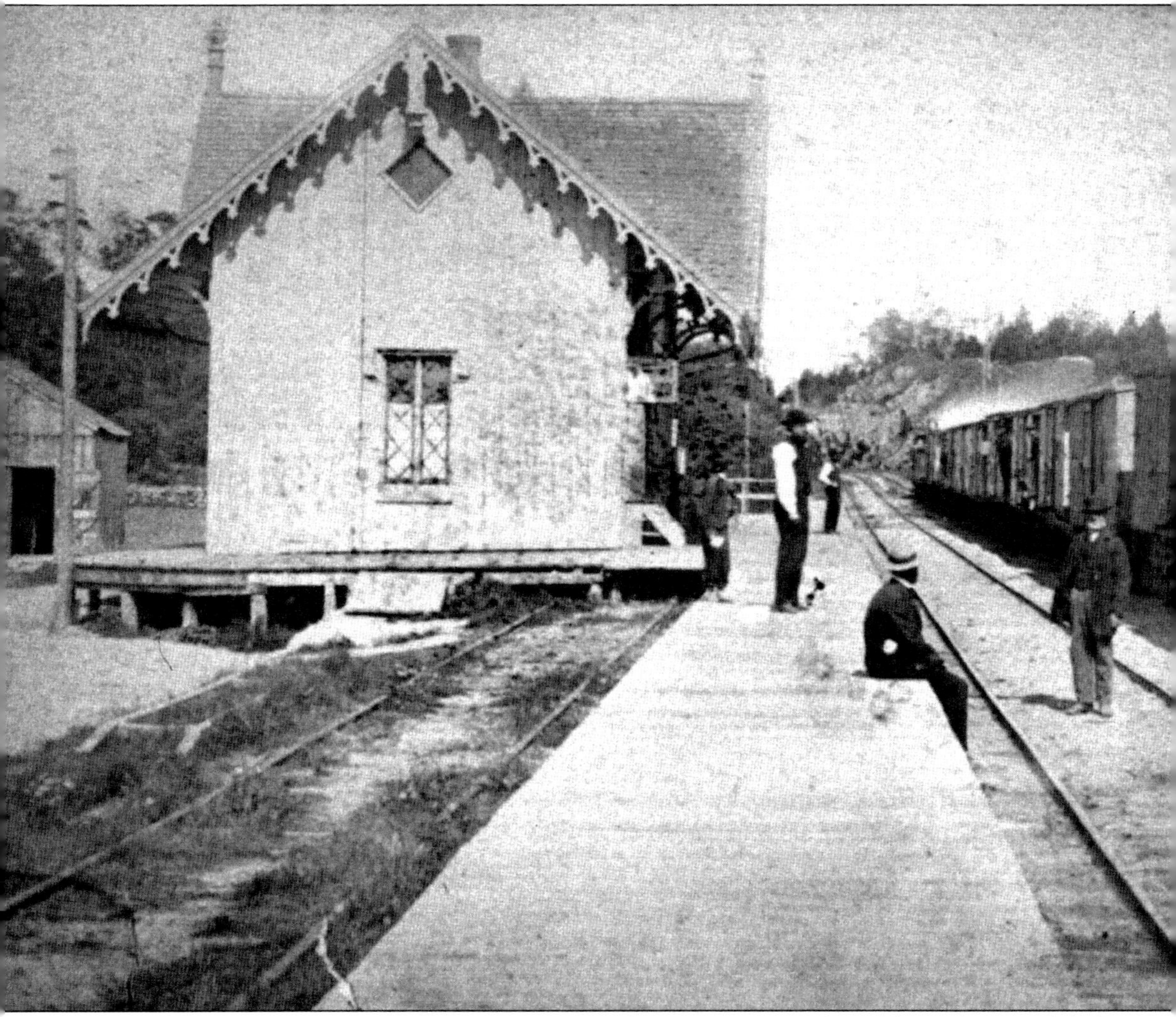

Hanging out at the railroad station in Greenwich *c.* 1870 was nothing like today's mad dash to reach the station on time for a hitch into Grand Central Station. Here, a man sits on the platform in front of the station building while a few others stand on the tracks and the platform with train cars on the tracks at the right. (Courtesy Thomas J. Dodd Research Center, University of Connecticut.)

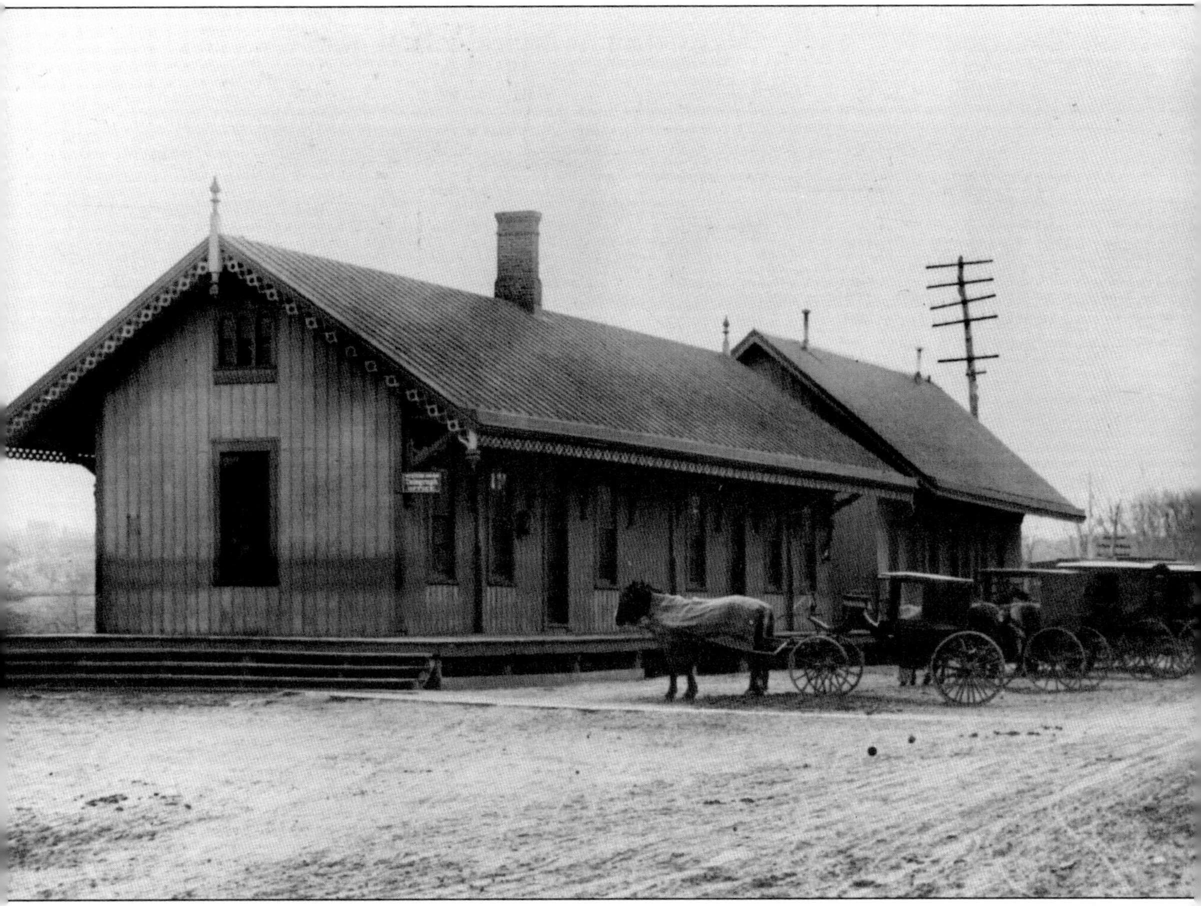

A view of the Greenwich Station building shows horse-and-wagon taxis lined up in front of the Western Union telegraph office in the 1880s. (Courtesy Historical Society of the Town of Greenwich.)

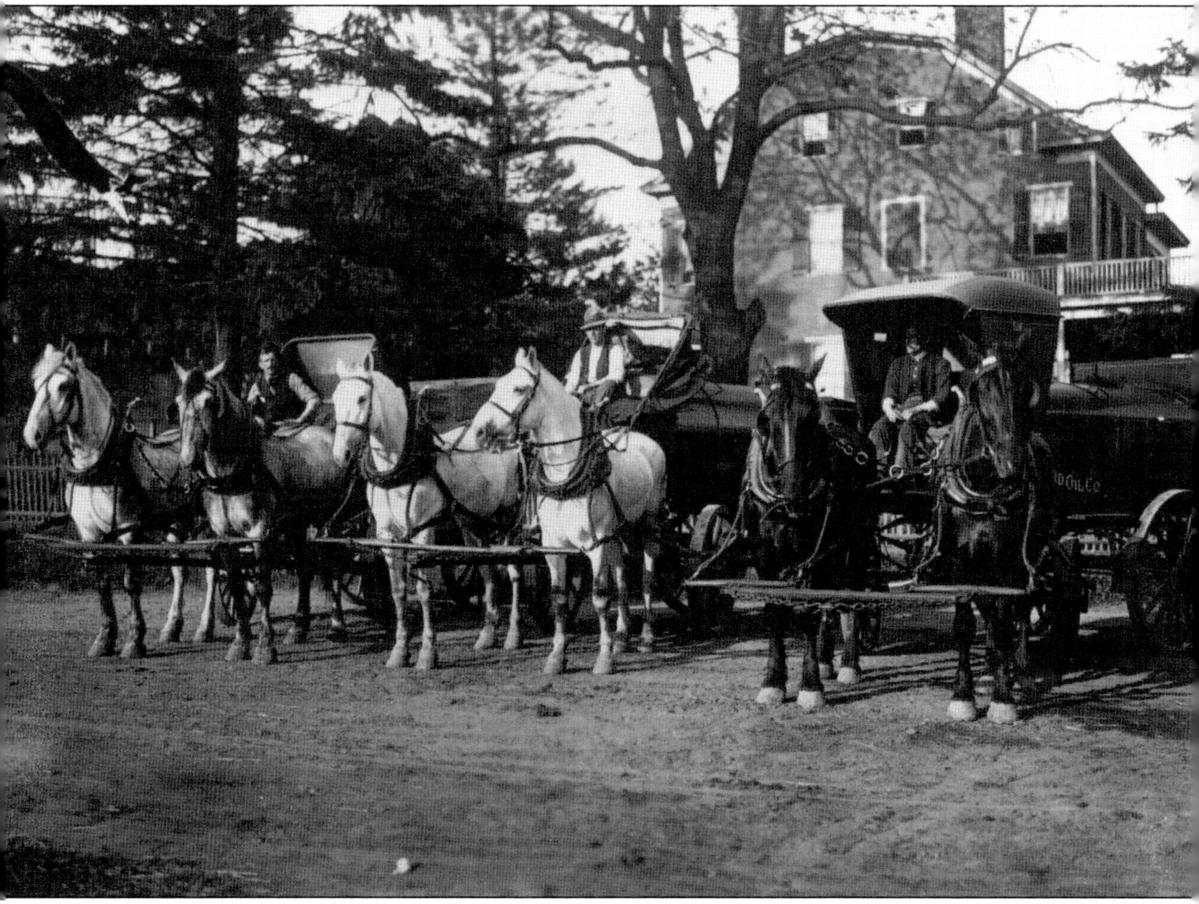

There is always time for picture taking in the Gay Nineties in Greenwich. Shown are delivery wagons for the Standard Oil Company, taking a break in front of the Daniel Merritt house on South Arch Street at Greenwich Station. (Courtesy Historical Society of the Town of Greenwich.)

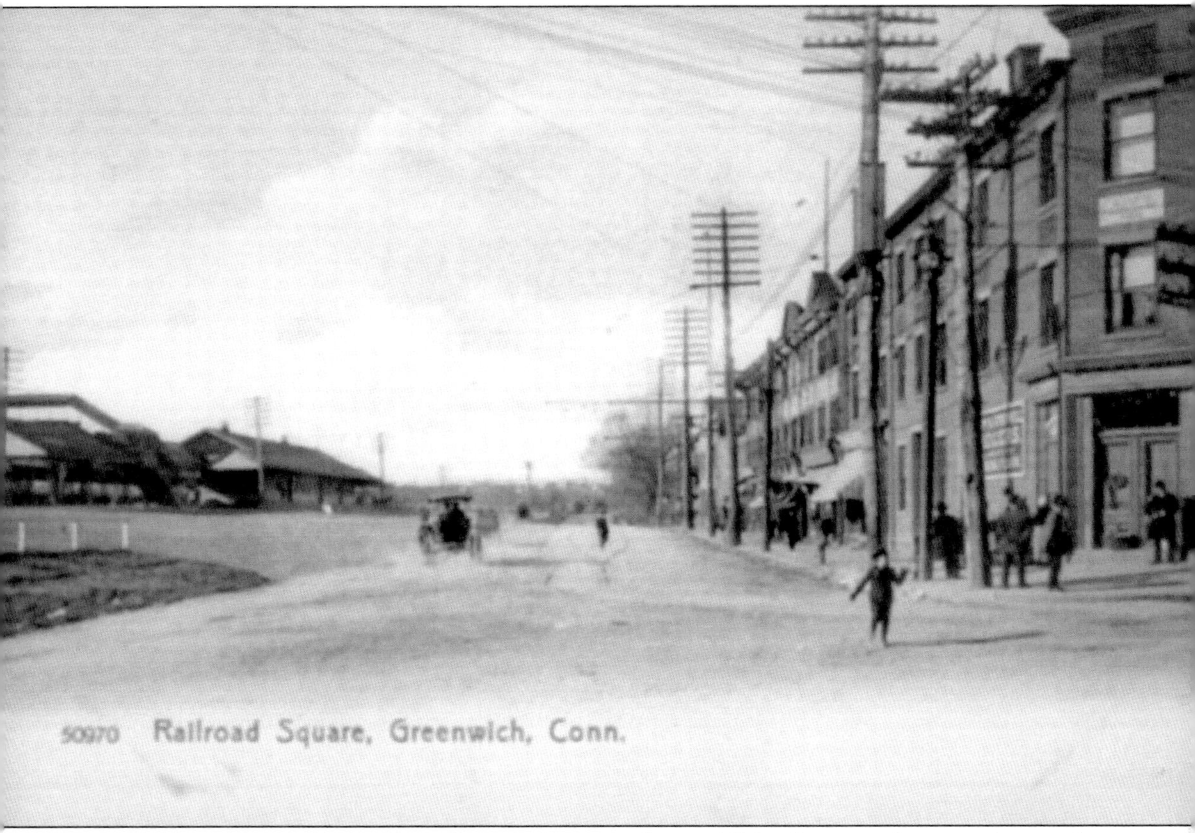

Forget about BMWs and Mercedes in Greenwich *c.* 1900. Greenwich is a dirt-road, horse-and-carriage community along Railroad Square. It is hard to say whether the youngster at the right is running to catch a train or running from a truant officer. (Courtesy Thomas J. Dodd Research Center, University of Connecticut.)

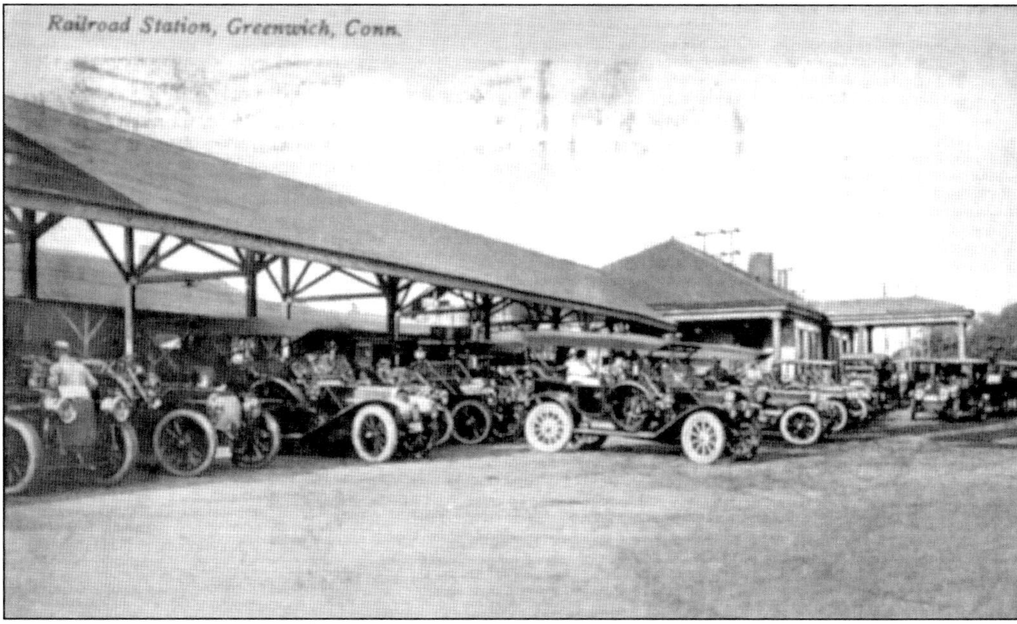

Okay, this is starting to look a little like the Greenwich we know and love. The *c.* 1913 view above has luxury automobiles parked in front of a covered platform attached to the station building. Below, for those unable to obtain the extravagance of an open-air vehicle, the old reliable horse and carriage makes the day. (Courtesy Thomas J. Dodd Research Center, University of Connecticut.)

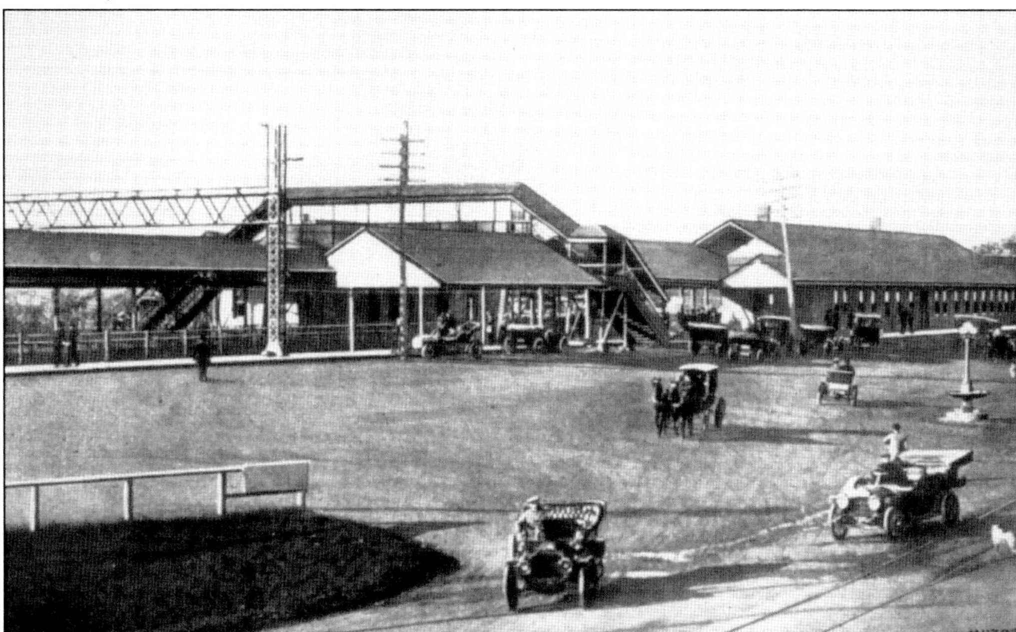

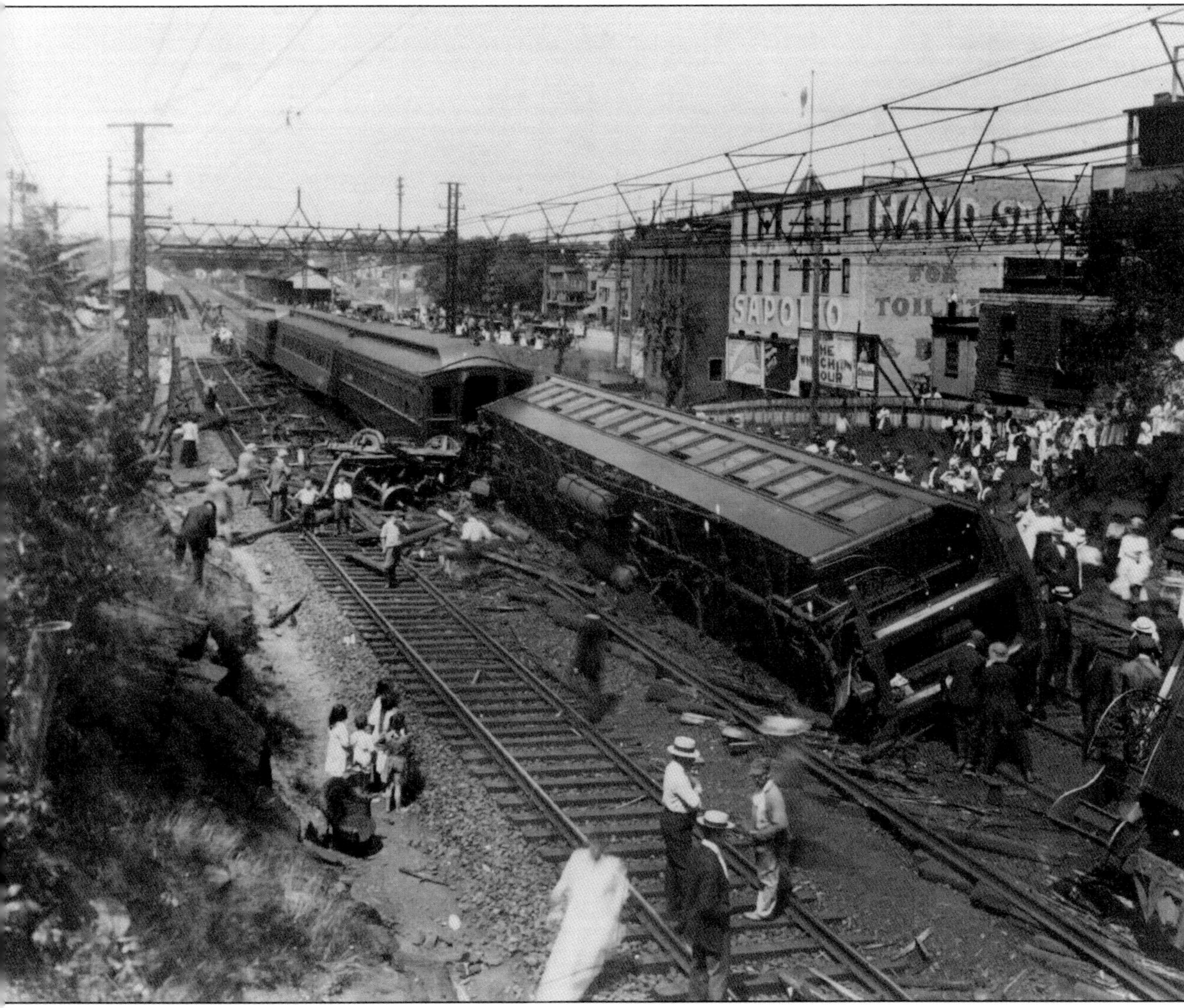

The New Haven Line was cursed by accidents *c*. 1910, and train wrecks drew spectators from miles around. This scene shows wooden cars of the *White Mountain Express* in a derailment that spewed wood and iron everywhere. Note the overhead wires that mark the beginning of the New Haven's revolutionary track electrification, a seven-year process that began in 1905. The train was heading to Boston from Grand Central Station when it derailed in Greenwich. One problem was that early electric trains were not equipped with the guiding wheels that made travel easier for the conductor. This could be an issue at 70 miles per hour. (W. Zekias collection, courtesy J.W. Swanberg.)

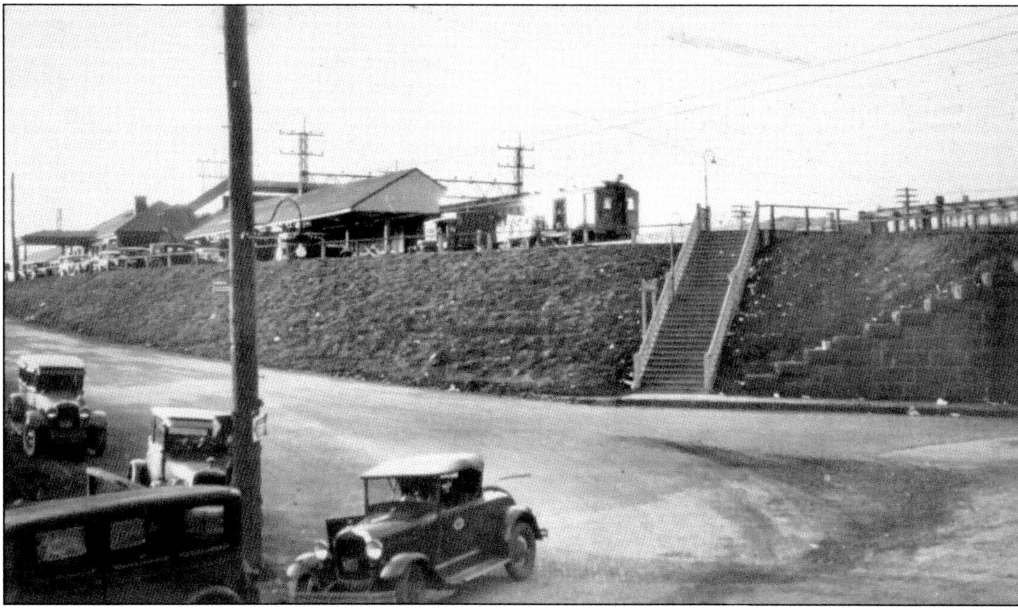

These two views show Greenwich Station in 1928. Above, automobiles are parked downhill from the eastbound side, with an electric train accessible by stairs. Below, cars are parked curbside near the station platform. (Courtesy Thomas J. Dodd Research Center, University of Connecticut.)

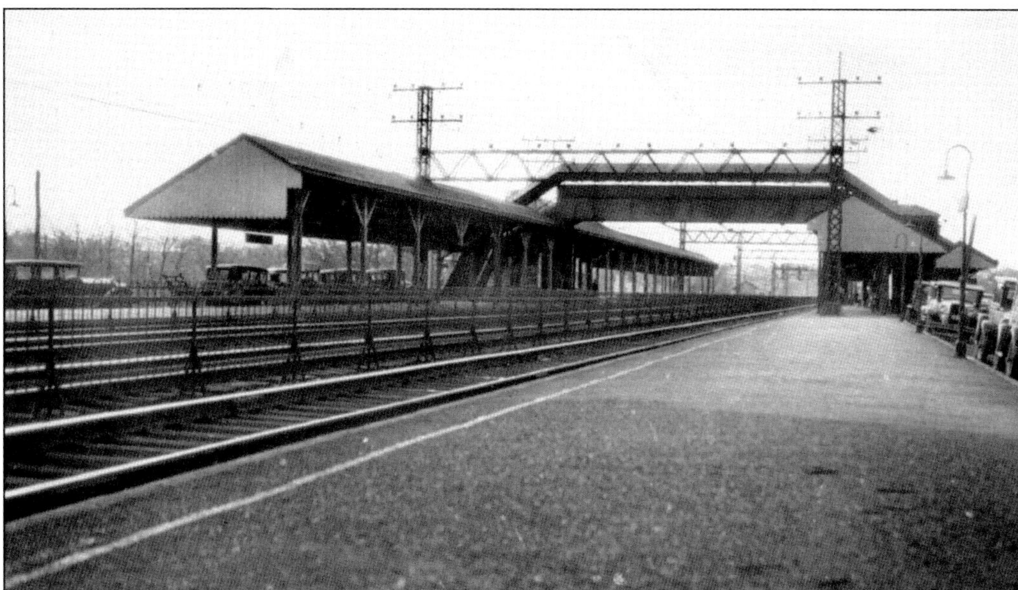

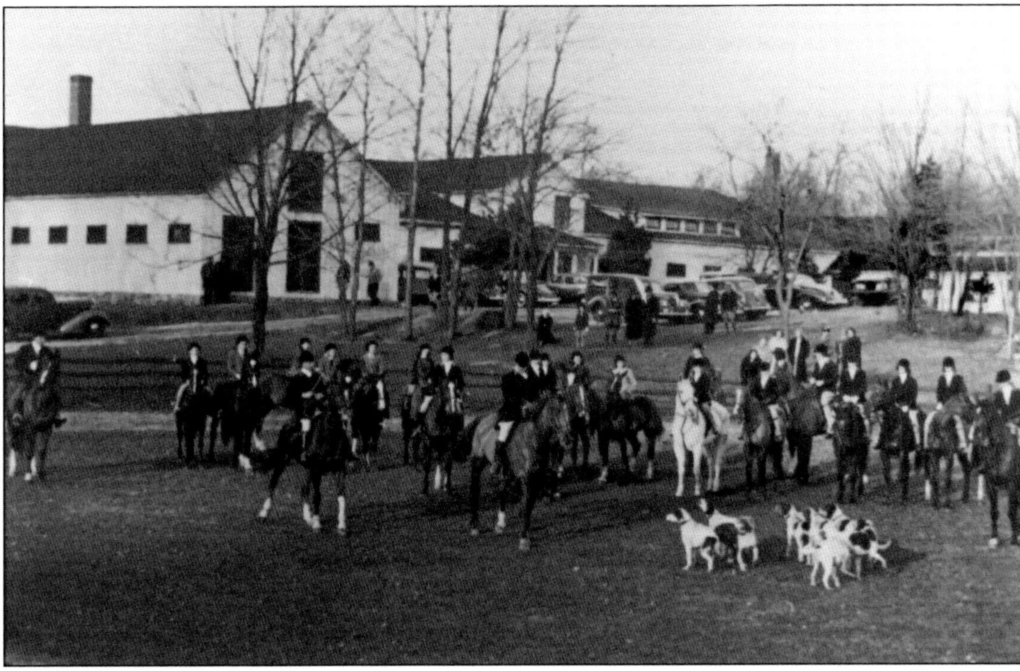

Here is a little weekend fox run to get the juices flowing. On horseback at Conyers Farm, in the back country of Greenwich c. 1930, a couple of dozen men and women are ready to ride. Release the hounds! Poor little foxes. (Courtesy Historical Society of the Town of Greenwich.)

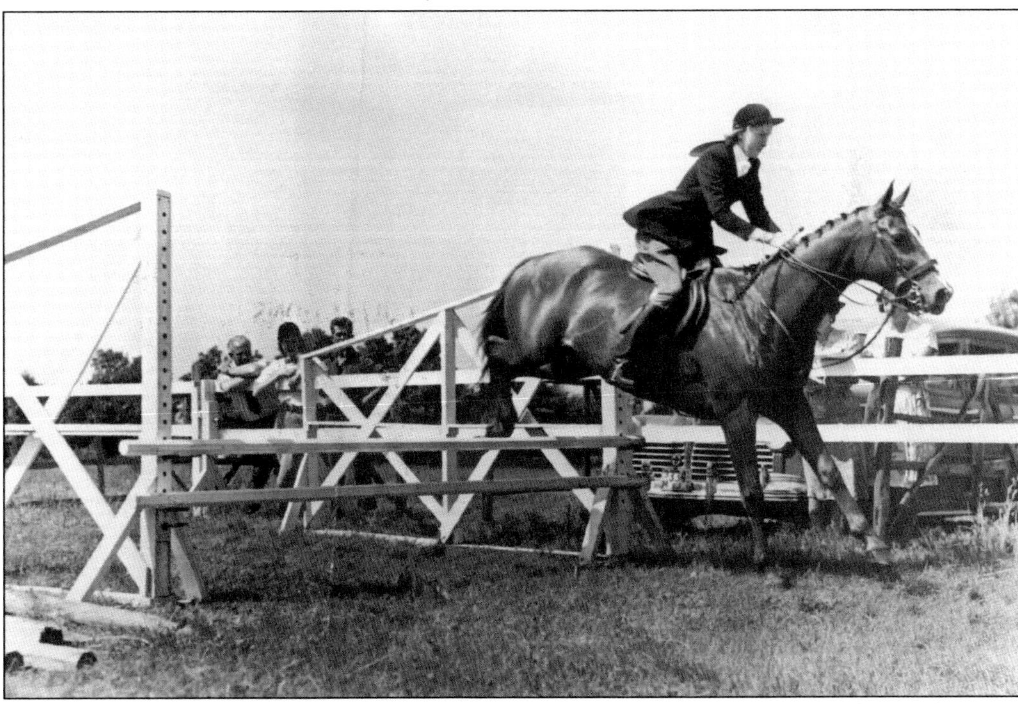

Most amateur riders would be flying off of the saddle, but not Hedda W. von Goeben, a champion rider showing her skills at a Greenwich horse show in 1946. Horses, foxes, hunting dogs, mansions, and money—that is Greenwich. (Courtesy Historical Society of the Town of Greenwich.)

NEW YORK TO GREENWICH

EASTERN STANDARD TIME

Schedule symbols should be checked carefully against "REFERENCES" at bottom of tables

MONDAY THRU FRIDAY		SATURDAY		SUNDAY	
Leave G.C.T.	Due Greenwich	Leave G.C.T.	Due Greenwich	Leave G.C.T.	Due Greenwich
au12:10AM	12:52AM	.....	.....	.....	.....
12:25	1:24	12:25AM	1:24AM	12:25AM	1:24AM
1:25	2:24	1:25	2:24	1:25	2:24
ux3:00	5:02	ux3:00	5:02	u3:25	4:29
Eu3:25	4:29	.....	.....	.....	.....
Au4:45	5:41	.....	.....	.....	.....
Au5:42	6:38	.....	.....	.....	.....
Du5:55	6:50	u5:55	6:50	u5:55	6:50
C6:30	7:28	6:30	7:28	.....	.....
A6:50	7:48	.....	.....	.....	.....
7:31	8:28	7:31	8:28	7:31	8:28
B7:50	8:52	.....	.....	.....	.....
8:28	9:42	8:28	9:42	8:28	9:42
9:55	10:54	9:55	10:54	9:55	10:54
10:20	11:19	10:20	11:19	10:20	11:19
A10:55	11:54	.....	.....	10:55	11:54
11:25	12:32PM	11:25	12:32PM	.....	.....
12:20PM	1:24	12:20PM	1:24	12:20PM	1:24PM
.....	.....	12:55	1:54	.....	.....
1:25	2:24	1:25	2:24	1:25	2:24
A1:55	2:54	1:55	2:54	.....	.....
2:25	3:24	2:25	3:24	2:25	3:24
A2:55	3:54	2:55	3:54	.....	.....
3:22	4:21	3:22	4:21	3:22	4:21
Au3:30	4:14	u3:30	4:14	.....	.....
A3:55	4:54	3:55	4:54	.....	.....
Au4:15	5:03	.....	.....	.....	.....
4:28	5:32	4:28	5:32	4:28	5:32
Au4:42	5:27	.....	.....	.....	.....
A5:14	5:59	u5:05	5:45	.....	.....
D5:23	6:22	5:23	6:22	5:23	6:22
AHux5:29	6:20	.....	.....	.....	.....
Du5:32	6:12	.....	.....	.....	.....
Gu5:34	6:14	.....	.....	.....	.....
A5:51	6:44	5:54	6:54	.....	.....
.....	.....	u6:02	6:47	.....	.....
Aux6:08	6:54	.....	.....	.....	.....
Gu6:08	6:54	.....	.....	.....	.....
6:25	7:24	6:25	7:24	6:25	7:24
A6:55	7:54	.....	.....	.....	.....
u7:02	7:49	u7:02	7:49	u7:02	7:49
7:25	8:24	7:25	8:24	7:25	8:24
Ku8:02	8:45	.....	.....	u8:02	8:45
Aux8:09	8:52	8:25	9:24	8:25	9:24
8:25	9:24	.....	.....	.....	.....
9:25	10:24	9:25	10:24	9:25	10:24
u10:00	10:44	.....	.....	u10:00	10:44
10:25	11:24	10:25	11:24	10:25	11:24
.....	.....	.....	.....	u11:00	11:42
11:25	12:24AM	11:25	12:24AM	11:25	12:24AM
u11:35	12:18	u11:35	12:18	.....	.....
A11:55	12:54	11:55	12:54	.....	.....

This is the official timetable for Greenwich and New York, dated September 28, 1952. On the opposite page, note the First National Bank's Commuter's Special, a branch bank located right at the station. (Courtesy Marc Frattasio collection.)

GREENWICH TO NEW YORK

EASTERN STANDARD TIME

Schedule symbols should be checked carefully against "REFERENCES" at bottom of tables

MONDAY THRU FRIDAY		SATURDAY		SUNDAY	
Leave Greenwich	Due G.C.T.	Leave Greenwich	Due G.C.T.	Leave Greenwich	Due G.C.T.
a12:23AM	1:22AM	.....	.....	.....	.....
b12:30	u1:35	12:30AM	u1:35AM	12:23AM	1:22AM
A5:03	6:00	.....	.....	.....	.....
6:42	7:40	6:42	7:40	6:42	7:40
A7:03	8:02	.....	.....	.....	.....
A7:13	u7:55	7:15	8:16	.....	.....
A7:28	8:18	.....	.....	.....	.....
D7:42	8:40	7:40	u8:24	7:42	8:40
A7:47	u8:32	.....	.....	.....	.....
A7:52	uy8:36	.....	.....	.....	.....
A8:00	8:58	8:00	8:58	.....	.....
A8:17	9:07	8:19	u9:17	.....	.....
8:42	9:40	8:42	9:40	8:42	9:40
A8:55	u9:42	.....	.....	.....	.....
9:21	u10:04	9:21	u10:04	.....	.....
9:52	10:50	9:52	10:50	9:52	10:50
10:09	u10:53	10:09	u10:53	.....	.....
10:47	11:45	10:47	11:45	10:47	11:45
11:45	12:48PM	11:45	12:48PM	11:45	12:48PM
.....	.....	.....	.....	12:52PM	1:50
12:52PM	1:50	12:52PM	1:50	.....	.....
1:43	2:45	1:43	2:45	1:43	2:45
A2:42	3:40	2:42	3:40	2:42	3:40
3:12	4:10	3:12	4:10	3:12	4:10
3:42	4:40	.....	.....	.....	.....
A4:12	5:10	4:12	5:10	4:12	5:10
4:47	5:47	4:47	5:47	4:47	5:47
A5:22	6:20	5:22	6:20	5:22	6:20
5:47	6:45	.....	.....	.....	.....
6:22	7:20	6:22	7:20	6:22	7:20
7:17	u8:00	7:17	u8:00	7:17	u8:00
7:42	8:43	7:42	8:43	7:42	8:43
8:17	9:15	8:17	9:15	8:17	9:15
9:17	10:15	9:17	10:15	9:17	10:15
M9:40	u10:25	.....	.....	9:40	u10:25
10:12	11:10	.....	.....	10:12	11:10
N10:34	u11:15	10:12	11:10	10:34	u11:15
10:43	11:40	10:43	11:40	11:12	12:12AM
11:12	12:12AM	11:12	12:12AM	.....	.....

REFERENCES

A—Will not run Nov. 27, Dec. 25, Jan. 1 and Feb. 23.
B—Will not run Oct. 13, Nov. 4, 11 and 27, Dec. 25, Jan. 1, Feb. 12 and 23.
C—Will not run Nov. 27, Dec. 25 and Jan. 1.
D—Runs only Nov. 27, Dec. 25, Jan. 1 and Feb. 23.
E—Runs only Jan. 1.
G—Runs only Wednesday, Dec. 24.
H—Will not run Wednesday 24.
K—Runs only Monday, Feb. 23.
M—Runs only Oct. 13, Nov. 27, Dec. 25, Jan. 1 and Feb. 23.
N—Runs only Nov. 27 and Feb. 23.
a—Runs only on Monday mornings.
b—Will not run Monday mornings.
u—Trains that arrive on or depart from the upper level, Grand Central, are marked with a "u".
x—All trains except those marked "x" stop at 125th St. Station approximately 10 minutes after leaving G. C. T.
y—All trains except those marked "y" stop at 125th St. Station approximately 10 minutes before arrival at G. C. T.

COMMUTER'S SPECIAL

Take care of your banking in the morning—before you get to the city. Our Commuter's Branch makes it simple. Open at 7:30 A.M. in the railroad station Monday through Saturday.

FIRST NATIONAL BANK
IN GREENWICH
MEMBER FEDERAL RESERVE SYSTEM
Member Federal Deposit Insurance Corporation
P.S. At your service also, our Main Office
1 EAST PUTNAM AVENUE

PHONE 8-3130 EST. 1936

Craig Electric Co., Inc.
SMITH BLDG.
GREENWICH - CONNECTICUT

WESTINGHOUSE
BENDIX - CARRIER
CAPEHART - MAGNAVOX
APPLIANCES - TELEVISION
ELECTRICAL CONTRACTING

Inside the September 28, 1952 official timetable for Greenwich and New York are advertisements for the First National Bank's Commuter's Special, a branch bank located right at the station, and for Radio City Music Hall. (Courtesy Marc Frattasio collection.)

RADIO CITY MUSIC HALL
World Famous Rockettes
Corps de Ballet
Symphony Orchestra
•
Finest Motion Pictures
•
Showplace of the Nation
Rockefeller Center

Curtain Rises 7 p. m. Mondays

On the following plays as advertised at Suburban Stations:

GUYS & DOLLS
MRS. McTHING
NEW FACES OF 1952
PAL JOEY
POINT OF NO RETURN
WISH YOU WERE HERE

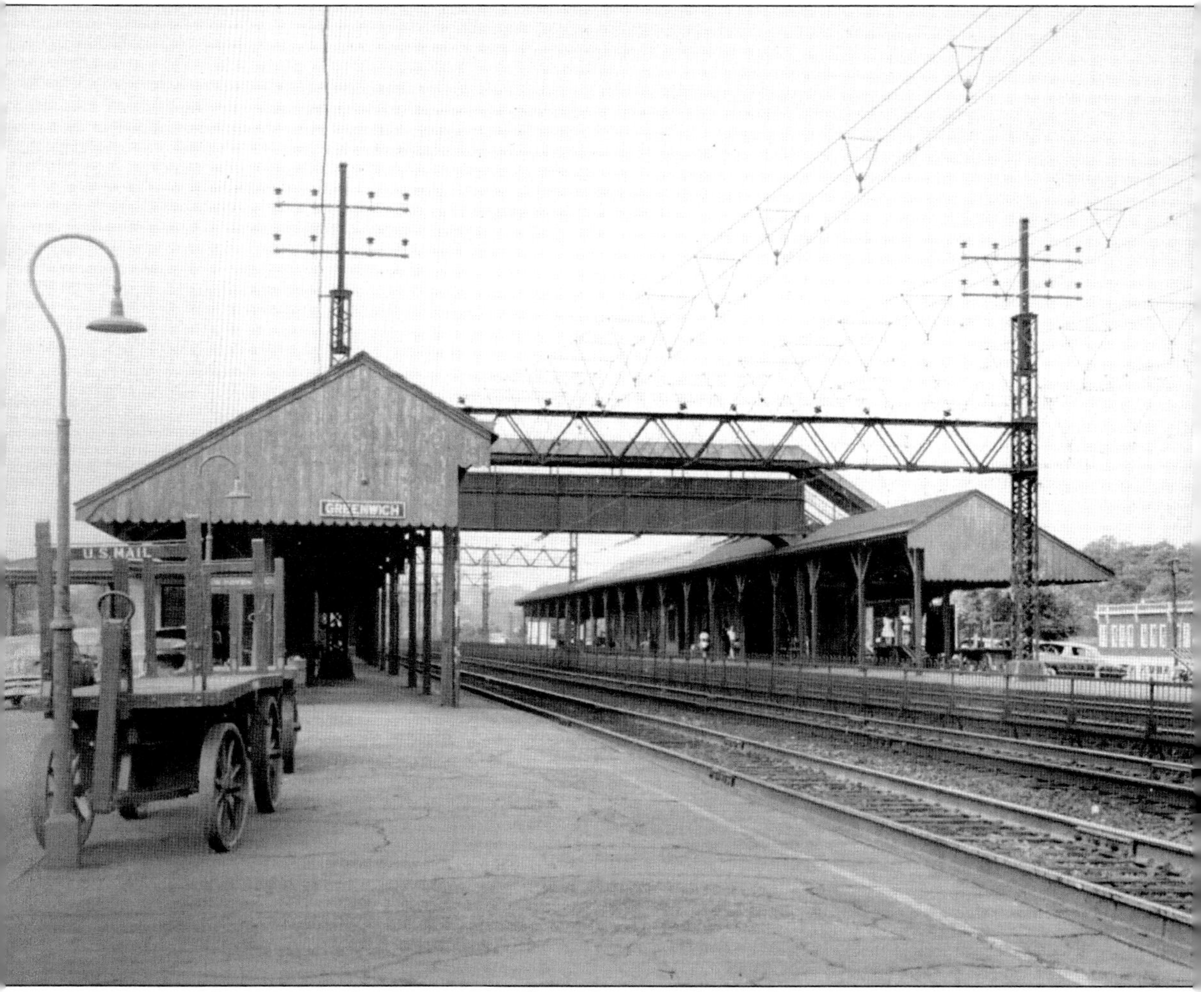

Greenwich Station is shown *c.* 1950. The railroad tracks are divided by a metal fence, between two covered platforms with baggage carts. (Courtesy Thomas J. Dodd Research Center, University of Connecticut.)

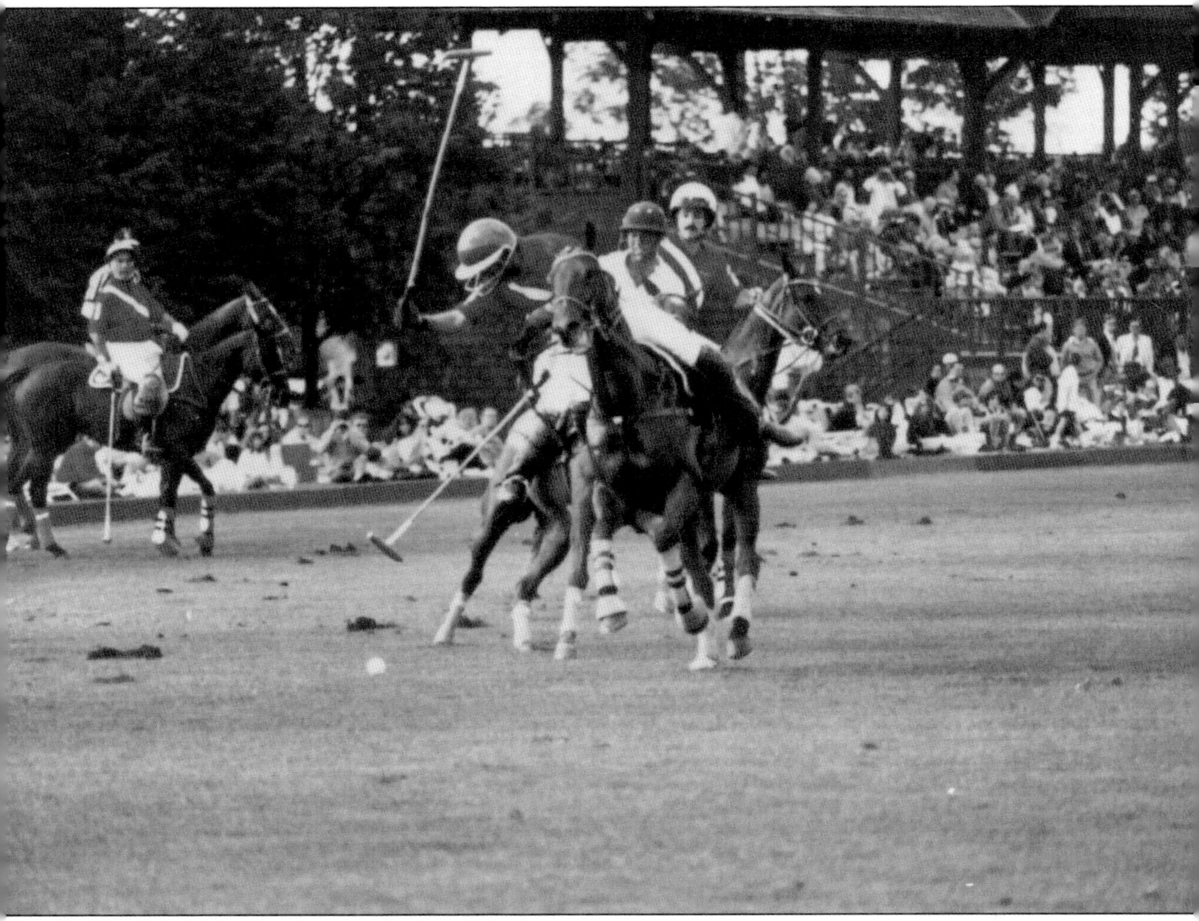

Will someone please explain how anyone can play this sport without disconnecting an entire body? Polo matches in the Greenwich back country attract thousands of enthusiasts each year to watch these 1,000-pound polo ponies. (Courtesy Historical Society of the Town of Greenwich.)

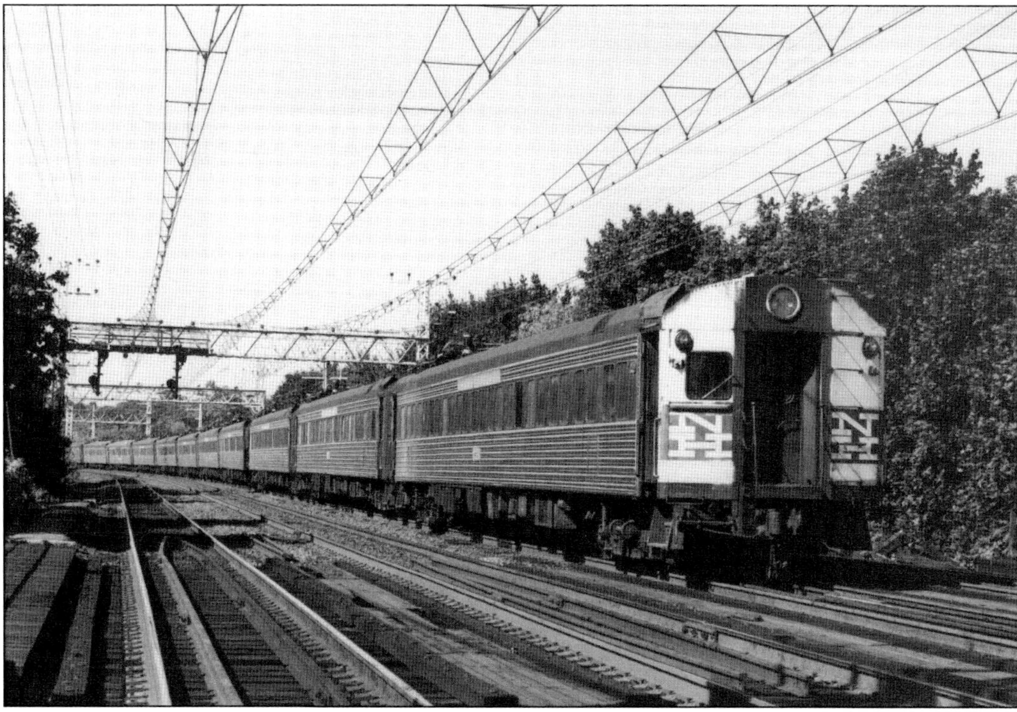

This is 1980, above, with the New Haven Line in the Conrail era. We are looking west from Greenwich Station at self-propelled electric cars. Note the original triangular overhead power wires of 1907. Below is a 1986 view of a dual-powered FL-9 locomotive, New York bound. (Courtesy J.W. Swanberg collection.)

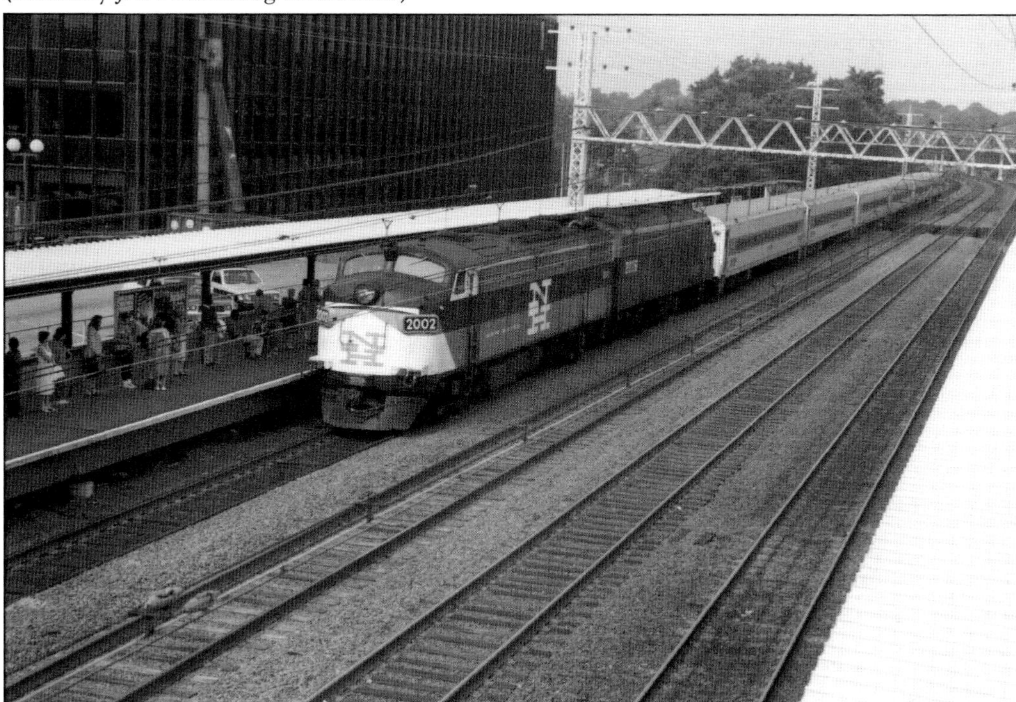

Three

STAMFORD STATION

Stamford is Connecticut's corporate capital, the third largest home of Fortune 500 Corporations in the country, including Xerox, Pitney Bowes, and International Paper.

Back in the 1960s, town fathers decided to rip apart the city center and start over with visions of shiny corporate offices and regional shopping attractions. Stamford's proximity to New York, and Connecticut's lack of a personal income tax, made Greenwich's neighbor desirable for big business, mall mania, job creation, and rail commuters. City planners accomplished pretty much what they set out to do. Yes, Connecticut implemented a personal income in 1991, and the executives meow about the state's tax burden, but Stamford still maintains its standing as one of the most active 9:00-to-5:00 commuter stops on the planet.

Bus service from Stamford's railroad station and transportation center along the Route 95 corridor provides plenty of access to downtown corporate buildings, restaurants, and the Town Center Mall, the center of downtown's activity, with all the major stores.

Downtown Stamford is all about business, and the Stamford Chamber of Commerce represents more than 1,400 business organizations. But if tranquility is on your mind, you can leave big business behind. Stamford's North End, above the Merritt Parkway, features the Stamford Museum and Nature Center, offering 118 acres of hiking trails, nature exhibits, and fine art attractions. Here, far removed from the corporate skyline, Stamford's Colonial heritage comes alive with demonstrations of Native American lifestyle and current ways of turning sap from maples into syrup.

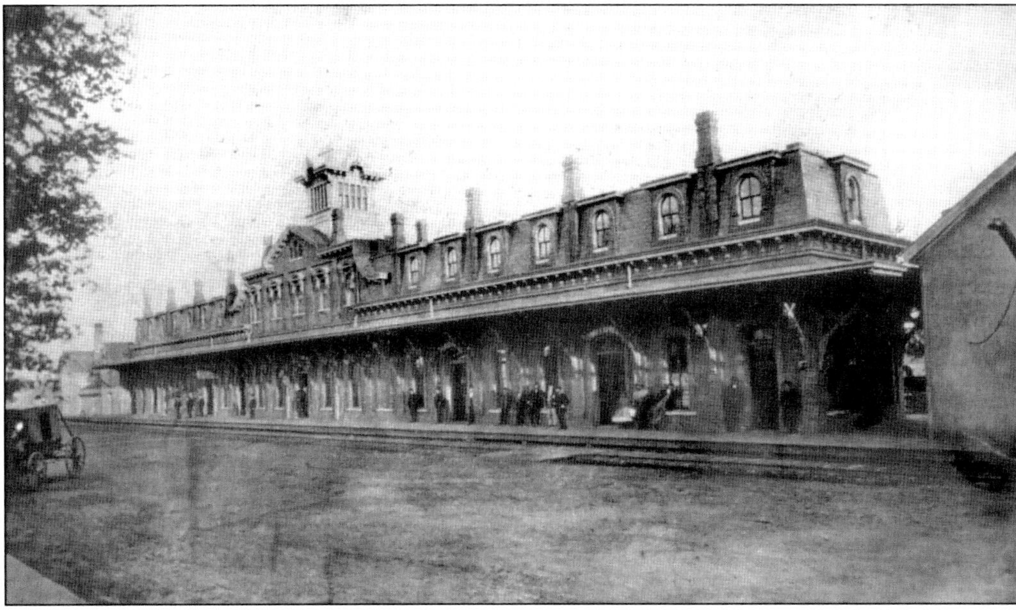

The majestic Stamford Station, shown in 1868, is an ornate, brick two-story building. People are visible on the station platform. This view was taken four years before the merger of the two major lines into the Consolidated. (Courtesy Thomas J. Dodd Research Center, University of Connecticut.)

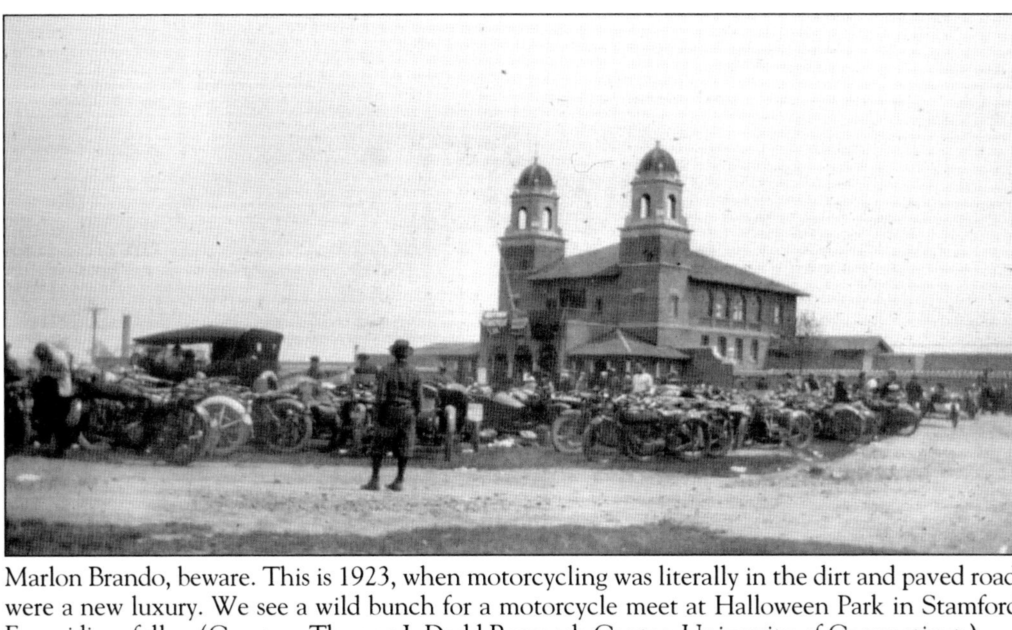

Marlon Brando, beware. This is 1923, when motorcycling was literally in the dirt and paved roads were a new luxury. We see a wild bunch for a motorcycle meet at Halloween Park in Stamford. Easy riding, fellas. (Courtesy Thomas J. Dodd Research Center, University of Connecticut.)

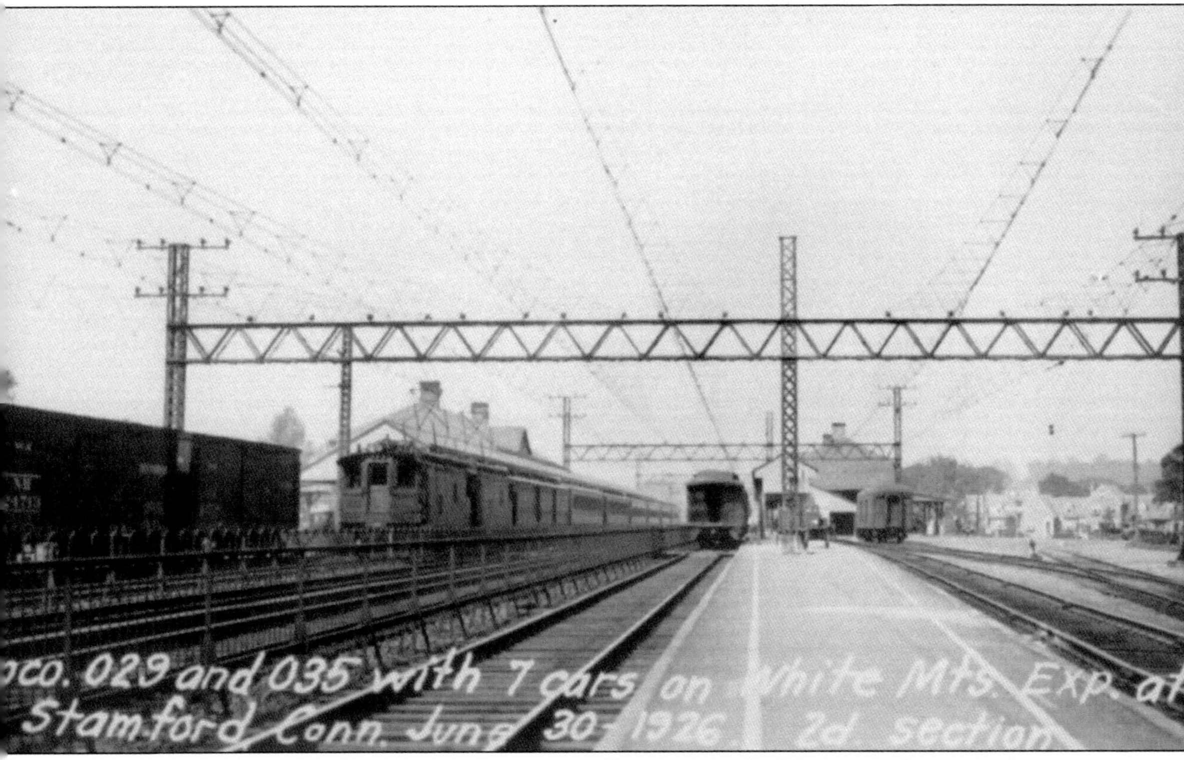

In 1926, the seven-car *White Mountain Express* pulls into Stamford Station, adjacent to boxcars on tracks. Above, this image provides a broad view of the New Haven Line's electrification. (Courtesy Thomas J. Dodd Research Center, University of Connecticut.)

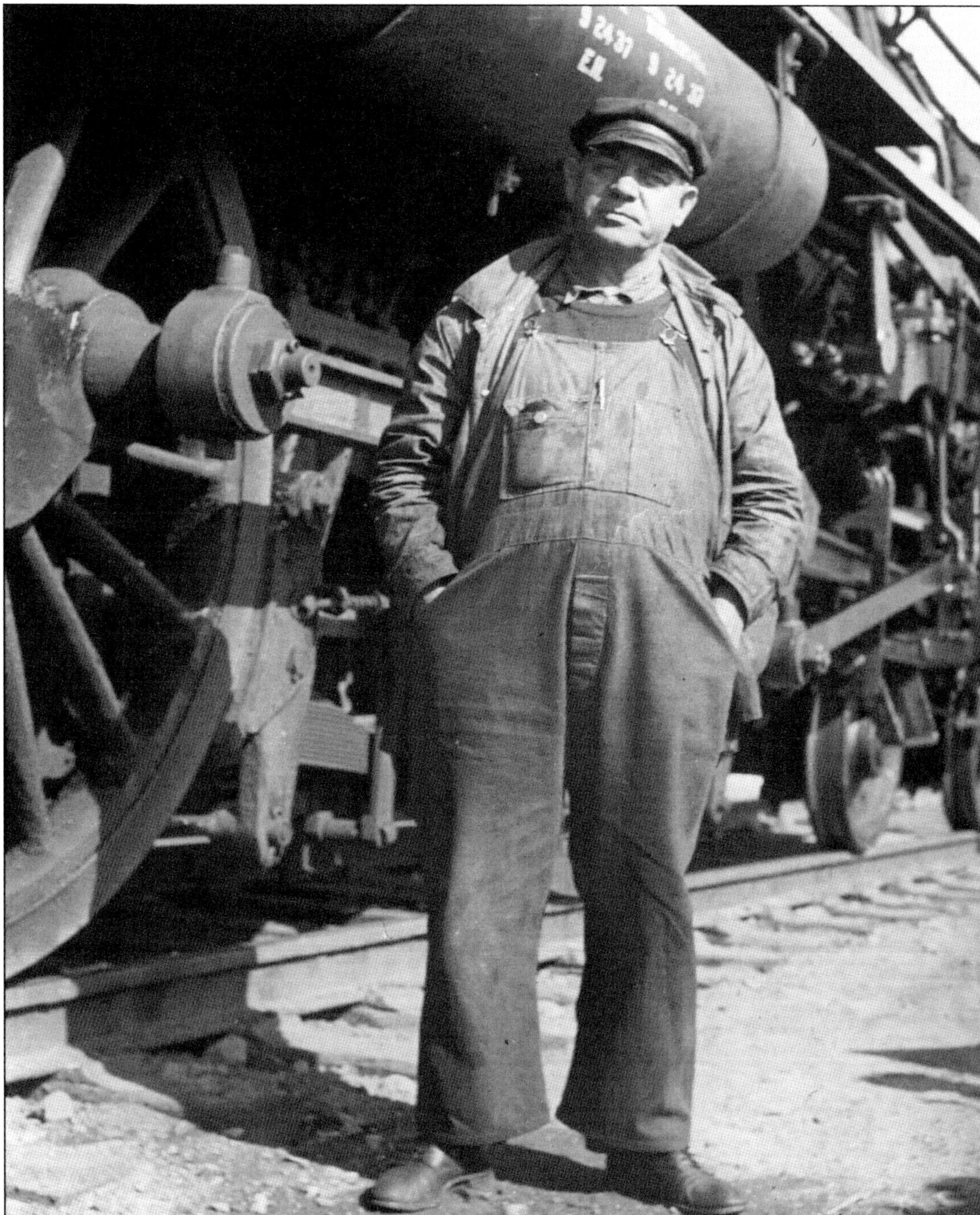

In Stamford in 1937, an engineer's work is never done, but it is always nice to see a face behind the engine. A sturdily built craftsman who kept the trains running on time was a godsend for commuters, tourists, and businesses. Not a whole lot has changed. Timing is everything. (Photograph by Charles A. Schrade, courtesy J.W. Swanberg collection.)

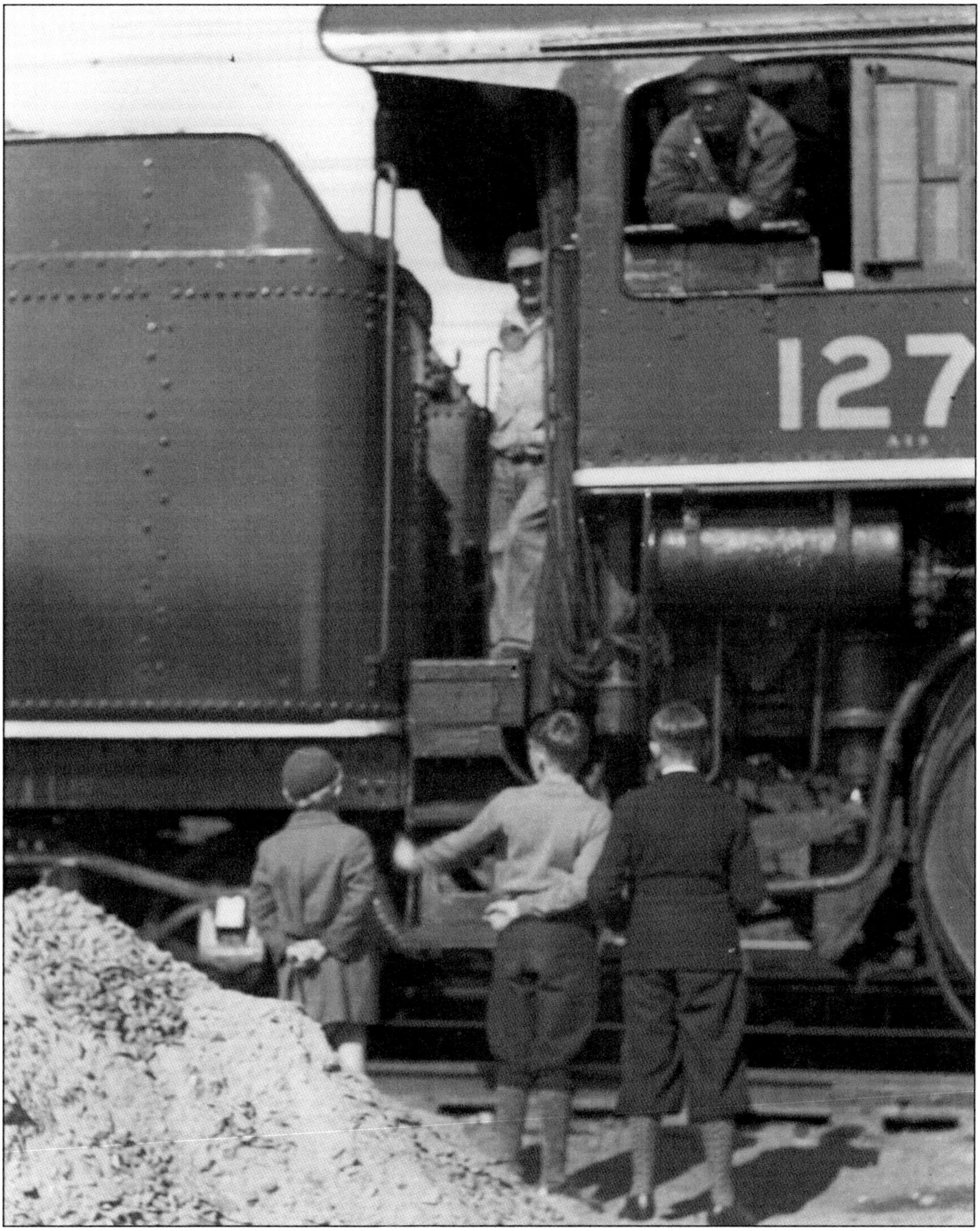

"C'mon, Mr. Railroad Man, let us on the train." So, what is wrong with a little harassment from kids after a day at school, and such nattily nickered boys? This wire train fascinates three Stamford boys c. the 1930s. (Photograph by Charles A. Schrade, courtesy J.W. Swanberg collection.)

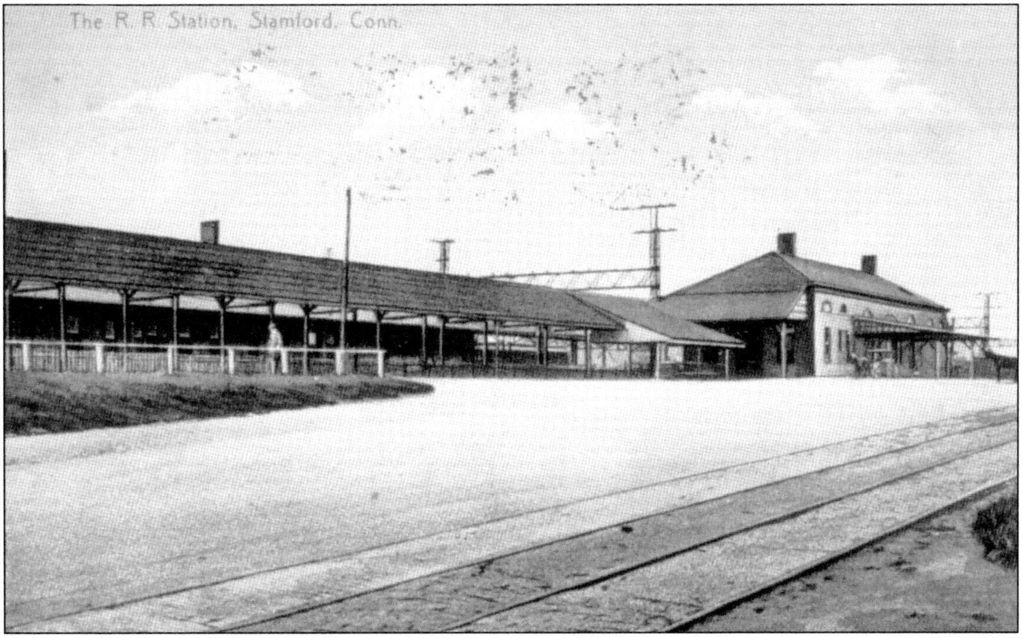

Shown is Stamford Station in the 1930s. A man stands on a covered platform extending from the two-story brick station building. The open area in front of the building shows trolley tracks. (Courtesy Thomas J. Dodd Research Center, University of Connecticut.)

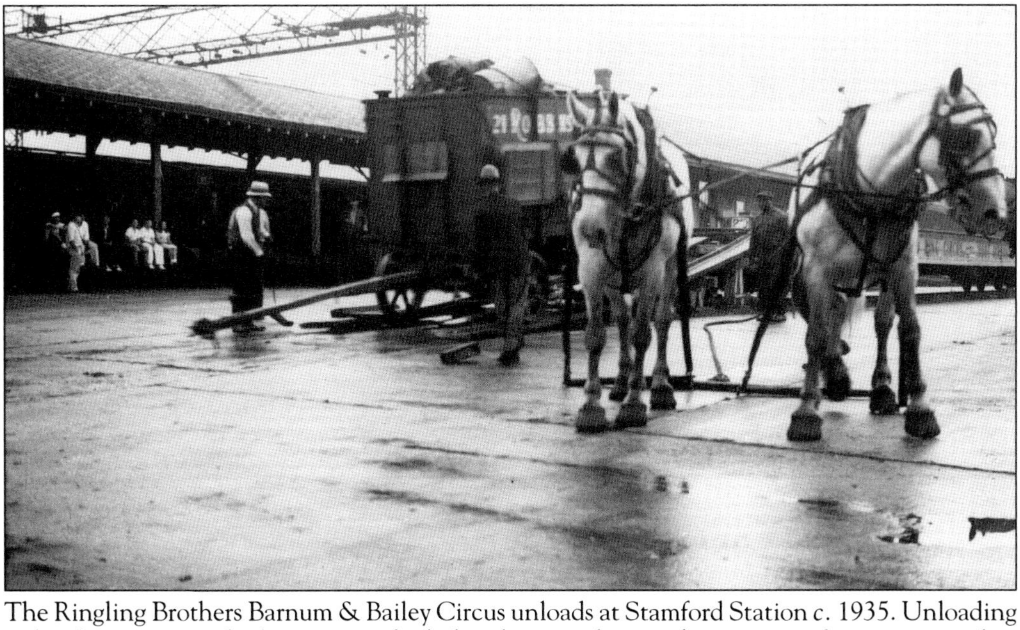

The Ringling Brothers Barnum & Bailey Circus unloads at Stamford Station *c.* 1935. Unloading at local stations is a little appetizer for kids, who can glimpse the circus performers unwind in a procession leading to the paid admission of the big top. These days, the circus preserves the traditional parade to the show, sans the big top, at arena venues. (Photograph by Charles A. Schrade, courtesy J.W. Swanberg collection.)

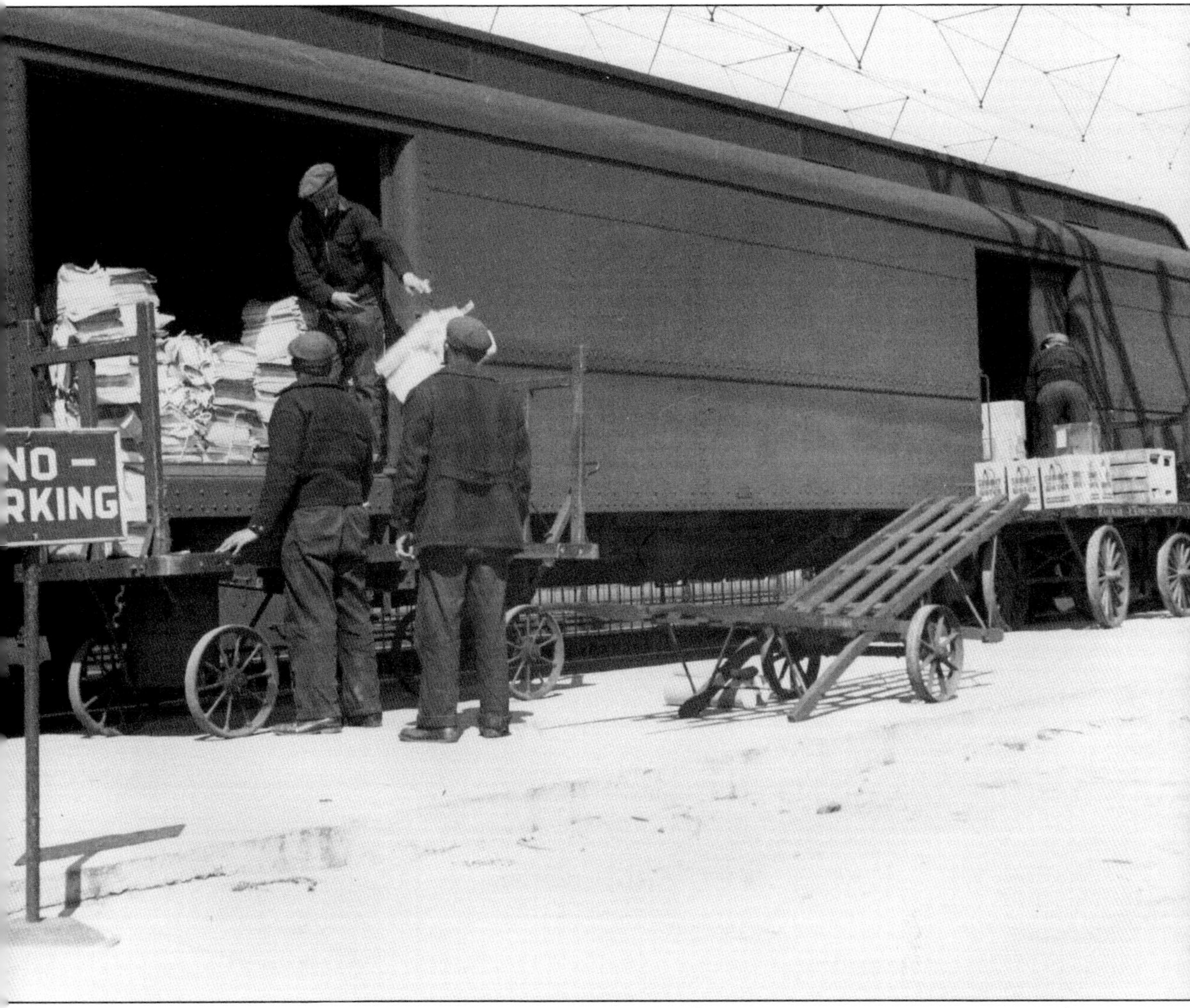

Now you know how your New York newspaper arrived in Connecticut. It is 1939, and a freighter stops in Stamford for the morning distribution point of New York papers. From here, distributors make local delivery runs. We hope that the guy throwing the papers out of the car did not drop his cigarette on the newspapers. (Photograph by Charles A. Schrade, courtesy J.W. Swanberg collection.)

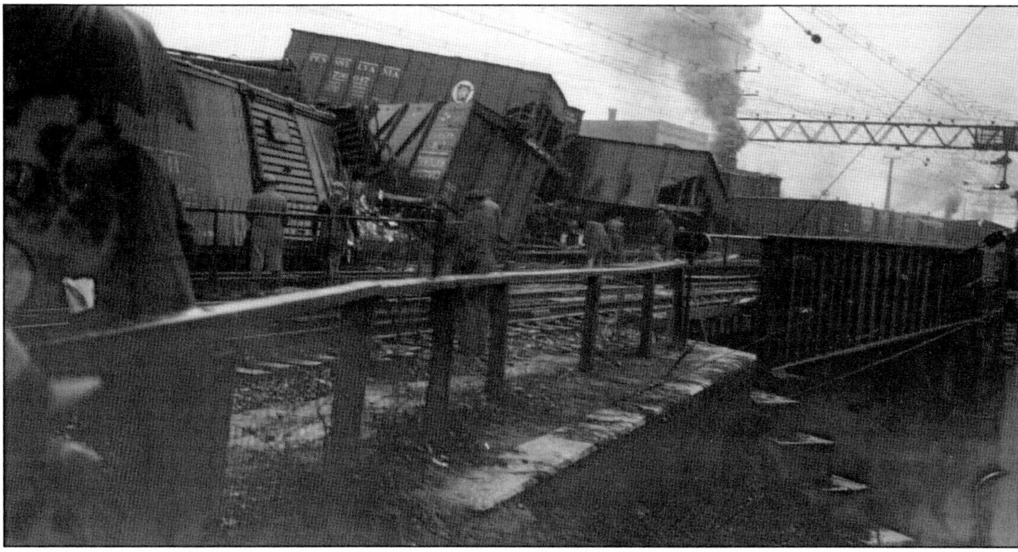

On April 30, 1935, a broken part causes a derailment of this New Haven Railroad freighter in Stamford. The wreckage pushes over into a New Canaan branch train. It is one of those raw and wet spring days, as the man at the left shields himself with an umbrella. (Photograph by Charles A. Schrade, courtesy J.W. Swanberg collection.)

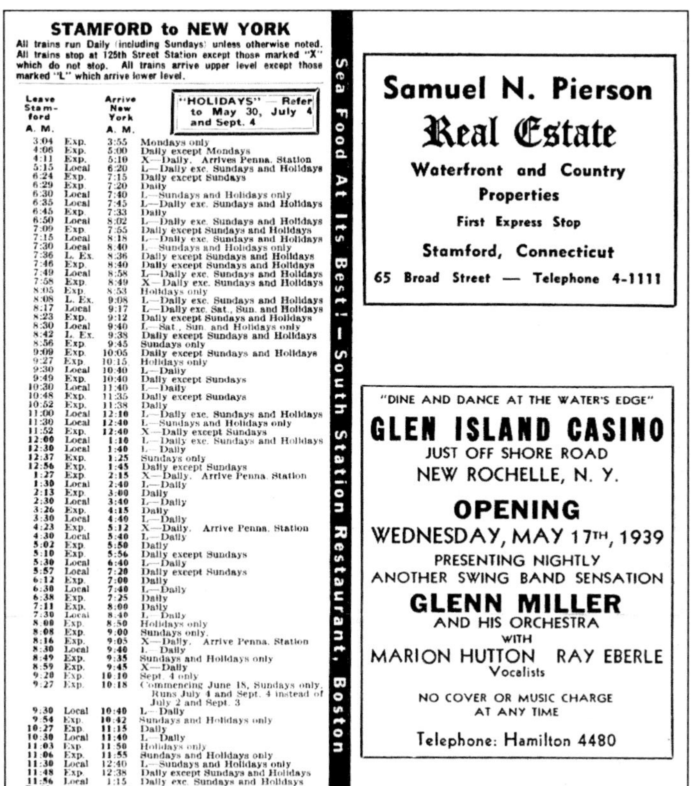

STAMFORD to NEW YORK

All trains run Daily (including Sundays) unless otherwise noted. All trains stop at 125th Street Station except those marked "X" which do not stop. All trains arrive upper level except those marked "L" which arrive lower level.

"HOLIDAYS" — Refer to May 30, July 4 and Sept. 4

Leave Stamford A. M.		Arrive New York A. M.	
3:04	Exp.	3:55	Mondays only
4:06	Exp.	5:00	Daily except Mondays
4:11	Exp.	5:10	X—Daily. Arrives Penna. Station
5:15	Local	6:20	L—Daily exc. Sundays and Holidays
6:24	Exp.	7:15	Daily except Sundays
6:29	Exp.	7:20	Daily
6:30	Local	7:40	L—Sundays and Holidays only
6:35	Local	7:45	L—Daily exc. Sundays and Holidays
6:45	Exp.	7:33	Daily
6:50	Local	8:02	L—Daily exc. Sundays and Holidays
7:09	Exp.	7:55	Daily except Sundays and Holidays
7:15	Local	8:18	L—Daily exc. Sundays and Holidays
7:30	Local	8:40	L—Sundays and Holidays only
7:36	L. Ex.	8:36	Daily except Sundays and Holidays
7:46	Exp.	8:40	Daily except Sundays and Holidays
7:49	Local	8:58	L—Daily exc. Sundays and Holidays
7:58	Exp.	8:49	X—Daily exc. Sundays and Holidays
8:05	Exp.	8:53	Holidays only
8:08	L. Ex.	9:08	L—Daily exc. Sundays and Holidays
8:17	Local	9:17	L—Daily exc. Sat., Sun. and Holidays
8:23	Exp.	9:12	Daily except Sundays and Holidays
8:30	Local	9:40	L—Sat., Sun. and Holidays only
8:42	L. Ex.	9:38	Daily except Sundays and Holidays
8:56	Exp.	9:45	Sundays only
9:09	Exp.	10:05	Daily except Sundays and Holidays
9:27	Exp.	10:15	Holidays only
9:30	Local	10:40	L—Daily
9:49	Exp.	10:40	Daily except Sundays
10:30	Local	11:40	L—Daily
10:48	Exp.	11:35	Daily except Sundays
10:52	Exp.	11:38	Daily
11:00	Local	12:10	L—Daily exc. Sundays and Holidays
11:30	Local	12:40	L—Sundays and Holidays only
11:52	Exp.	12:40	X—Daily except Sundays
12:00	Local	1:10	L—Daily exc. Sundays and Holidays
12:30	Local	1:40	L—Daily
12:37	Exp.	1:25	Sundays only
12:56	Exp.	1:45	Daily except Sundays
1:27	Exp.	2:15	X—Daily. Arrive Penna. Station
1:30	Local	2:40	L—Daily
2:13	Exp.	3:00	Daily
2:30	Local	3:40	L—Daily
3:26	Exp.	4:15	Daily
3:30	Local	4:40	L—Daily
4:23	Exp.	5:12	X—Daily. Arrive Penna. Station
4:30	Local	5:40	L—Daily
5:02	Exp.	5:50	Daily
5:10	Exp.	5:56	Daily except Sundays
5:30	Local	6:40	L—Daily
5:57	Local	7:20	Daily except Sundays
6:12	Exp.	7:00	Daily
6:30	Local	7:40	L—Daily
6:38	Exp.	7:25	Daily
7:11	Exp.	8:00	Daily
7:30	Local	8:40	L—Daily
8:00	Exp.	8:50	Holidays only
8:08	Exp.	9:00	Sundays only.
8:16	Exp.	9:05	X—Daily. Arrive Penna. Station
8:30	Local	9:40	L—Daily
8:49	Exp.	9:35	Sundays and Holidays only
8:59	Exp.	9:45	X—Daily
9:20	Exp.	10:10	Sept. 4 only
9:27	Exp.	10:18	Commencing June 18, Sundays only. Runs July 4 and Sept. 4 instead of July 2 and Sept. 3
9:30	Local	10:40	L—Daily
9:54	Exp.	10:42	Sundays and Holidays only
10:27	Exp.	11:15	Daily
10:30	Local	11:40	L—Daily
11:03	Exp.	11:50	Holidays only
11:06	Exp.	11:55	Sundays and Holidays only
11:30	Local	12:40	L—Sundays and Holidays only
11:48	Exp.	12:38	Daily except Sundays and Holidays
11:56	Local	1:15	Daily exc. Sundays and Holidays
P. M.		A. M.	

Sea Food At Its Best! — South Station Restaurant, Boston

Samuel N. Pierson
Real Estate
Waterfront and Country Properties
First Express Stop
Stamford, Connecticut
65 Broad Street — Telephone 4-1111

"DINE AND DANCE AT THE WATER'S EDGE"
GLEN ISLAND CASINO
JUST OFF SHORE ROAD
NEW ROCHELLE, N. Y.
OPENING
WEDNESDAY, MAY 17TH, 1939
PRESENTING NIGHTLY
ANOTHER SWING BAND SENSATION
GLENN MILLER
AND HIS ORCHESTRA
WITH
MARION HUTTON RAY EBERLE
Vocalists
NO COVER OR MUSIC CHARGE
AT ANY TIME
Telephone: Hamilton 4480

This is the official Stamford-to-New York timetable for April 30, 1939. Commuters could leave Stamford daily (except Mondays) at 4:06 a.m. and arrive at Grand Central at 5:00 a.m. Check out the advertisement for Glenn Miller: "No cover or music charge at any time." In the mood? (Courtesy Marc Frattasio collection.)

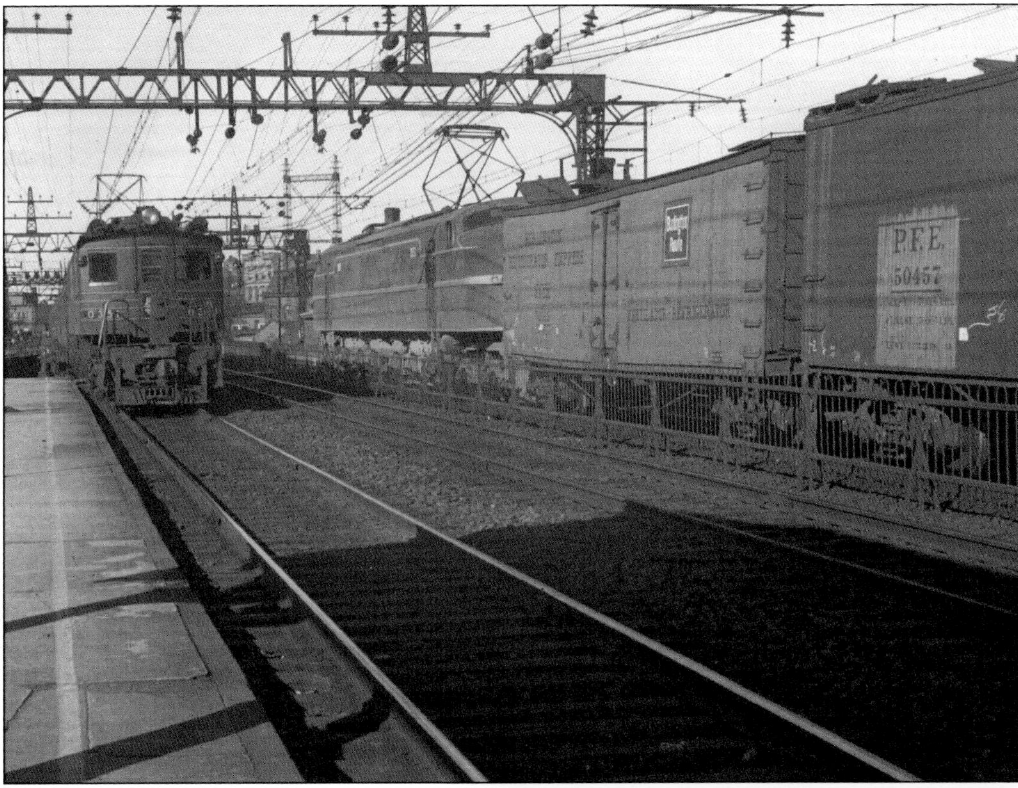

It is the late 1940s and, as rail historian Jack Swanberg notes, there is "always lots of action in Stamford." Above, the 0351 passenger train rolls into Stamford Station for its last stop before heading into Penn Station, while a new streamlined freight engine pulling "Burlington Route" cars heads east for New Haven. Right, a New Haven Railroad passenger train heads east out of Stamford. (Photographs by Charles A. Schrade, courtesy J.W. Swanberg collection.)

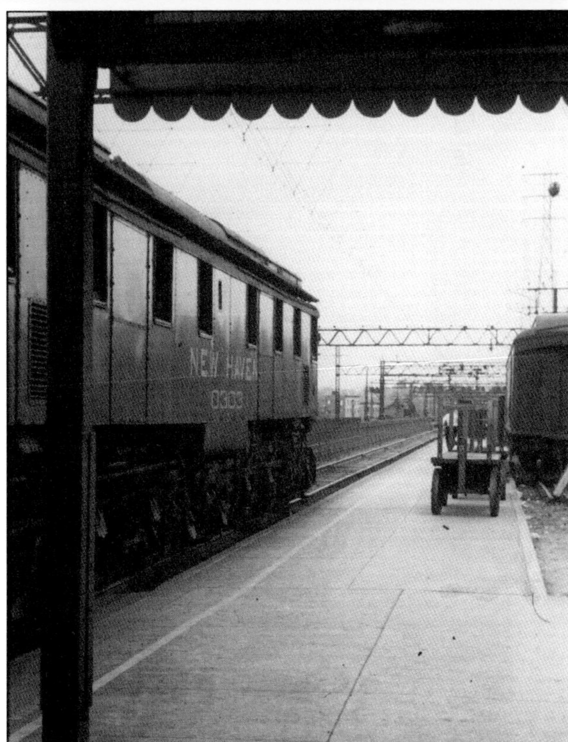

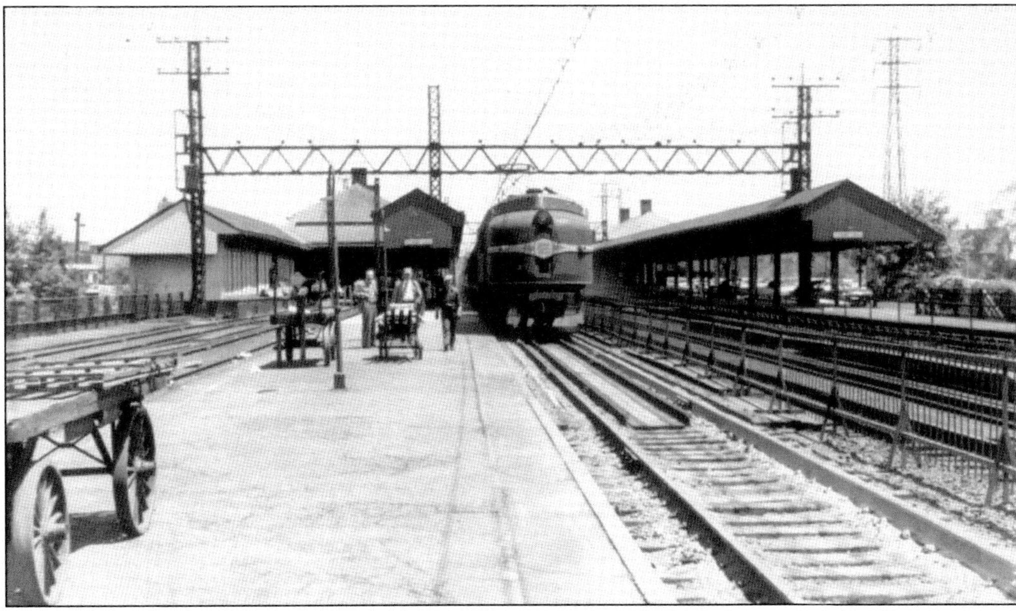

Shown is Stamford Station in 1950, with men on the platform near wooden baggage carts and an electric locomotive pulling in a passenger train. (Courtesy Thomas J. Dodd Research Center, University of Connecticut.)

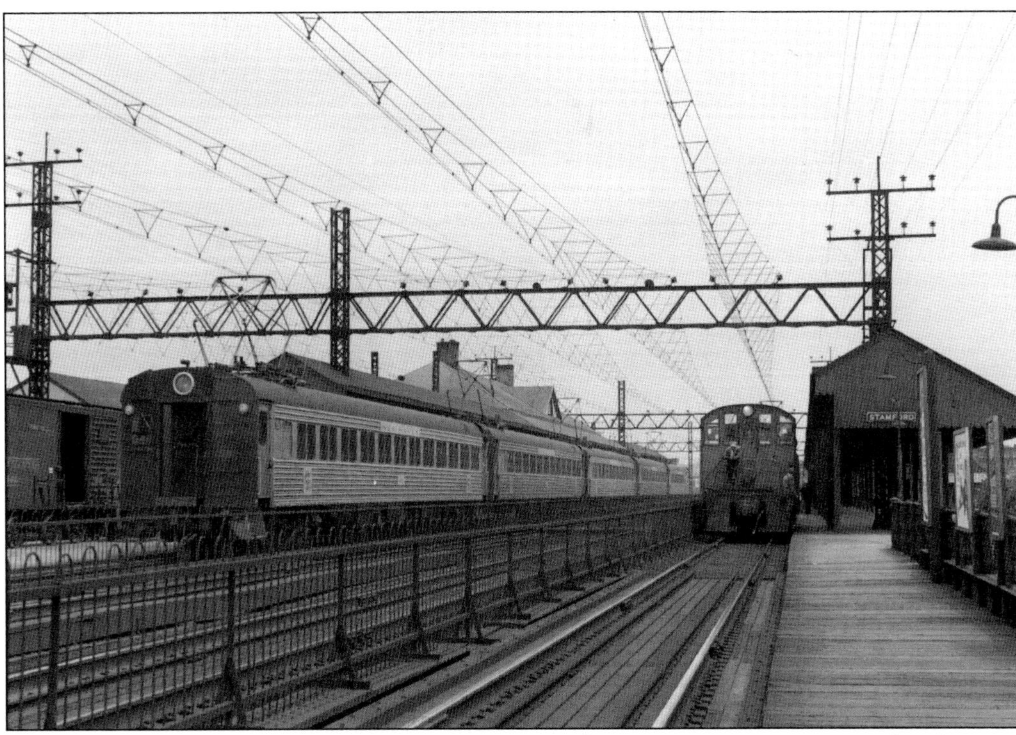

In May 1955, a five-car electric commuter train with a 120-passenger capacity heads out of Stamford toward Grand Central Station. At the right is a diesel train heading toward New Haven. (Photograph by George Votava, courtesy J.W. Swanberg collection.)

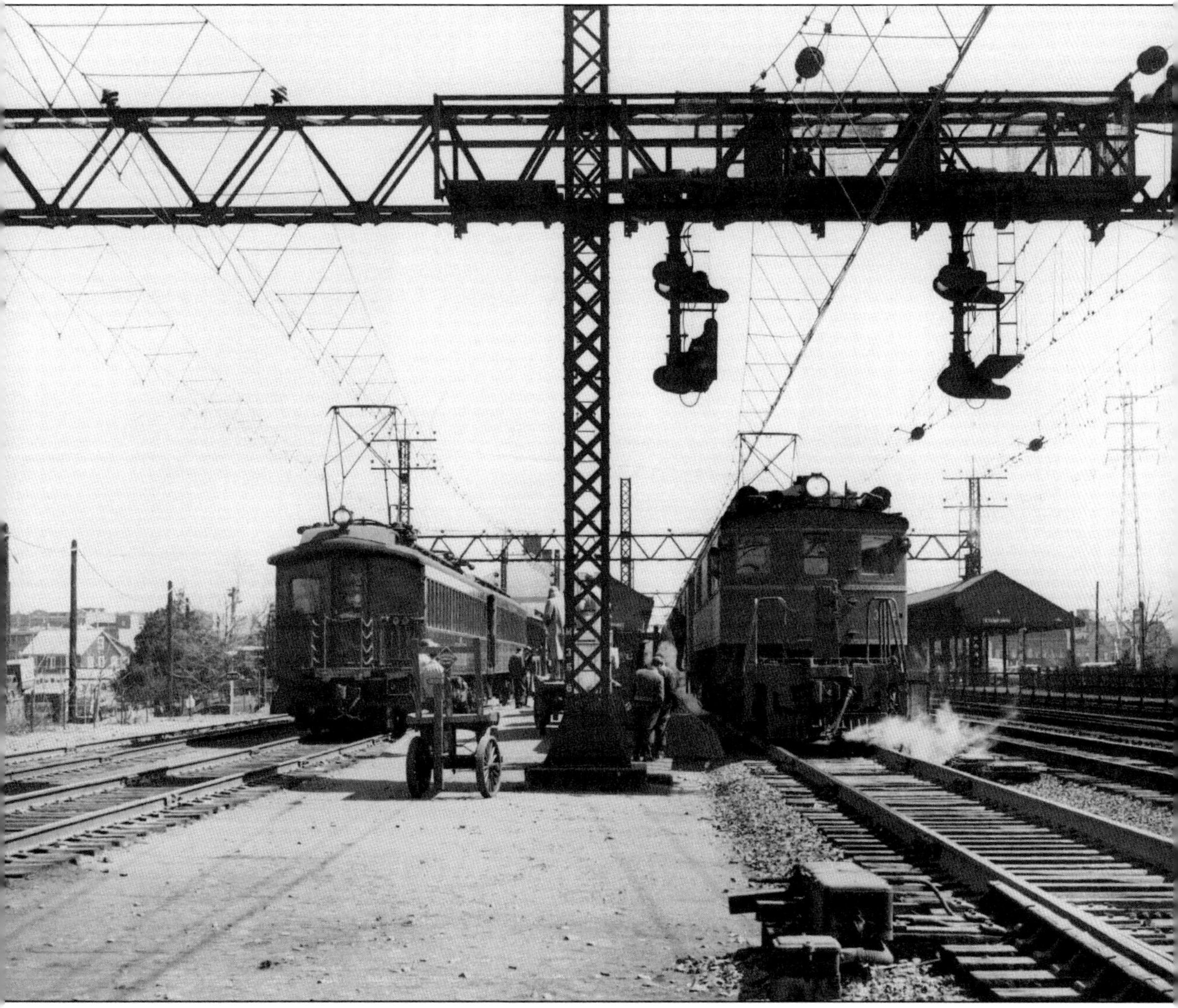

This is Stamford Station in April 1954. Cars at the left are part of the inland New Canaan branch service. At the right is an electric locomotive for a mainline passenger train. (Courtesy J.W. Swanberg collection.)

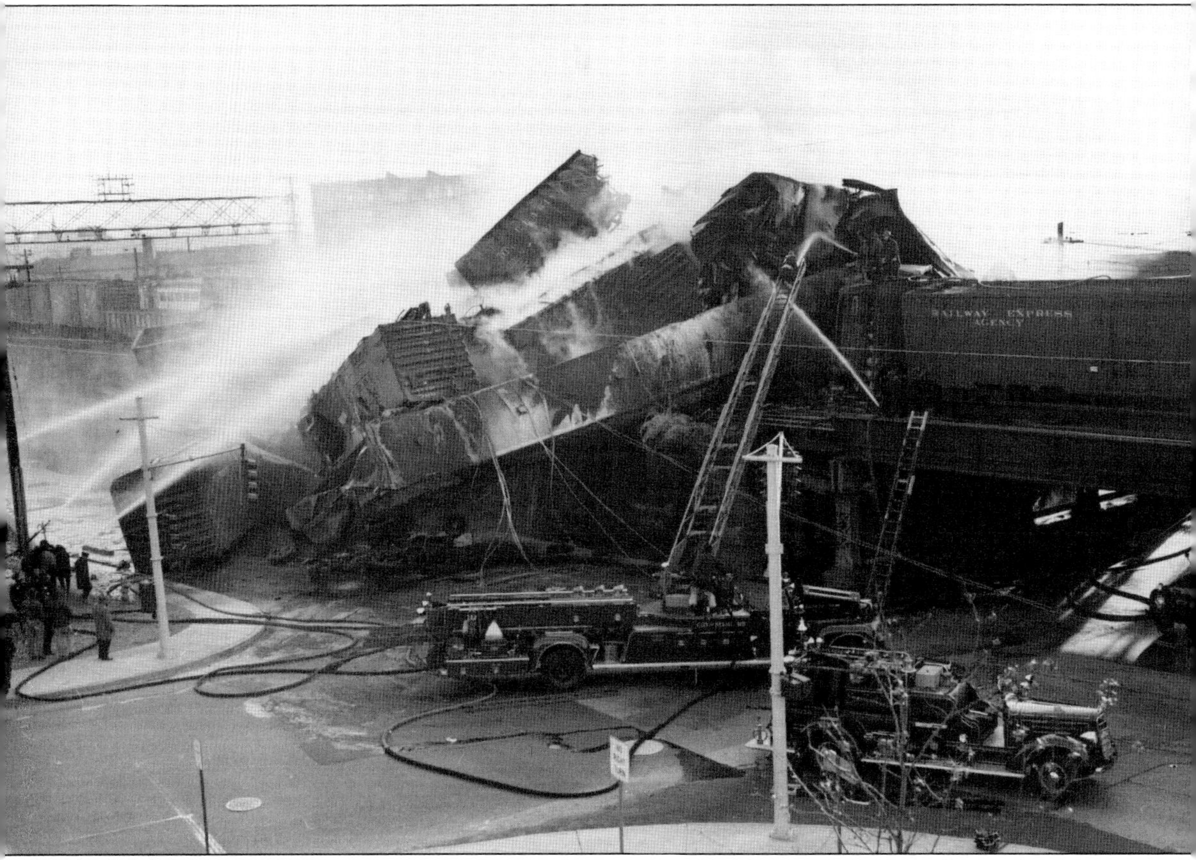

Talk about a chain-effect freighter topple: this is January 10, 1959, and Stamford firefighters are working from all angles to quickly hose down the wreckage. Notice the firefighter on the ladder at the top of the photograph and his engine company mates on top of the freighter car. (Courtesy J.W. Swanberg collection.)

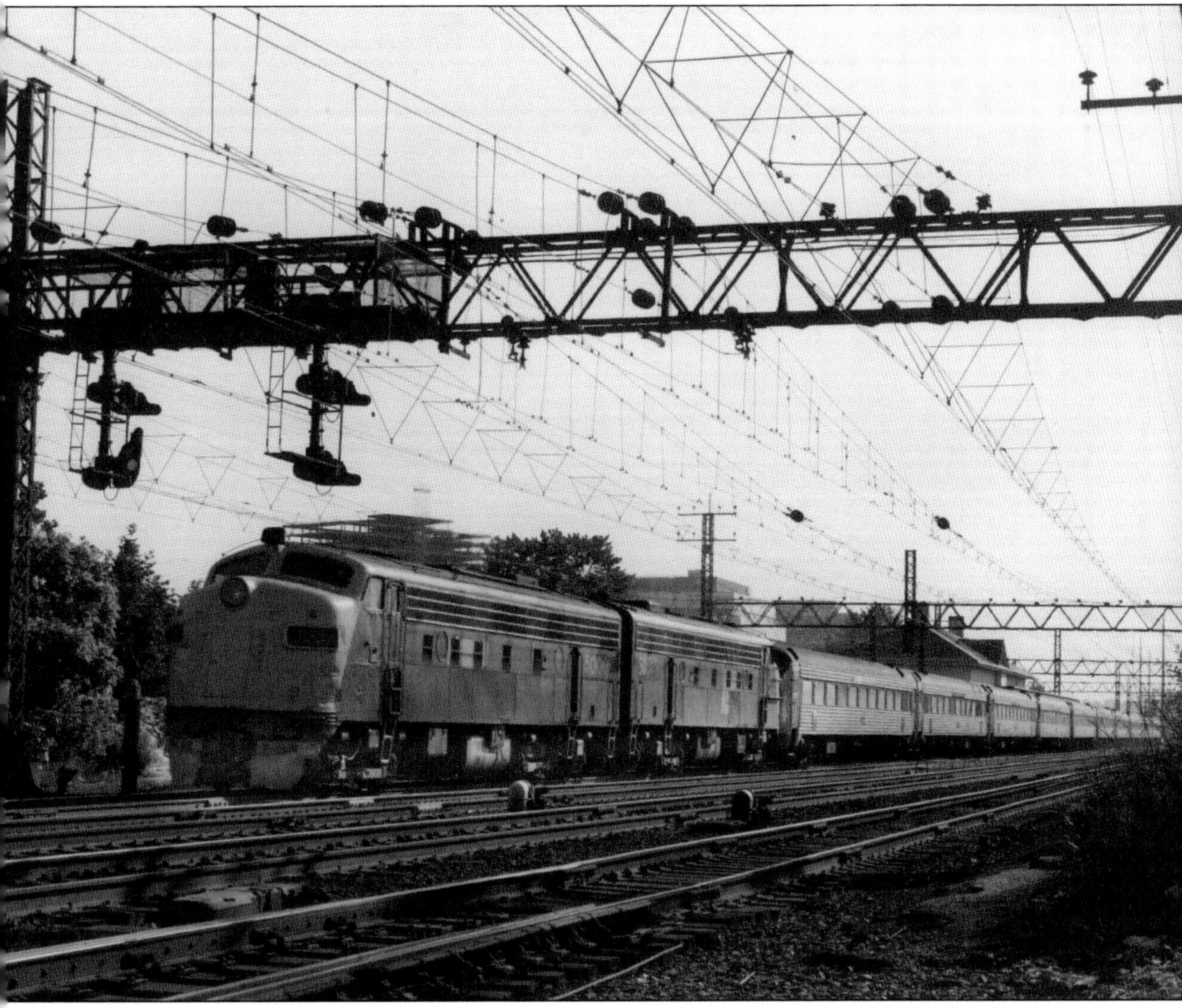

On June 27, 1979, historian Jack Swanberg took this photograph of two former New Haven Railroad dual-powered locomotives during the Conrail era. This Danbury commuter departure accelerates through Stamford en route for Grand Central. (Courtesy J.W. Swanberg collection.)

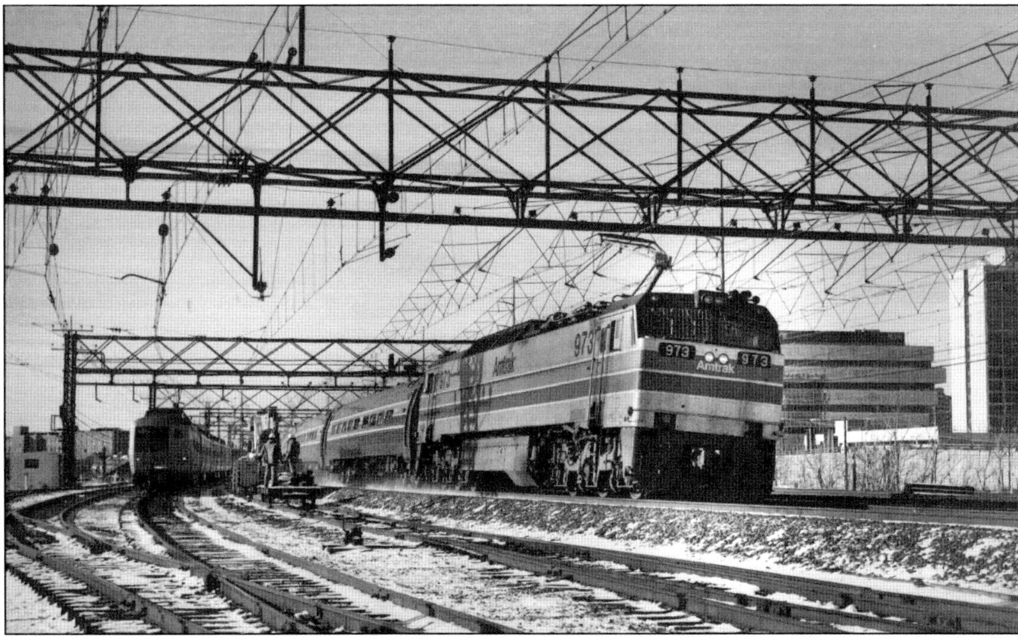

Benjamin Franklin, an Amtrak special originating in Washington, D.C., heads through Stamford en route to Boston on January 5, 1981. To the right of the Amtrak electric locomotive is the GTE building, followed by the Marriott tower. Ben Franklin must be thinking that all this electrical stuff is a long way from flying kites. (Courtesy J.W. Swanberg collection.)

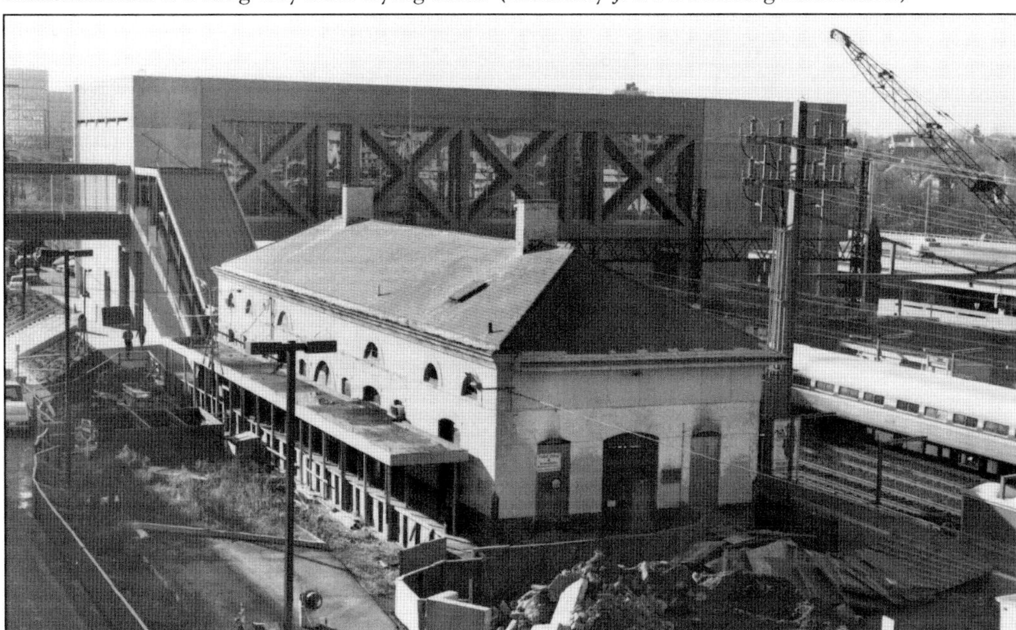

Shown in this November 13, 1987 view, the new Metro-North–Amtrak overpass station modernizes commuter facilities in Stamford. The old eastbound station below is poised for demolition to make way for a parking lot and taxi pick-up area. Commuters know the existing facility is not an architectural jewel. So long as the trains run on time, who cares? (Courtesy J.W. Swanberg collection.)

Four

Darien Station

They say George Washington often traveled under cover through the town to avoid capture from this Tory stronghold on his way to northern encampments. Darien is a place to live incognito. It has "private" written all over the roads, beaches, and parks. Charles Lindbergh managed to live in Darien for many years without much commotion, as did the philosopher and inventor Buckminster Fuller.

Darien's quaint shopping district lies within walking distance of its charming red railroad station, located on the New York–bound side. The eastbound side fell victim to a fire in the 1930s. The district includes antiques, consignments, and gourmet foods.

If you want to mingle with the horsey set, the Ox Ridge Hunt Club is the place to be. Each June, the club hosts a week-long event featuring Olympic medallists. Bring your red pants and blue blazer.

Let us not forget the other clubs in Darien, such as the Wee Burn and Woodway Country Clubs, along Long Island Sound, and the Country Club of Darien. Good luck trying to get in.

Noroton Heights, with a limited-stop station, is a subsection of Darien with some splendid old mansions. Don't expect to be invited in for tea, traveler James G. Clark added. This is, after all, a private town with private homes and private boats. This leads to the question of how Noroton and Rowayton, a section of neighboring Norwalk, got their names. Clark uncovered that, back in the 19th century, when the ships brought their cargo to the area, boats would row out to the ships, pick up a ton of cargo, and row back up the Five Mile River—*Row-a-ton*. Noroton got its name because the Noroton River was too shallow to row a ton—*No-ro-ton*.

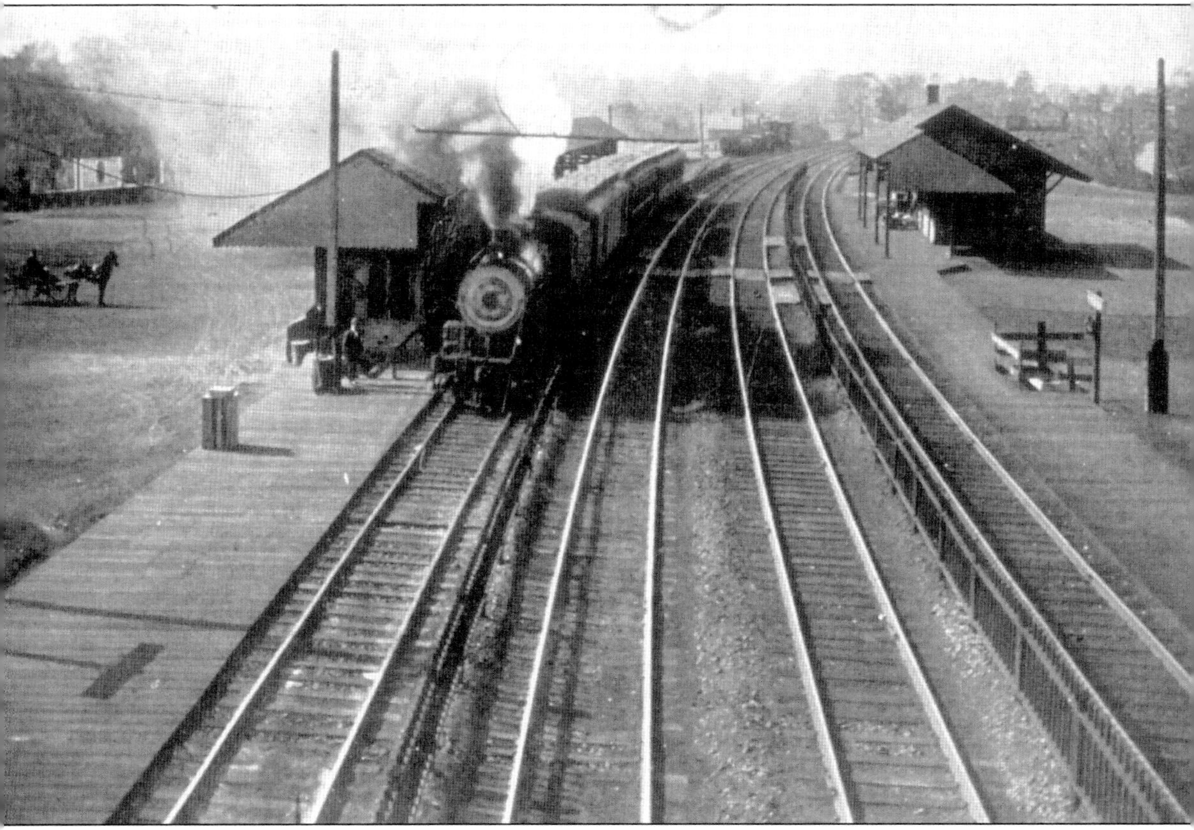

This view shows a steamer at the exclusive Noroton Heights Station *c.* 1900, before electrification. The engine and train cars are stopped on the tracks in front of a covered platform. A horse and carriage waits in an open area. (Courtesy Thomas J. Dodd Research Center, University of Connecticut.)

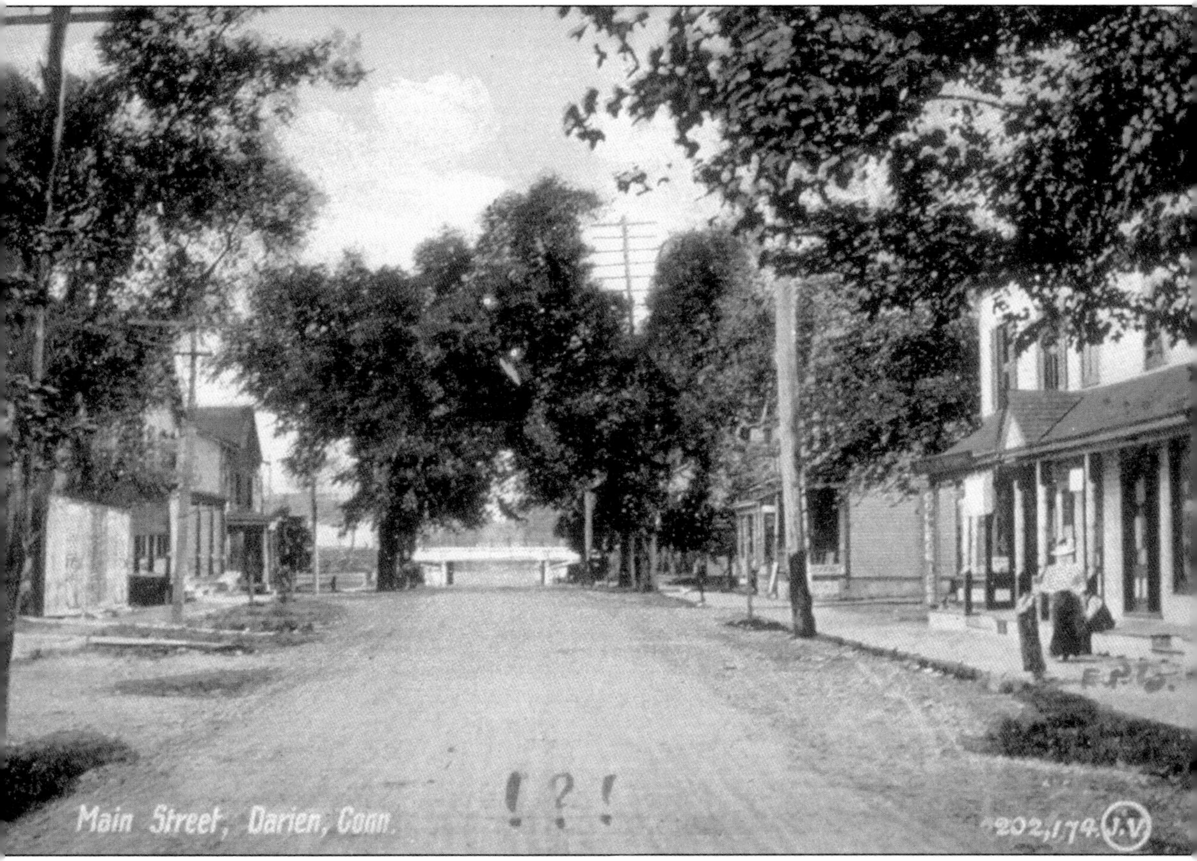

Shown is Main Street in Darien *c.* 1907, a sleepy bedroom community of New York. Has a whole lot really changed? Trees and telephone poles line the dirt road. A woman walks on the sidewalk in front of the building at the right. (Courtesy Thomas J. Dodd Research Center, University of Connecticut.)

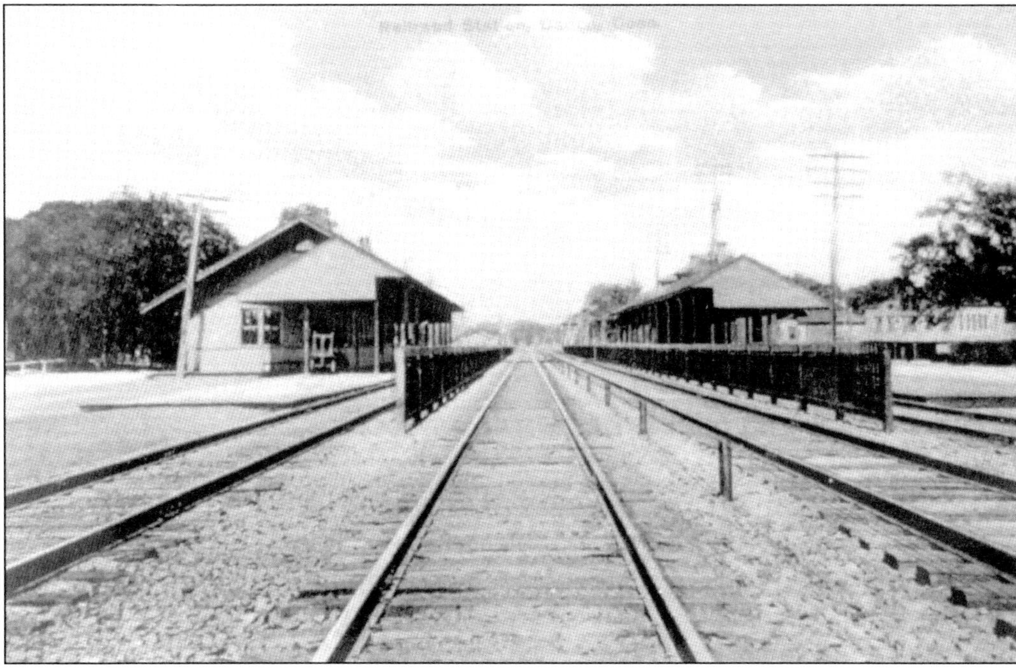

These two views show Darien before and after electrification. Above is Darien Station during the steamer era. Below, the view looks toward New York at the overhead electrical system. The eastbound building at the left was destroyed in a fire shortly after this *c.* 1930 photograph was taken. Today, Darien Station relies solely on a westbound station. (Above courtesy Thomas J. Dodd Research Center, University of Connecticut; below courtesy J.W. Swanberg collection.)

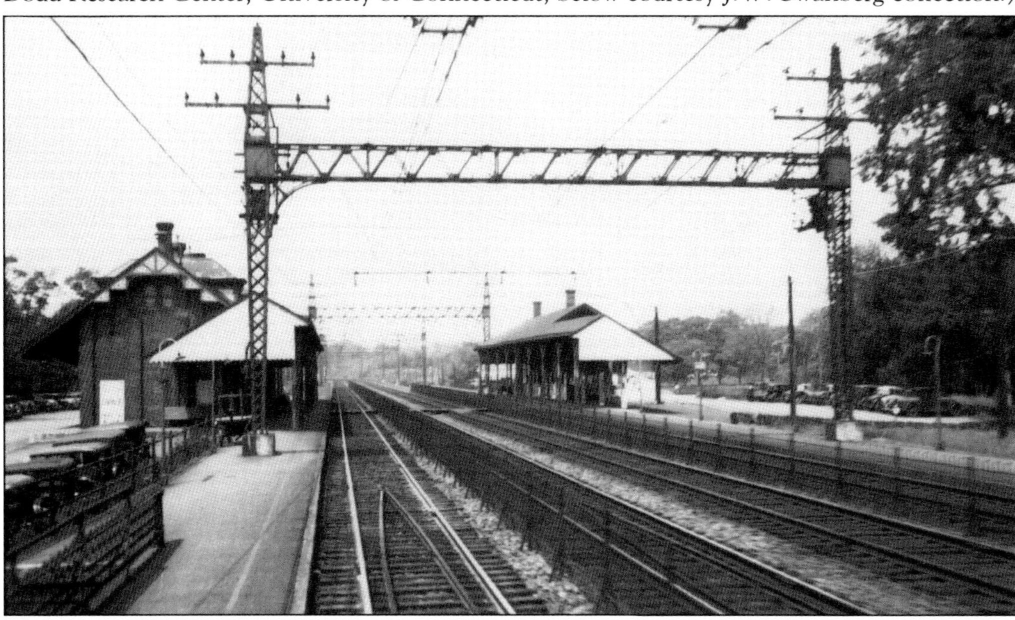

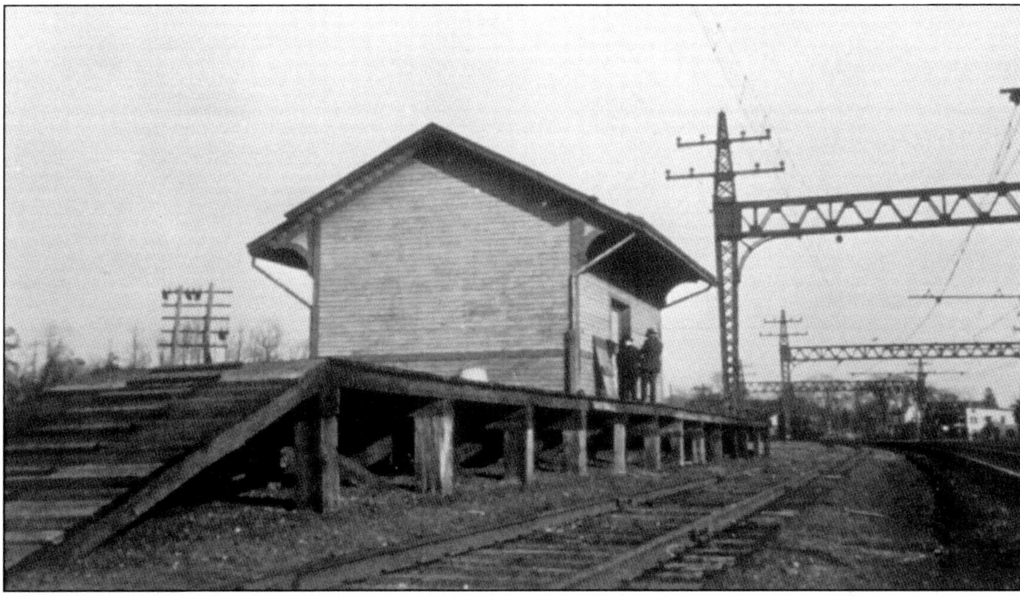

This is Noroton Heights after electrification. Two men stand on a platform in front of a freight house near the railroad tracks. Metal towers support electrical cables over the tracks. (Courtesy Thomas J. Dodd Research Center, University of Connecticut.)

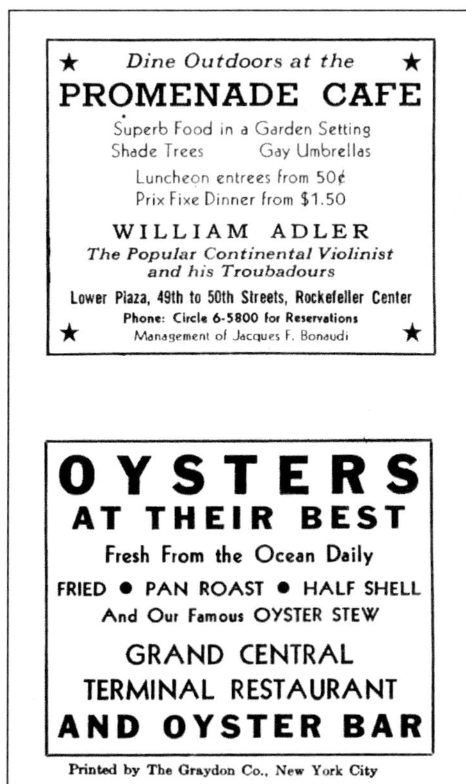

This is an advertisement from a New York, New Haven & Hartford Railroad timetable for New Canaan and Darien in 1939. How about the outdoor dining prices at the Promenade Café at Rockefeller Center: a cool $1.50. Today, you might have to mortgage your house for a meal in Manhattan. (Courtesy Marc Frattasio collection.)

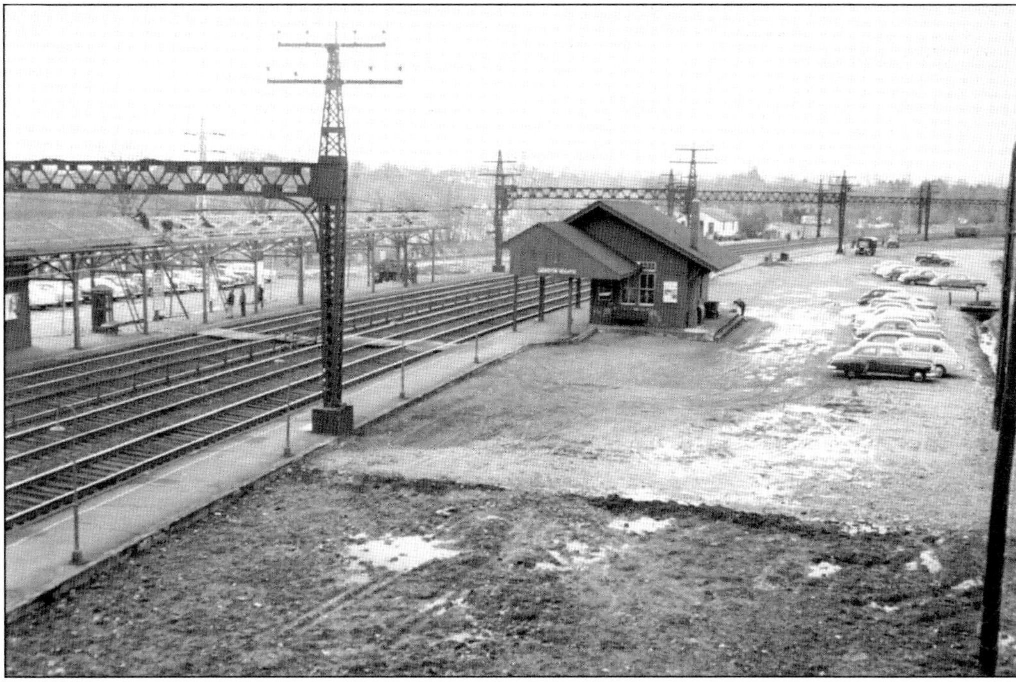

Parking at Noroton Heights Station was not an issue when this photograph was taken in the 1950s. Just pull into the station and hop aboard. Try that today at most Metro-North stops, and you would be lucky to find a parking spot with a skateboard. (Courtesy Thomas J. Dodd Research Center, University of Connecticut.)

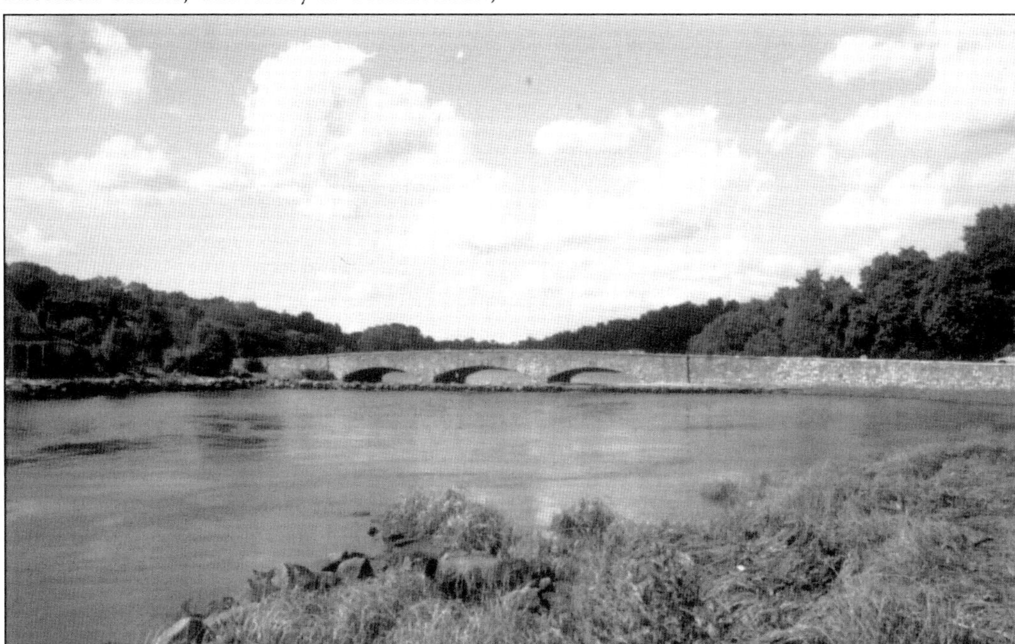

This scene of pure serenity is quintessential Darien. Shown is the Rings End Bridge over Gorhams Pond in 1990. (Courtesy Thomas J. Dodd Research Center, University of Connecticut.)

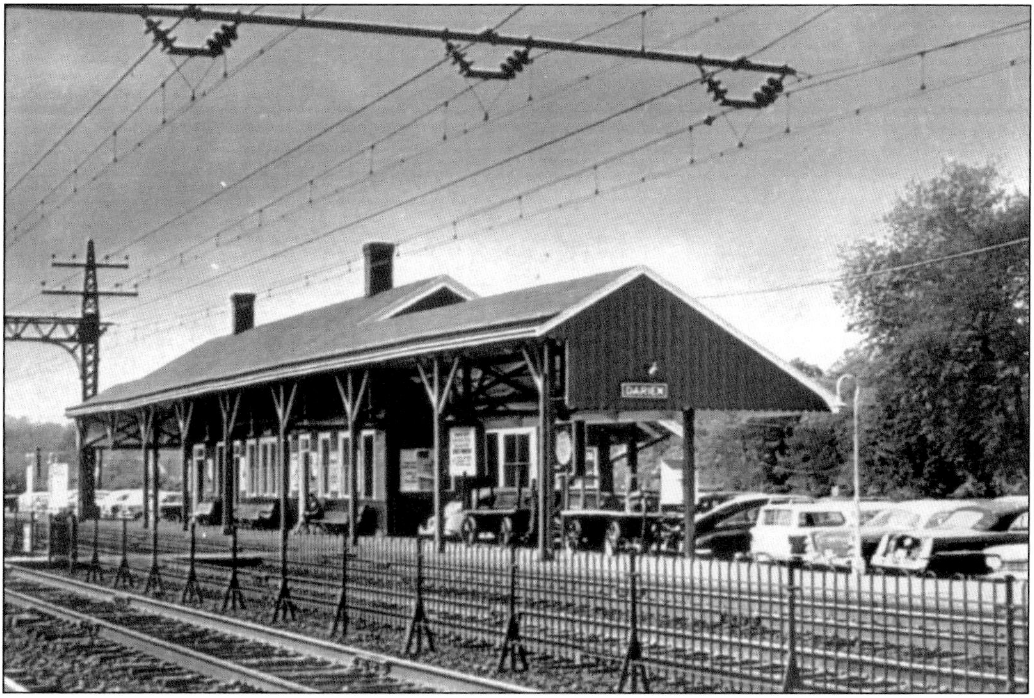

Shown are two stations. Above is the little red train station in Darien *c.* 1955, with cars pushed right against the station platform. Below is the tiny Noroton Heights Station in the same era. (Courtesy Thomas J. Dodd Research Center, University of Connecticut.)

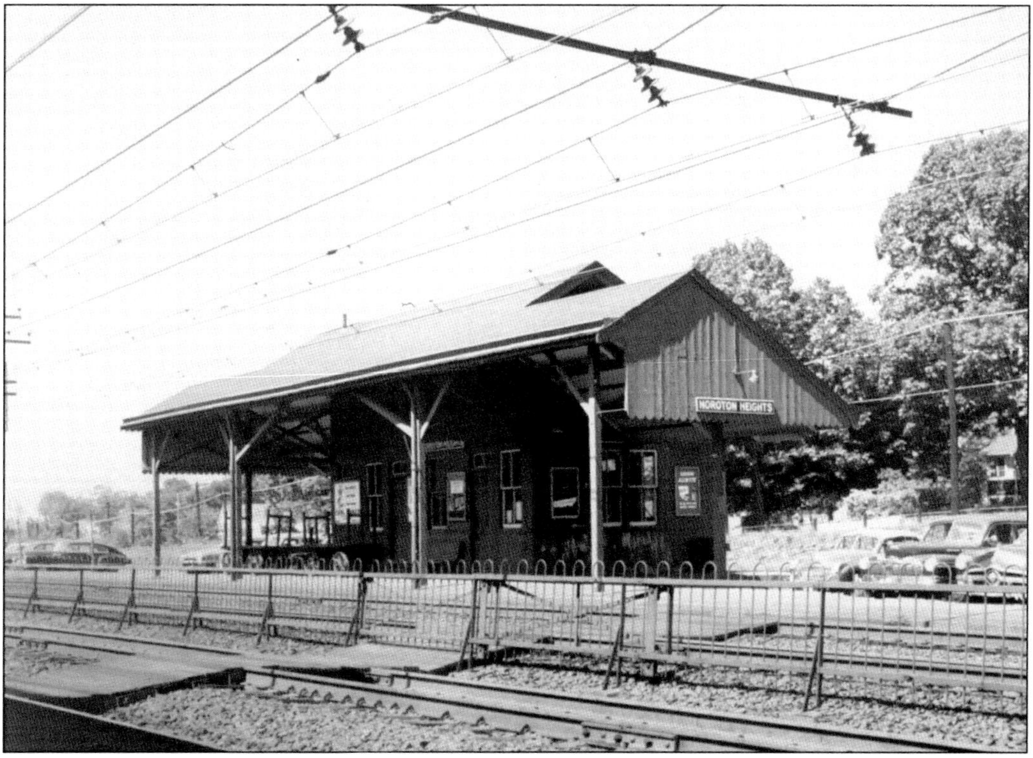

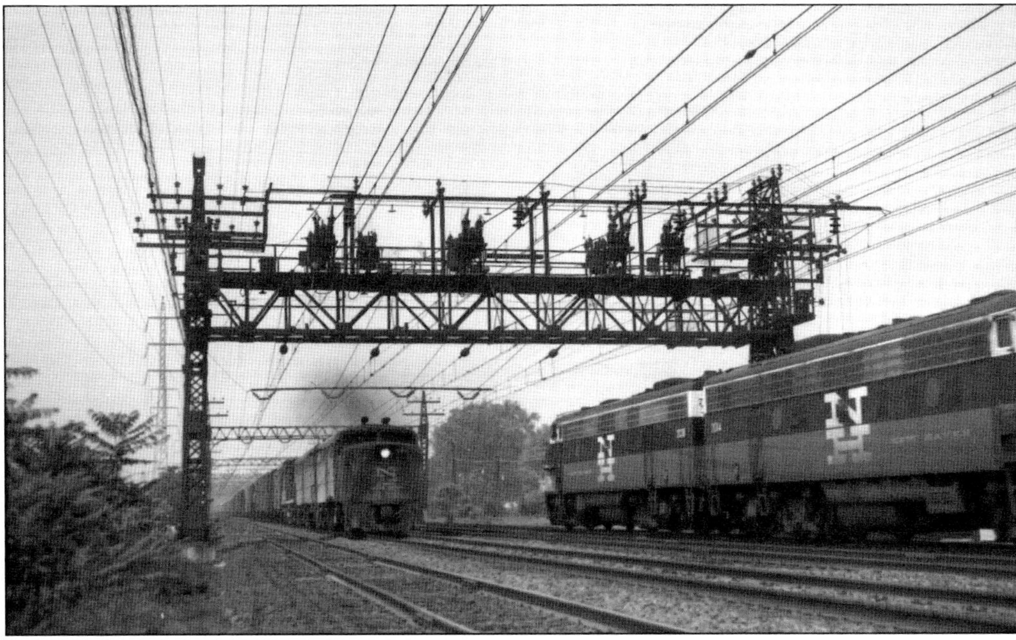

Historian Jack Swanberg took these two photographs. The one above, on June 19, 1961, shows a New Haven Railroad diesel train, at the left, meeting a passenger train with dual-powered FL-9 locomotives. The one below, on September 18, 1986, provides a view from the locomotive cab of an Amtrak train heading for New York and Washington, D.C. The push-pull train at the right is heading away from the camera toward Danbury. The electrical network overhead is a catenary anchor bridge in Darien. (Courtesy J.W. Swanberg collection.)

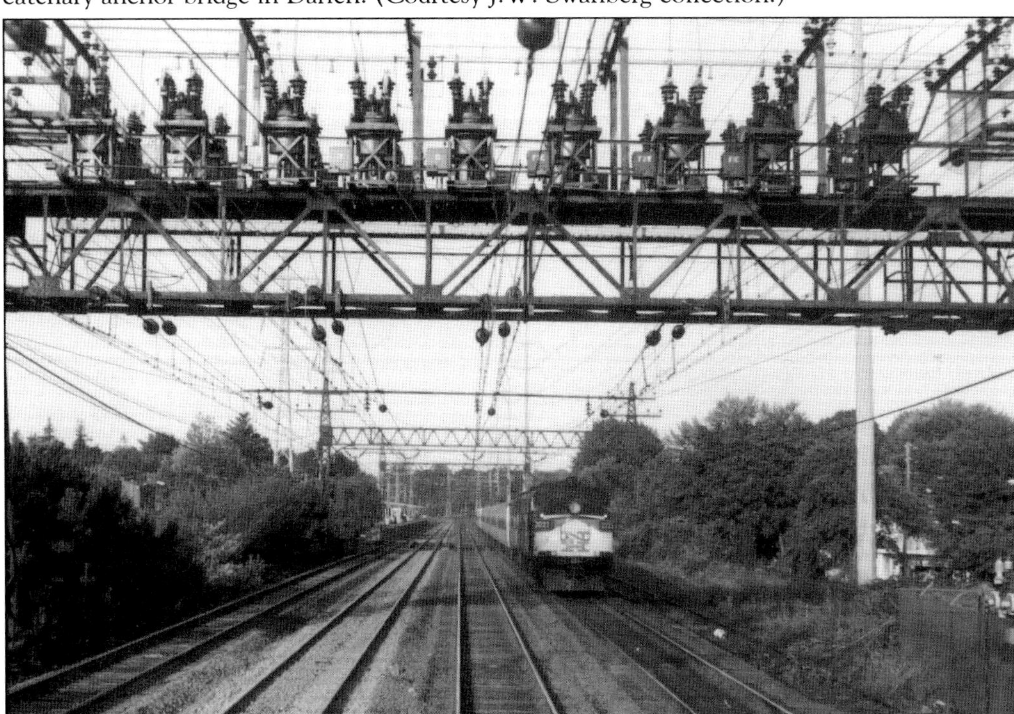

Five

South Norwalk Station

"Let's get one thing straight," traveler James G. Clark emphasized. "There is South Norwalk, there is East Norwalk and there is a place called Rowayton, all located in the city of Norwalk." There is no Norwalk stop on Metro-North. To ask for a ticket to Norwalk is to show geographic unfamiliarity.

The destination of most travelers is South Norwalk, where you can catch the branch train to western Connecticut towns such as Redding, Bethel, and Danbury. In the 1970s, South Norwalk was slowly slipping into urban blight. Then, developers transformed a strip of the neighborhood into SoNo, a trendy mix of restaurants, bars, and boutiques on Washington Street, between South Main Street and Water Street, that runs along the Norwalk River, anchored by the Maritime Center at Norwalk—one of the state's largest tourist attractions. One of the main attractions at the Maritime Center is the IMAX Theater, a giant three-dimensional screen that shows movies and documentaries from life in the Antarctic to the life of the Rolling Stones.

If there is one summer festival to attend, it must be the Norwalk Oyster Festival, a spectacular three-day affair held the first weekend after Labor Day. It is filled with boat parades, fireworks, huge arts-and-crafts shows, and enough food to feed the sharks in the 110,000-gallon Norwalk Aquarium. Buses take you directly from the train station to the festival at Veteran's Park, just over the bridge in East Norwalk, or you can walk through SoNo, which is about two blocks from the train station. The annual SoNo Arts Celebration, held the first weekend of August, is another major event. Jugglers and street artists take over Washington Street from morning to late at night.

The other major yearly event in Norwalk is the Round Hill Scottish Games, held on the first Saturday of July. According to Clark, a Scotsman himself, "Men are not afraid to wear skirts, and women wear sensible shoes." All Scotsmen and Scotswomen worth their brogue show up, Clark notes. Pipe band members from up and down the East Coast play the bagpipes all day long. During the event there are Scottish crafts, folk singers, history lessons on Scotland, and even meat pies. The amateur games are of particular interest. These are what Scots consider fun, like tossing a 25-pound bag over a high bar using a pitchfork and the hernia-producing tossing of the caber, which is something like trying to flip a telephone pole. Not bad for a country that gave us golf. All of these events take place at Cranberry Park in the north end of Norwalk. Buses take you to the park from the Perkin Elmer plant, on Route 7 near the Norwalk-Wilton town line.

Across the street from East Norwalk Station are several discount outlets that sell men's clothing, linens, china, and other goods, if you tire of the stylish wares in SoNo. You can also walk to the Oyster Festival from the station.

As for Rowayton, Clark reminds us that there is a private guard at the station during the week to make sure the BMW or Mercedes does not disappear while the owner is in the city making the big decision. So, try not to look too suspicious when getting off the train.

Boats, boats, and more boats are the topic of the day in Rowayton. If you do not have one, get one or say it is still down in St. Croix. Otherwise, you are going to be very left out at cocktail parties.

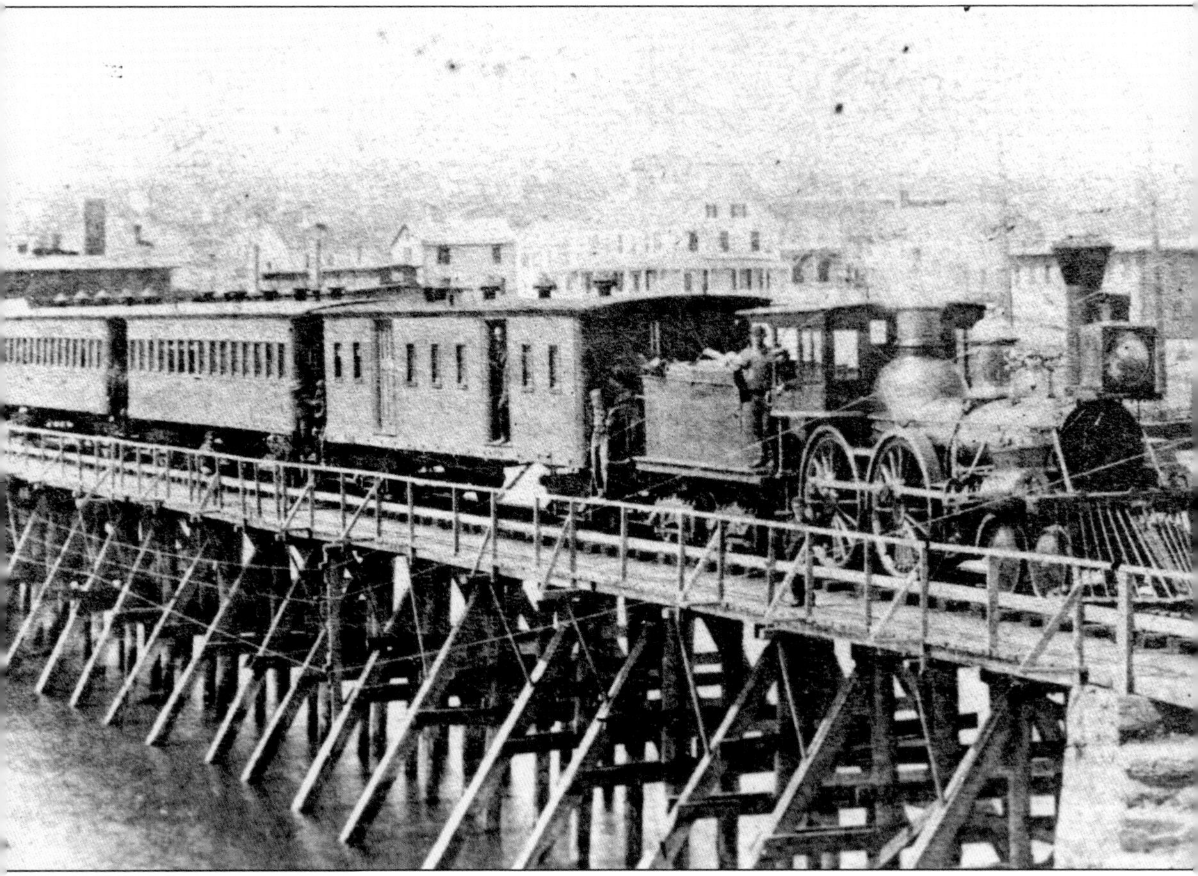

As photographs of the New York & New Haven Railroad go, this *c.* 1850s image of a steamer on the Norwalk Bridge is about as early as it gets. Just about everything shown is wood: the bridge, the cars, and the fuel to feed the steel steamer engine. Note the conductor standing by the woodpile. (Courtesy J.W. Swanberg collection.)

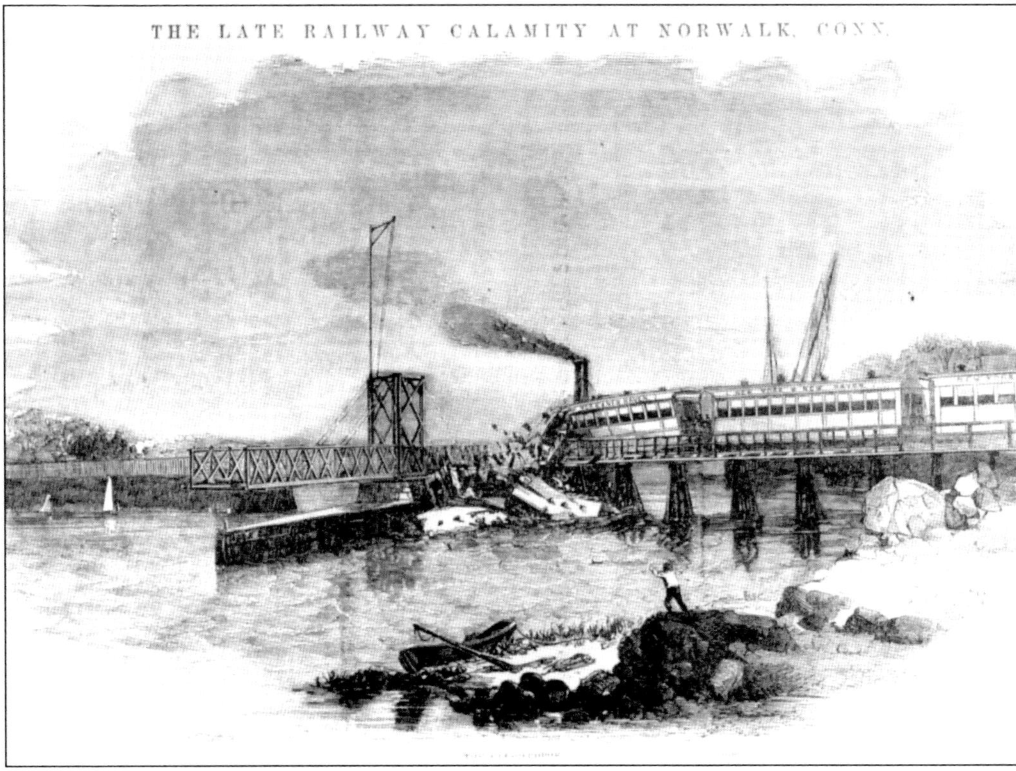

Shown here is an illustration of the most devastating train wreck in the history of the New York & New Haven Railroad. On May 6, 1853, the train sailed through a bridge signal, killing 46 people. (Courtesy J.W. Swanberg collection.)

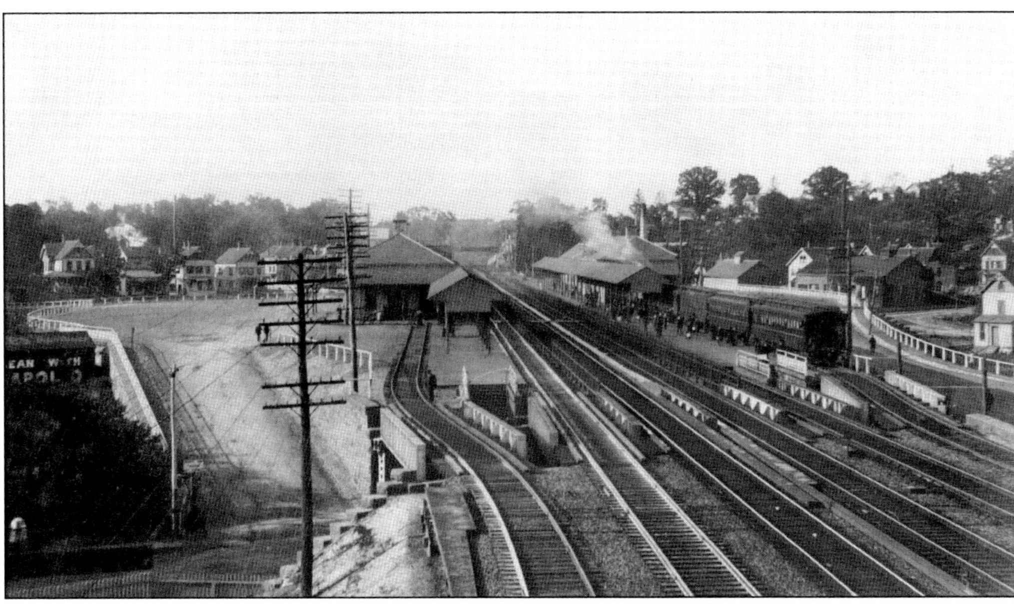

This is South Norwalk Station *c.* 1900, before electrification and shortly after the installation of the four-tracking system. (Courtesy J.W. Swanberg collection.)

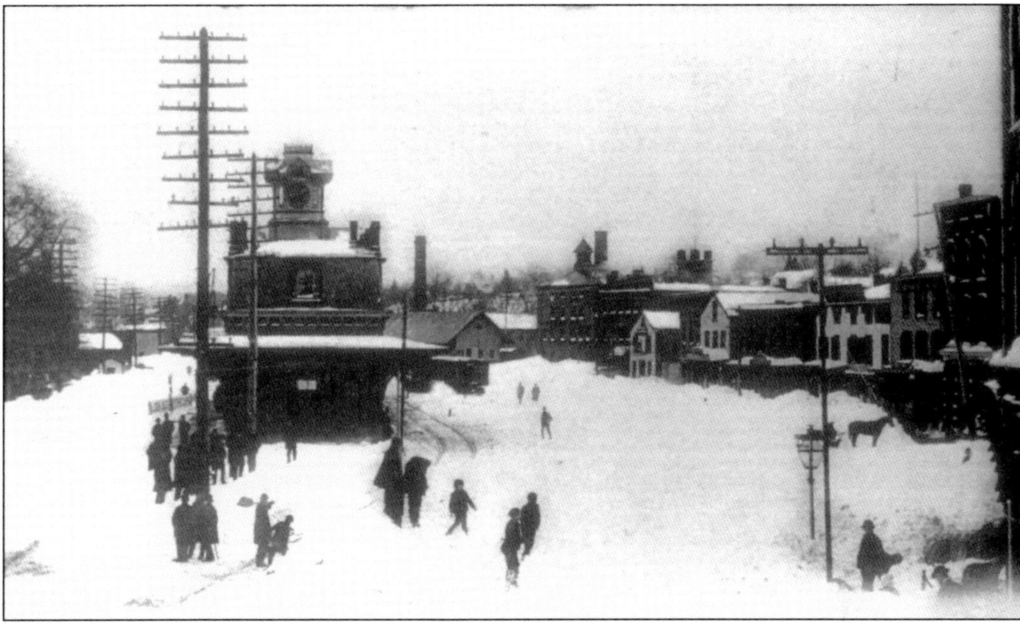

The Blizzard of 1888 buried South Norwalk Station in drifts of snow up to 14 feet high. The shovel brigades tried to clear the tracks, but many trains got trapped in the drifts. The storm, which began on March 12, dumped almost two feet of snow. Street lamps and electric lights all went black. (Courtesy Thomas J. Dodd Research Center, University of Connecticut.)

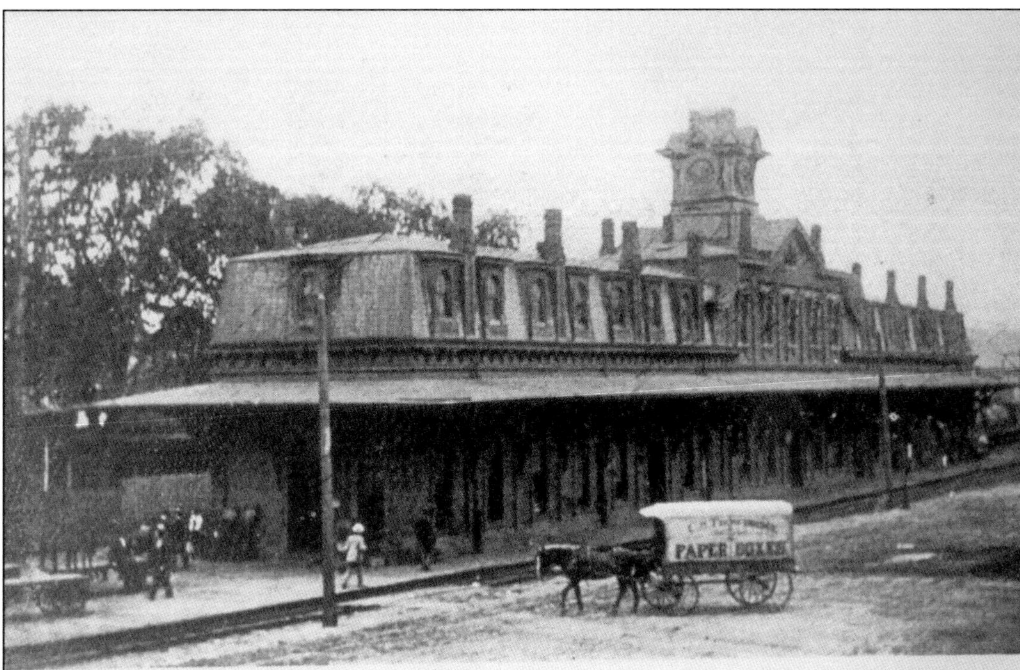

Things in South Norwalk are back to normal. A horse and wagon approaches the front of the station building *c.* 1890. (Courtesy Thomas J. Dodd Research Center, University of Connecticut.)

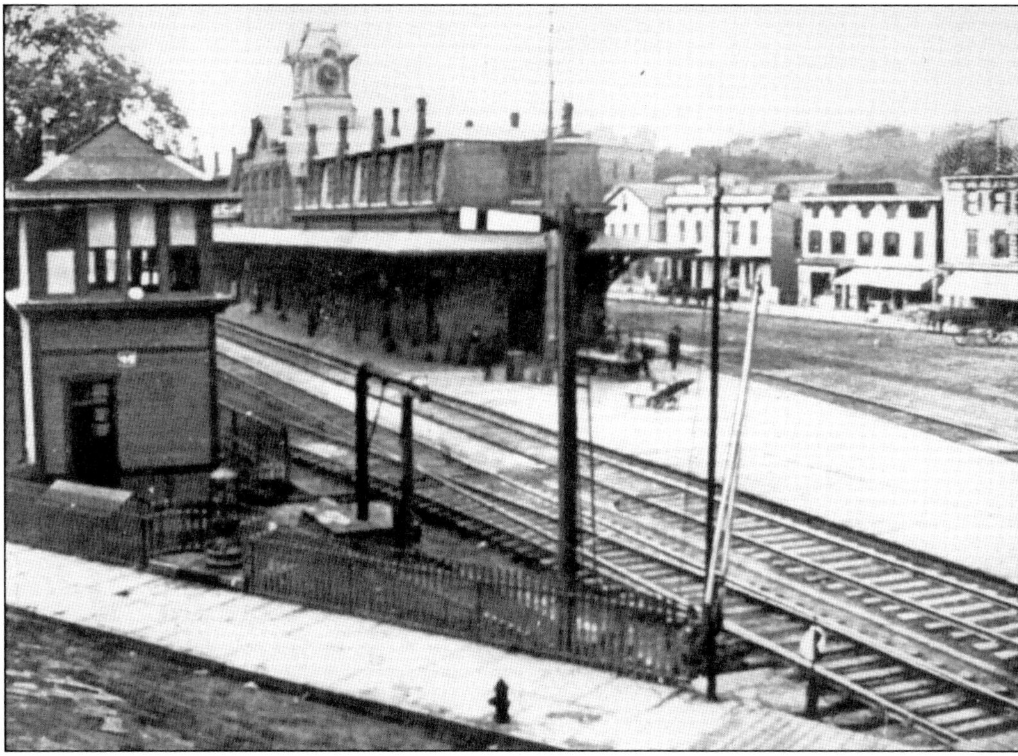

Another view of the old South Norwalk Station shows a horse-and-carriage town growing around the train station. (Courtesy Thomas J. Dodd Research Center, University of Connecticut.)

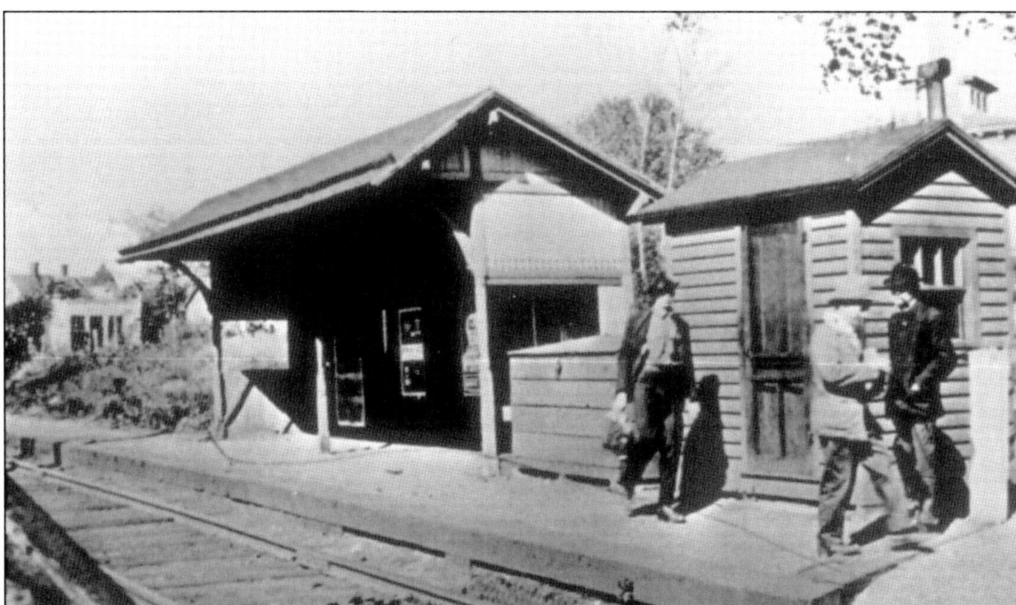

Three men stand on a platform in front of a woodshed near South Norwalk Station *c.* 1910. (Courtesy Thomas J. Dodd Research Center, University of Connecticut.)

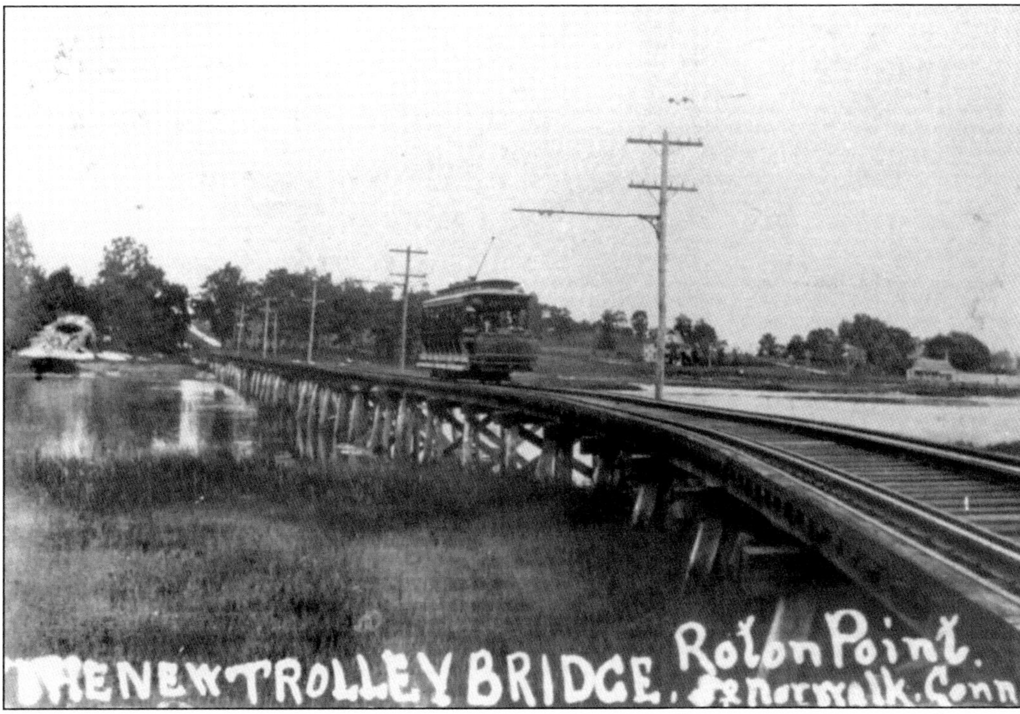

A trolley crosses a bridge over Roton Point in South Norwalk *c.* 1910. (Courtesy Thomas J. Dodd Research Center, University of Connecticut.)

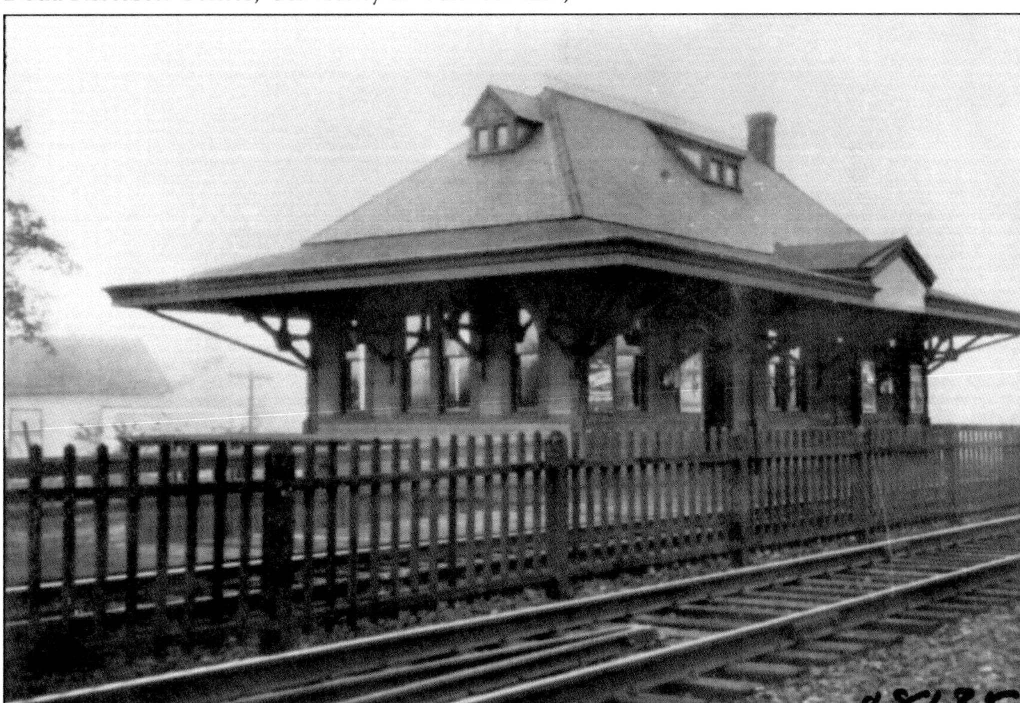

East Norwalk Station and the tracks are divided by a fence *c.* 1900. (Courtesy Thomas J. Dodd Research Center, University of Connecticut.)

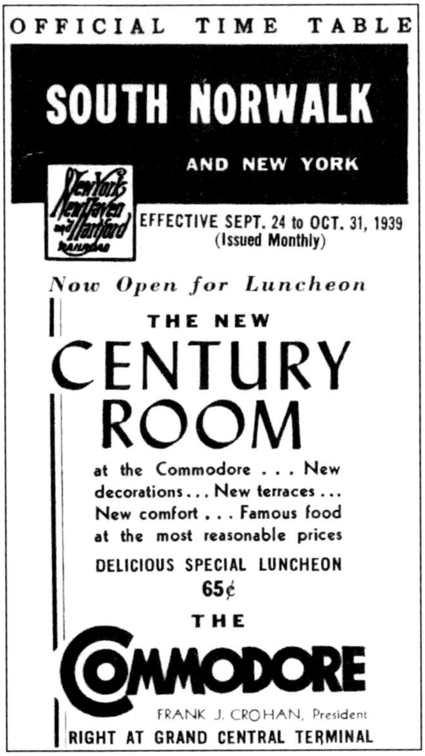

Boy, oh boy, oh boy. For 65¢ in 1939, you could have a good meal at the Century Room, right in Grand Central Station. These days, terminal restaurants charge you that much just to walk in and inhale deeply. (Courtesy Marc Frattasio collection.)

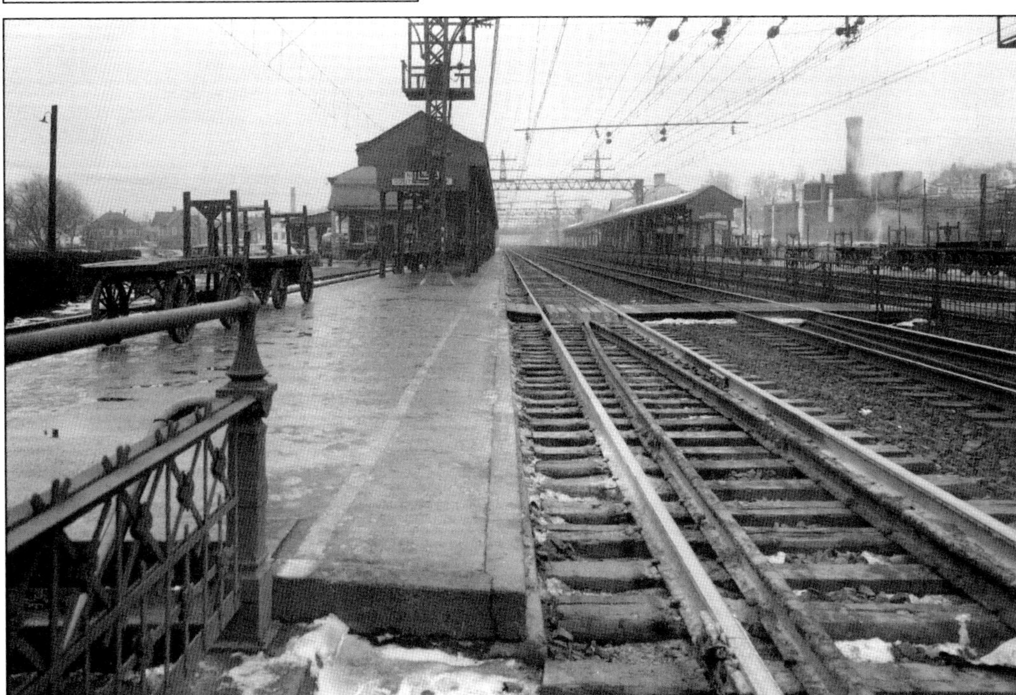

Shown is South Norwalk after electrification *c.* 1940, featuring baggage carts lined up on both platforms. (Courtesy J.W. Swanberg collection.)

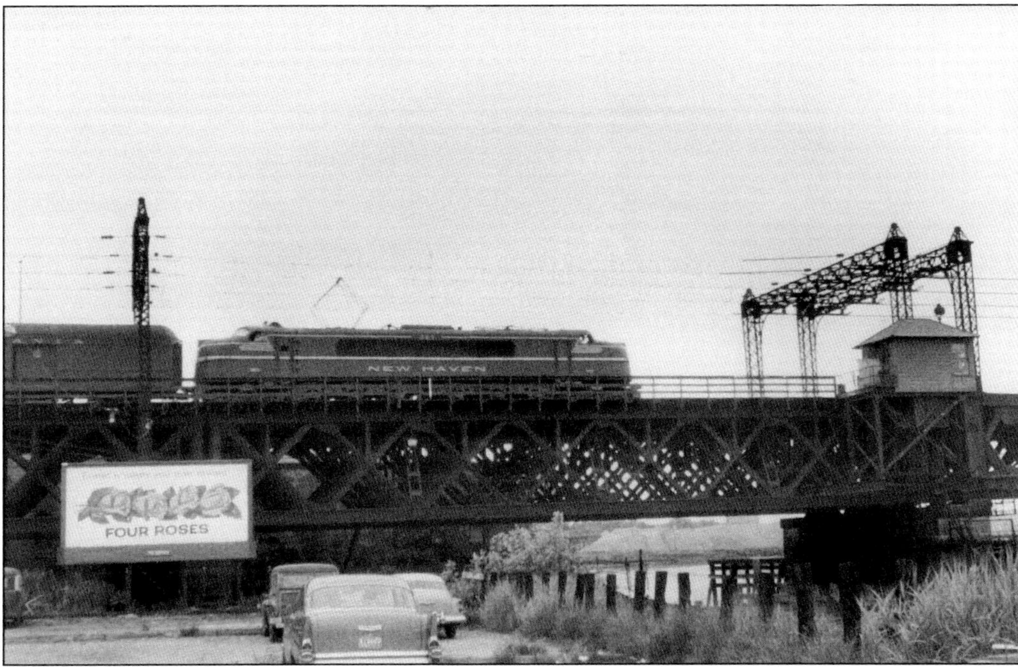

In the summer of 1957, a New Haven Railroad electric locomotive leads a passenger train through Norwalk, headed for Boston. (Courtesy J.W. Swanberg collection.)

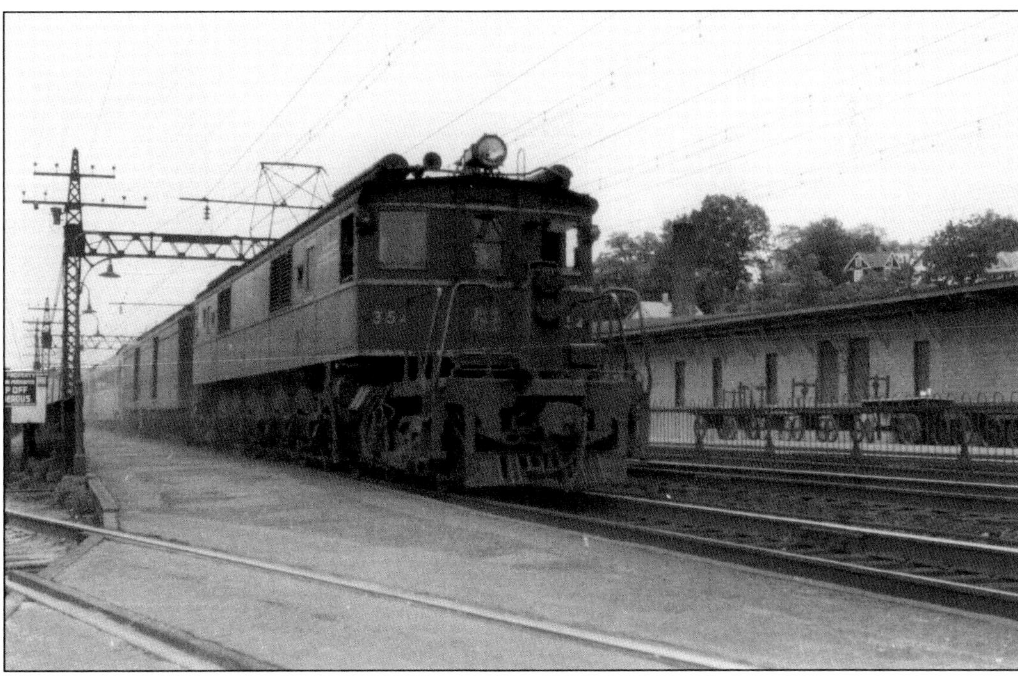

Another New Haven Railroad locomotive heads out of South Norwalk for New Haven. (Courtesy J.W. Swanberg collection.)

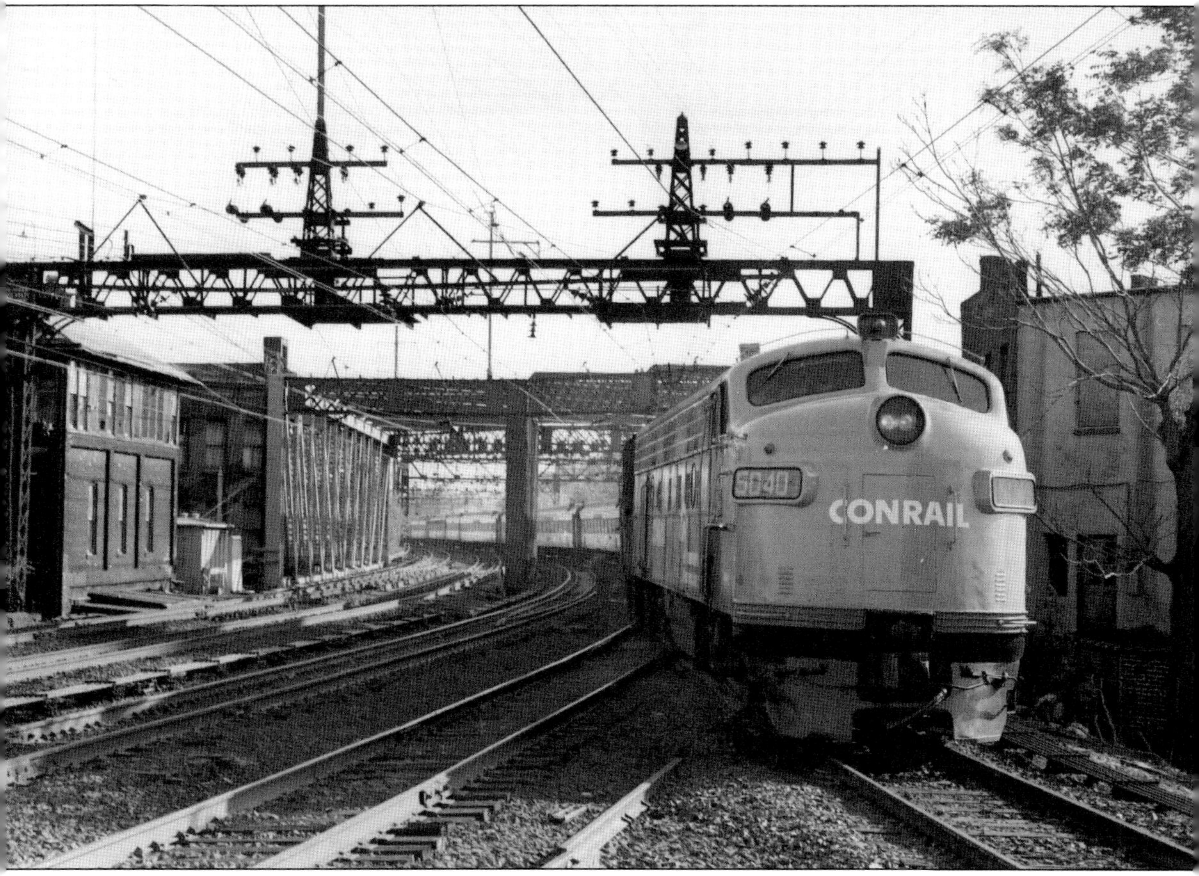

On June 9, 1978, historian Jack Swanberg captured a Conrail dual-powered locomotive diverging from South Norwalk toward Danbury. Conrail ran passenger service from 1976 to 1983, before Metro-North assumed control. (Courtesy J.W. Swanberg collection.)

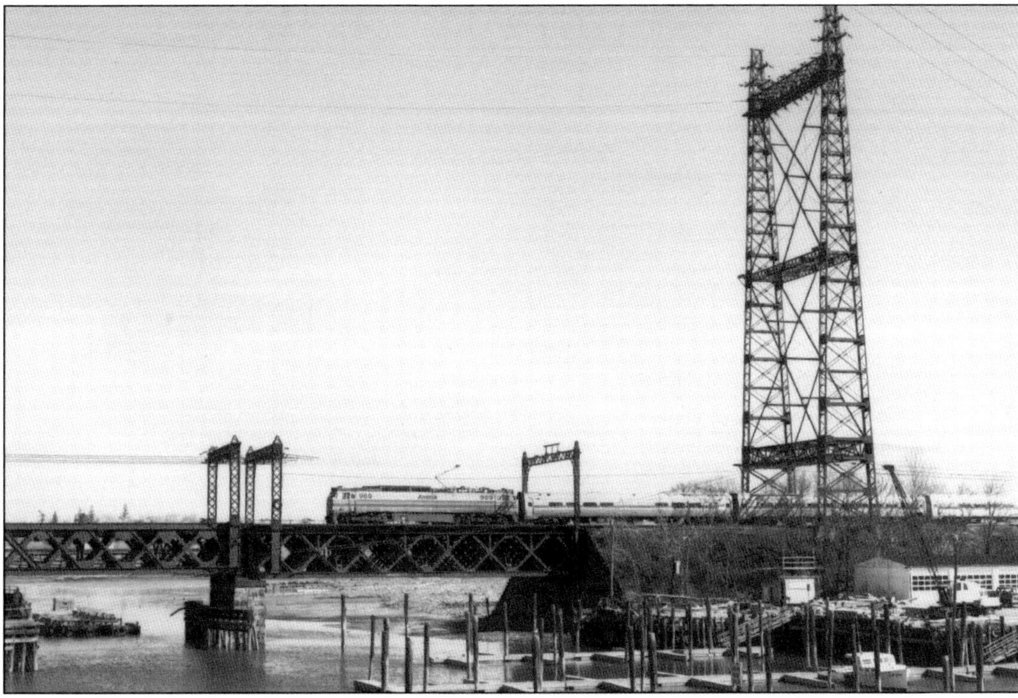

Another Swanberg photograph shows an Amtrak electric locomotive pulling a passenger train in Norwalk. Note the towers carrying high-tension wires over the drawbridge. (Courtesy J.W. Swanberg collection.)

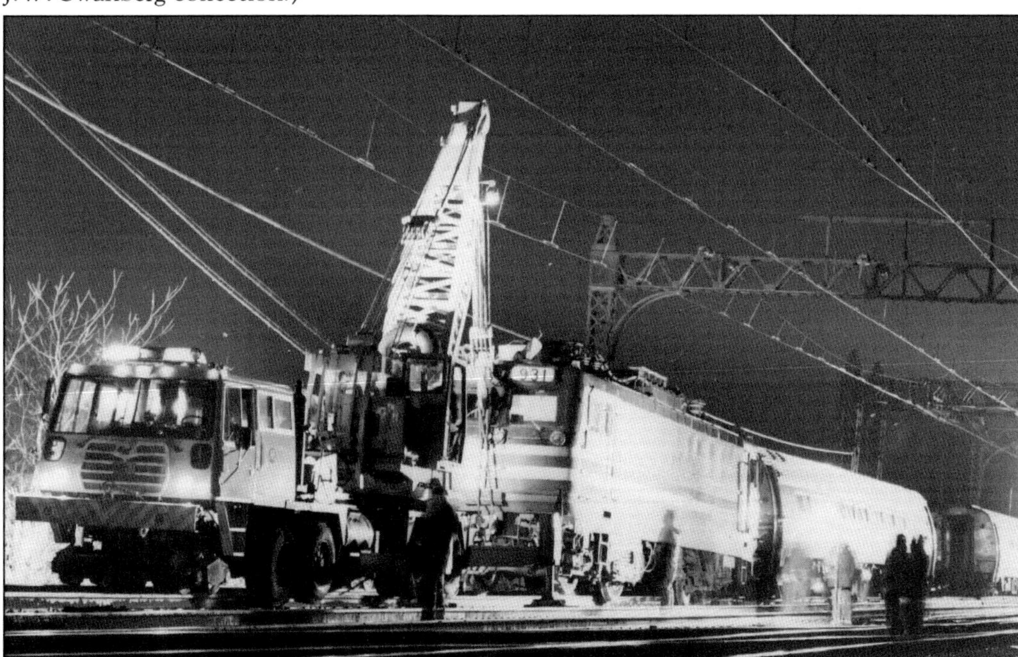

So, what happens when an Amtrak electric locomotive derails? A Metro-North crane rerails one in 1984. This Amtrak 931 locomotive was backed up by the five-car *Metroliner*. (Courtesy J.W. Swanberg collection.)

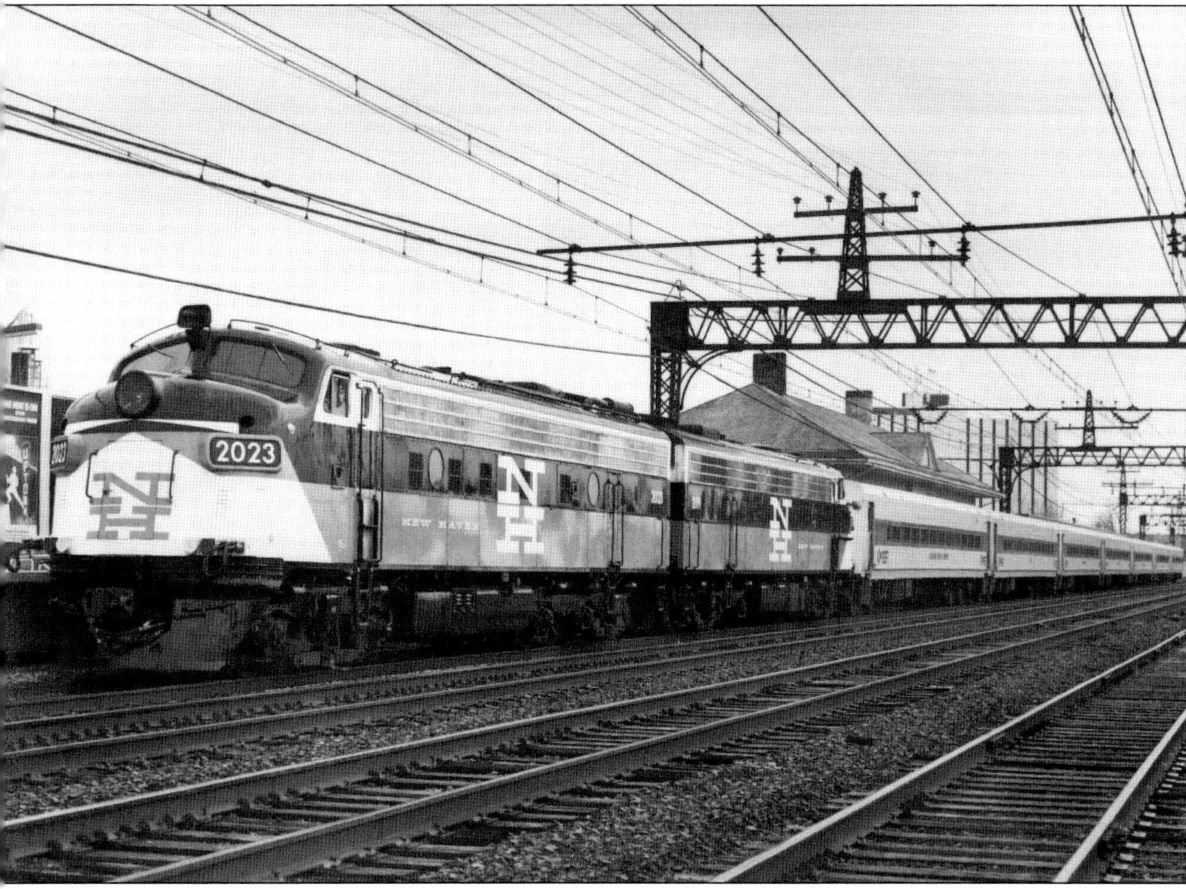

These FL-9 dual-powered New Haven Railroad locomotives did not end up on the scrap pile. They were rebuilt, as shown in 1986, for a demonstration on the Metro-North Danbury branch heading through South Norwalk. (Courtesy J.W. Swanberg collection.)

Six

Westport-Saugatuck Station

Westport is the tony stop along the New Haven Line. In fact, there might be enough Tony Awards in this town to fill the Westport Playhouse. It is home to Paul Newman and Joanne Woodward and Phil Donohue and Marlo Thomas. Westport is where Michael Bolton styles his angelic voice and where Martha Stewart showed us how to be fashionable, although she recently opted for a New York state of mind. Westport continues the artsy spirit from its days as a magnet for New York entertainers seeking a country getaway.

The main station is actually located in Saugatuck (there is the limited-stop Green's Farms Station also in Westport), a breezy hamlet along the shores of the Saugatuck River that is loaded with restaurants, shops, boutiques, and the centerpiece for summer festivals, Luciano Park. Every summer, tens of thousands gather at the park for Festival Italiano, sponsored by the Westport Sons of Italy. The park is a short walk from the train station. Try the pizza fritto, sausage and peppers and *porchetta*. Do not worry about missing a ride home. The trains run all night.

Westport features miles and miles of commercialization along the Post Road but offers the contrasting quaintness of shopping on Main Street with a variety of upscale stores, restaurants, and food for the common people. Westport preserves its past with multiple exhibits at its active historical society, a short distance from the Main Street shopping district. The town continues to draw artists and tourists to its galleries, theaters, shops, and beaches, including Sherwood Island State Park. There are magnificent waterfront mansions, country Colonials, and crews on the river—not a bad place to be.

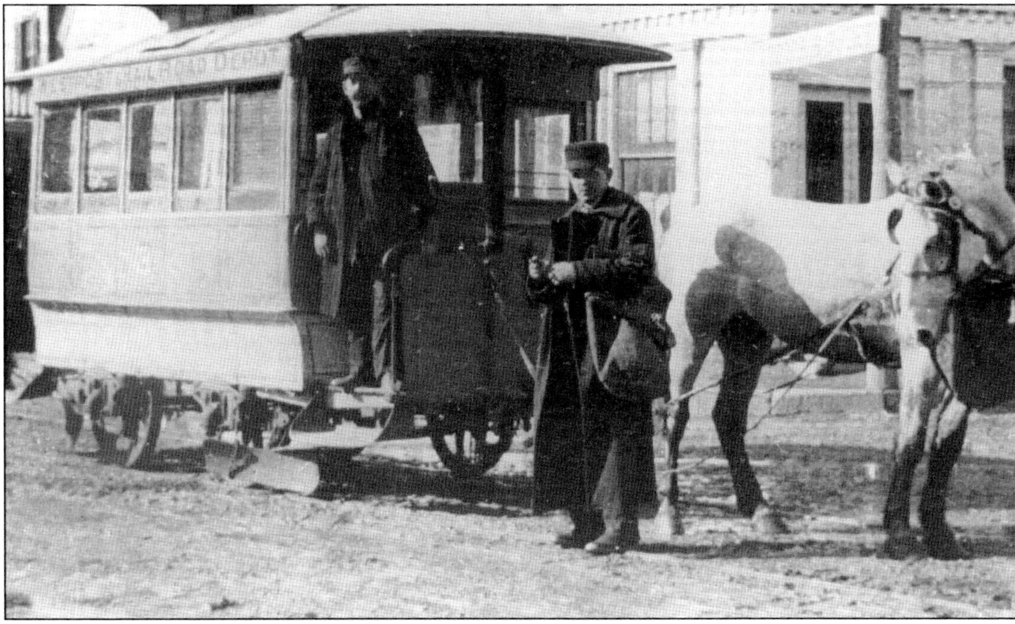

So, for all you Westport shopping lovers who want to know what the corner of Main Street and the Post Road (the former State Street) was like in 1894, here it is, courtesy of the horse-drawn Westport Railroad Depot taxi. The building behind the taxi housed a place for "boots and shoes." Judging from the dirt road, Westporters' boots needed lots of spit and polish. (Courtesy Westport Historical Society.)

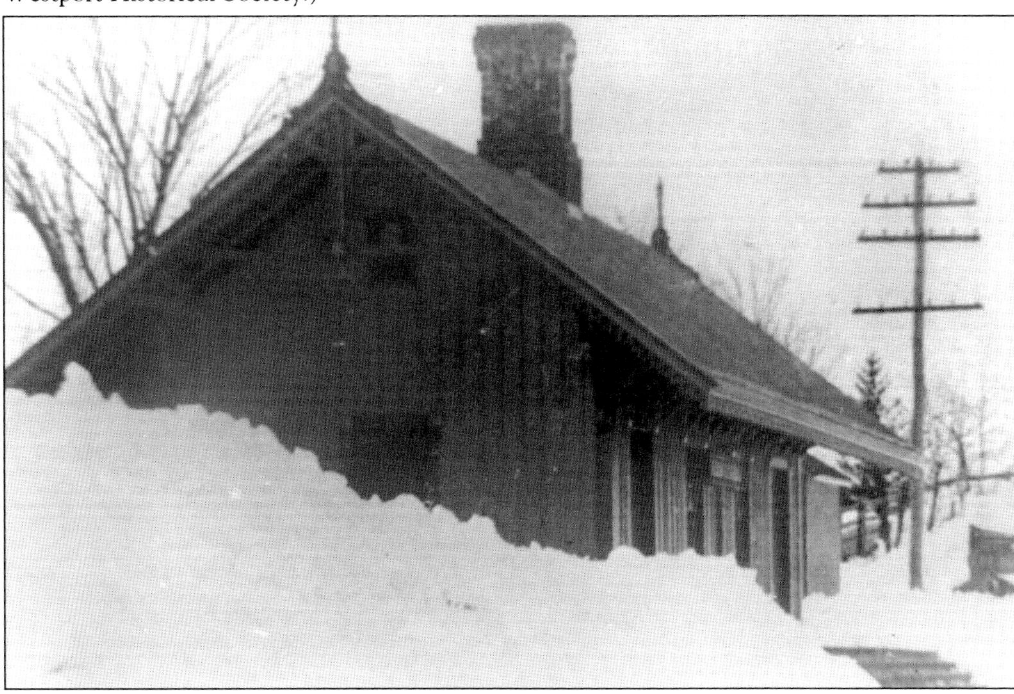

The Blizzard of 1888 discriminated against no train station along the New Haven Line, including the little Green's Farms depot, the stop before the main Westport station in Saugatuck. (Courtesy Westport Historical Society.)

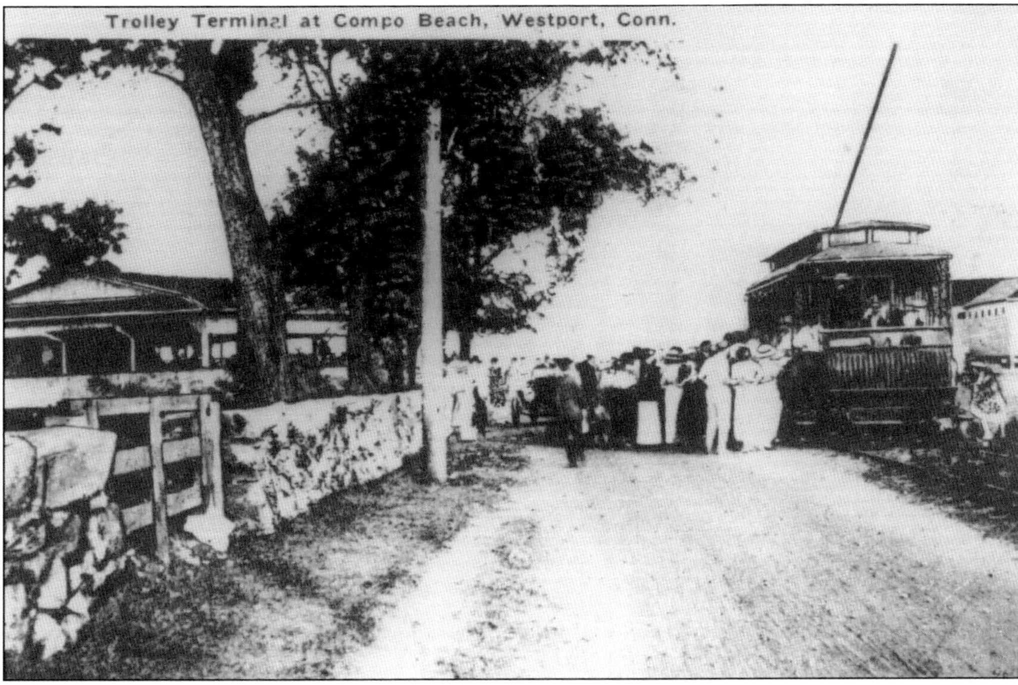

Westport's beaches, country roads, and rural character attracted New York's theatrical gentry for weekend excursions and then permanent residence. Shown here is the Westport trolley terminal at Compo Beach *c.* 1910. (Courtesy Westport Historical Society.)

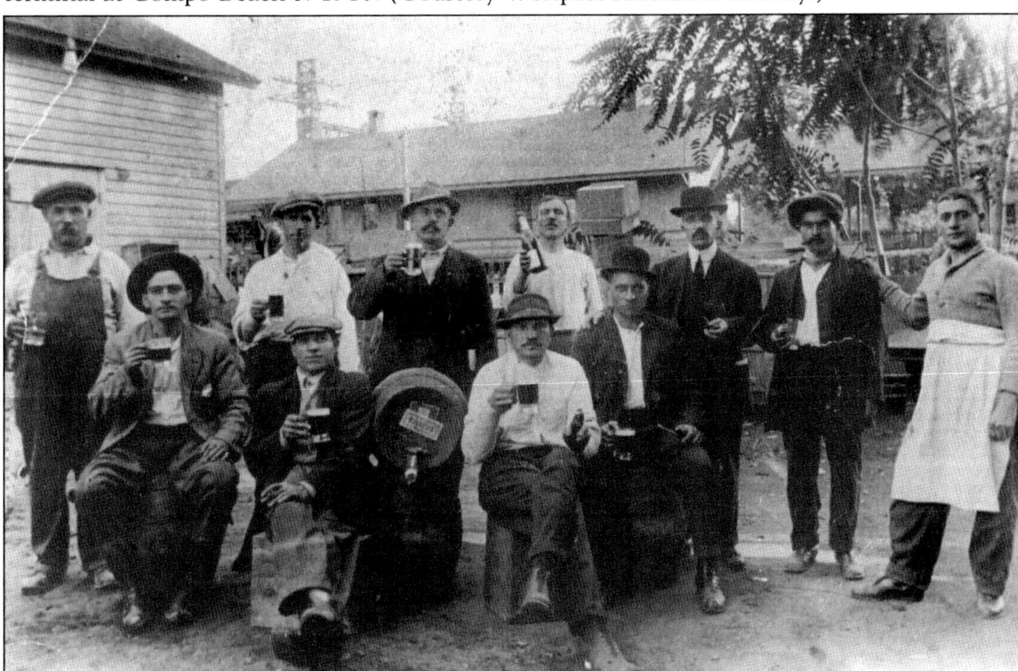

A hot summer day and a refreshing mugful satisfy this crowd in Saugatuck, with Westport Station in the background. The date of this photograph is likely *c.* 1915, with Prohibition looming. Do you think Prohibition put a damper on this group? (Courtesy Westport Historical Society.)

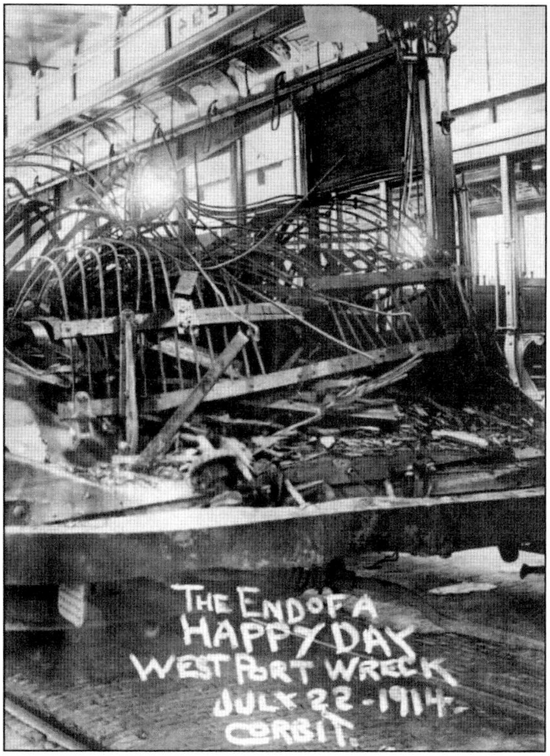

The "end of a happy day" shows this Westport trolley smashed to pieces on July 22, 1914. Much of the exciting action of this era was captured by the legendary Bridgeport-based photographer Lewis Corbit. (Courtesy Westport Historical Society.)

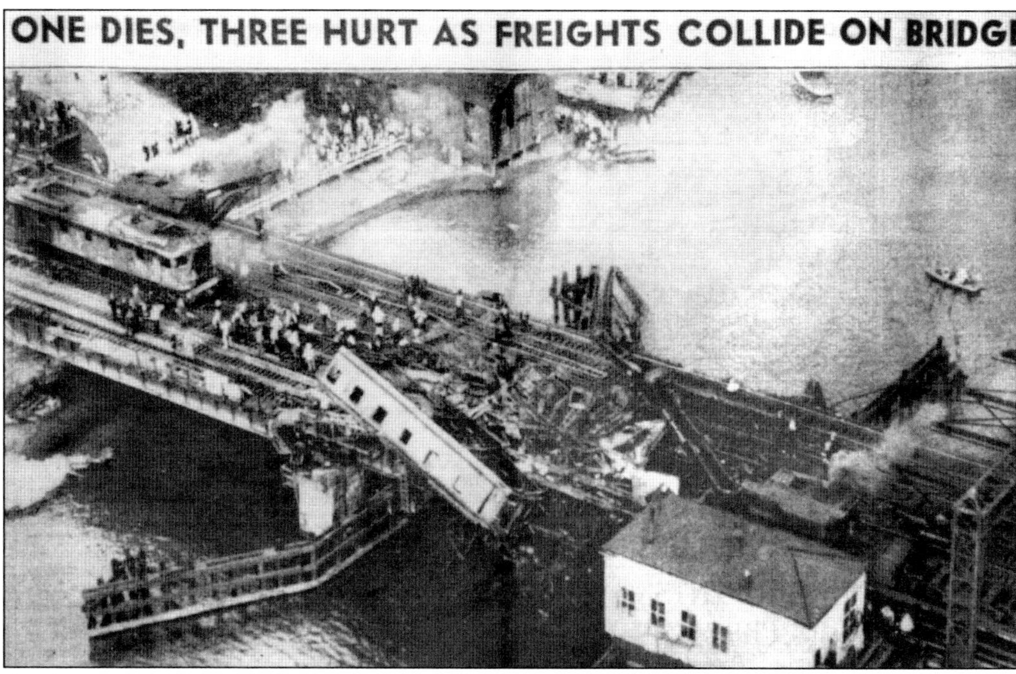

On September 27, 1935, freighters collide on the Saugatuck Bridge. Press accounts said it was a miracle that only one person died. This overhead view shows dozens of rail and rescue workers on the scene, with spectators at top in the distance along the Saugatuck River. (Courtesy J.W. Swanberg collection.)

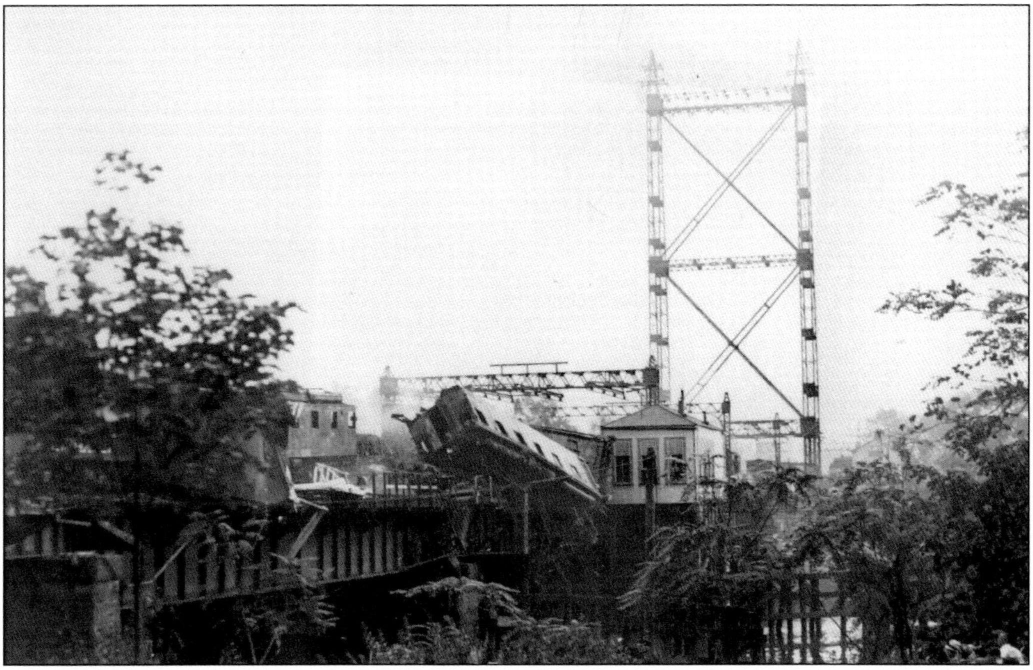

Two more views of the September 27, 1935 wreck show one car perched precariously over the bridge, with the tower carrying high-tension wires in the background. A crane was employed to keep the car from falling into the river. (Courtesy J.W. Swanberg collection.)

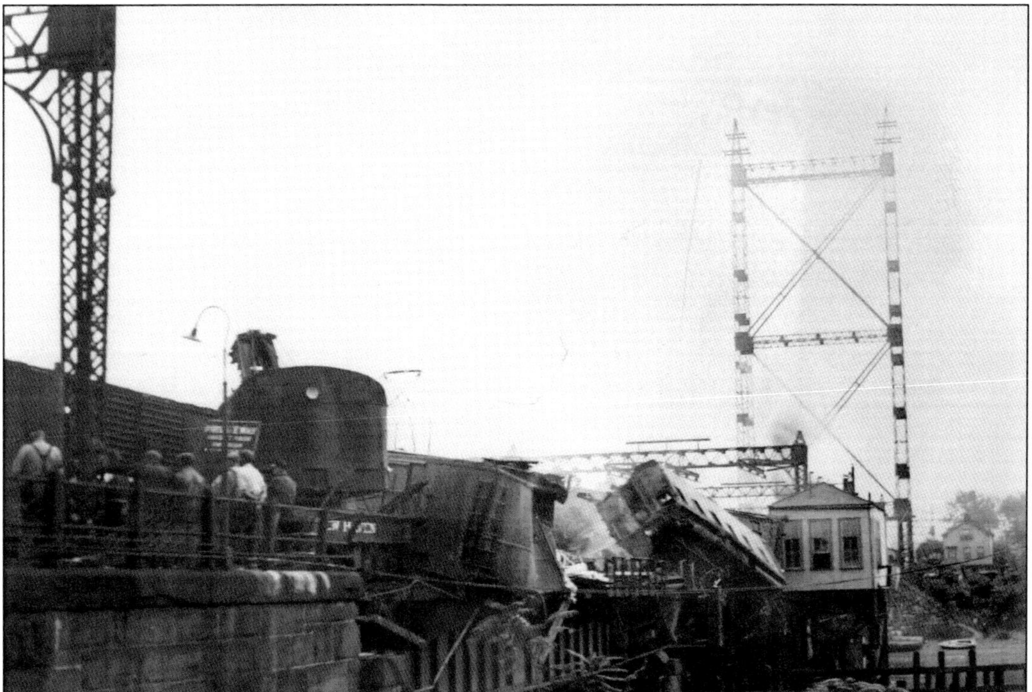

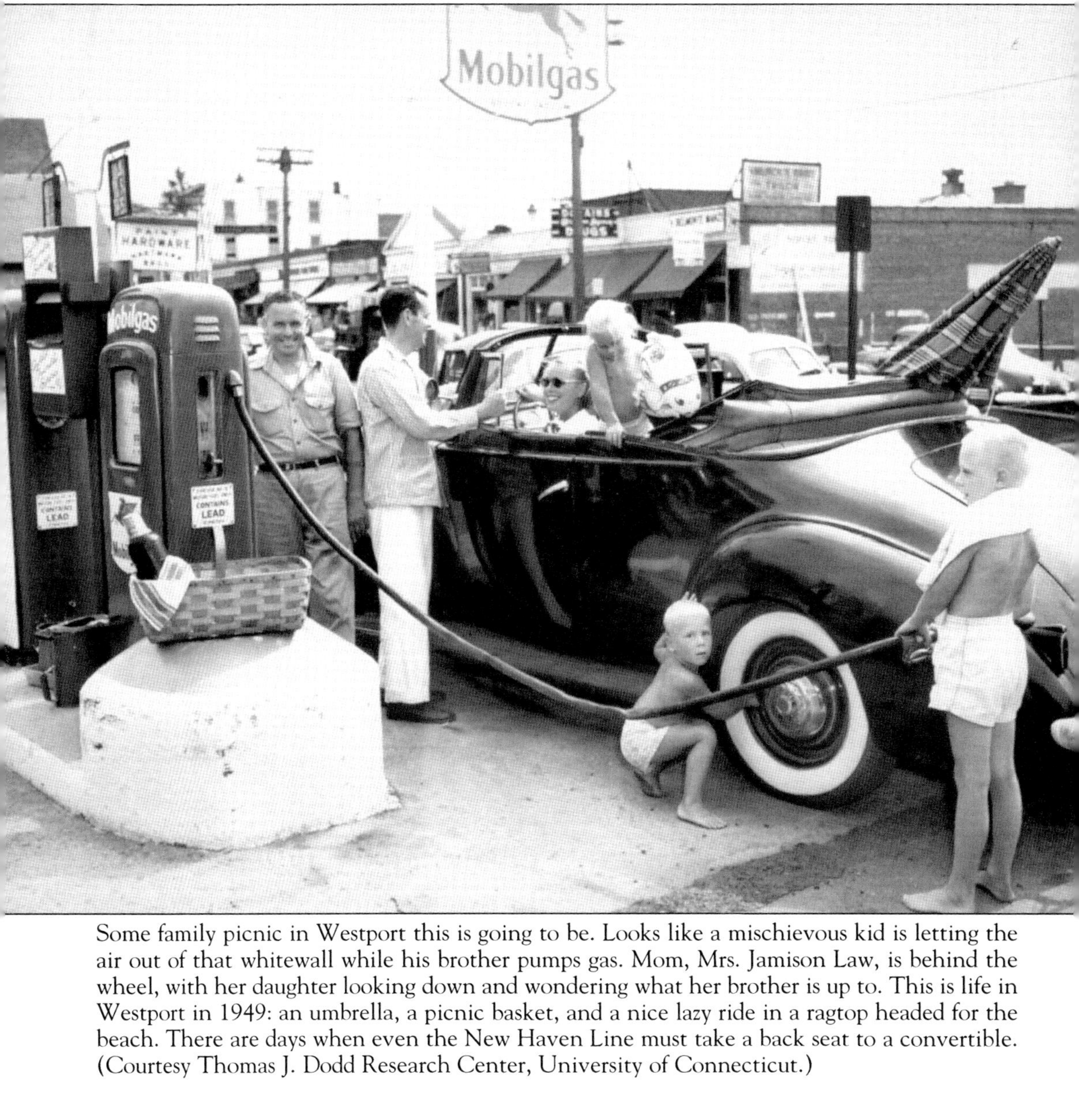

Some family picnic in Westport this is going to be. Looks like a mischievous kid is letting the air out of that whitewall while his brother pumps gas. Mom, Mrs. Jamison Law, is behind the wheel, with her daughter looking down and wondering what her brother is up to. This is life in Westport in 1949: an umbrella, a picnic basket, and a nice lazy ride in a ragtop headed for the beach. There are days when even the New Haven Line must take a back seat to a convertible. (Courtesy Thomas J. Dodd Research Center, University of Connecticut.)

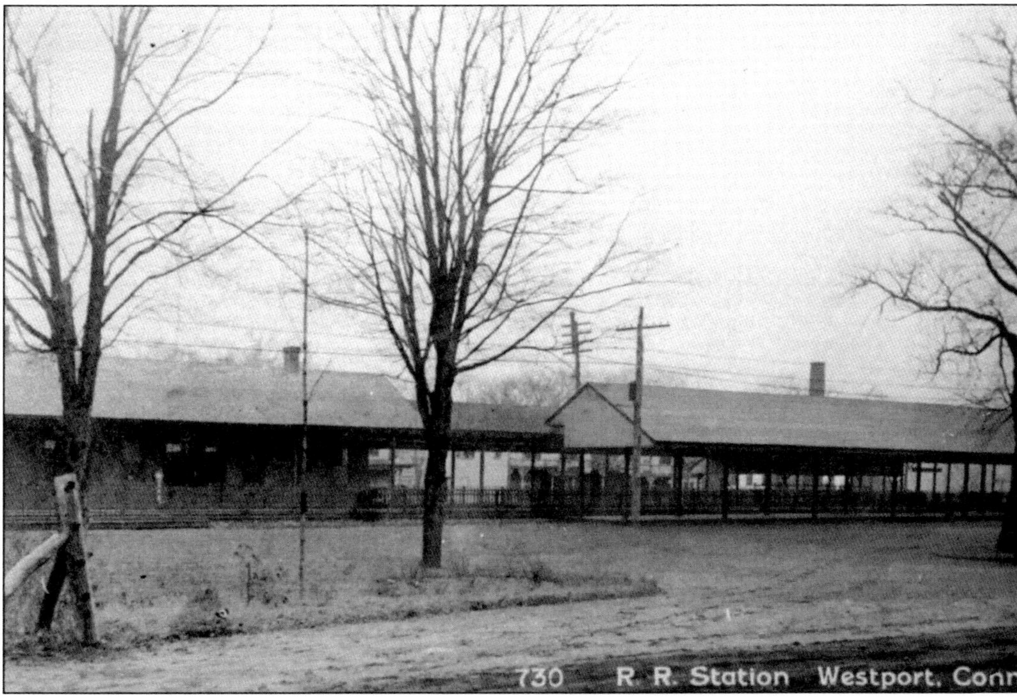

This *c.* 1940 scene shows Westport Station, with trees, a dirt road in front of the buildings, and a covered platform. (Courtesy Thomas J. Dodd Research Center, University of Connecticut.)

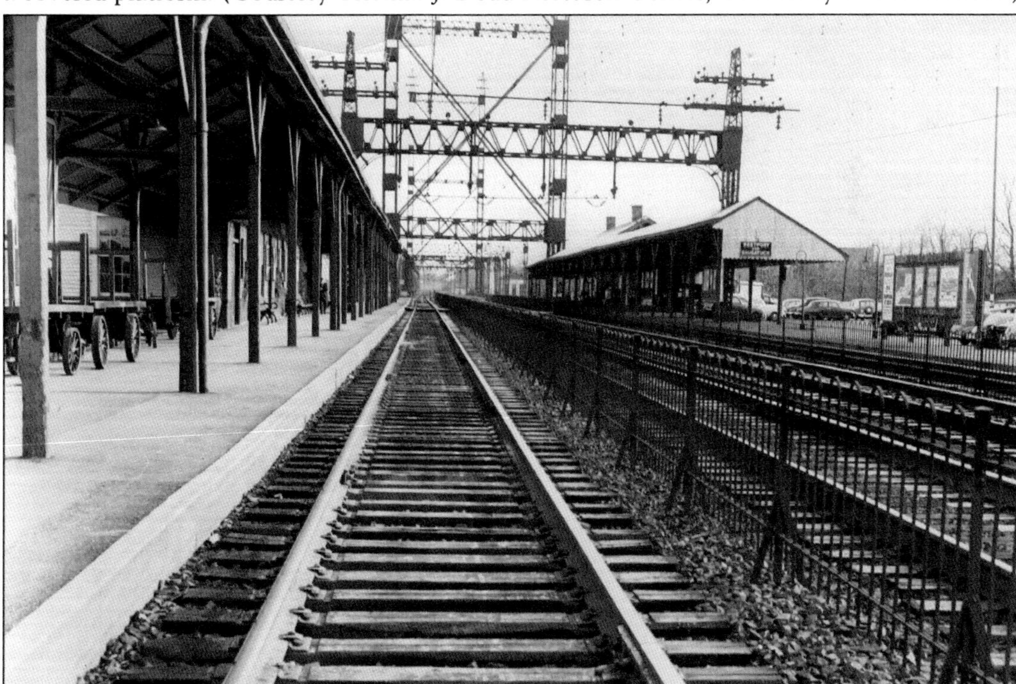

A 1954 view looks down the throat of the rails under the towering electrified tracks at Westport Station in 1954. Note the baggage carts on the platform at the left. (Courtesy J.W. Swanberg collection.)

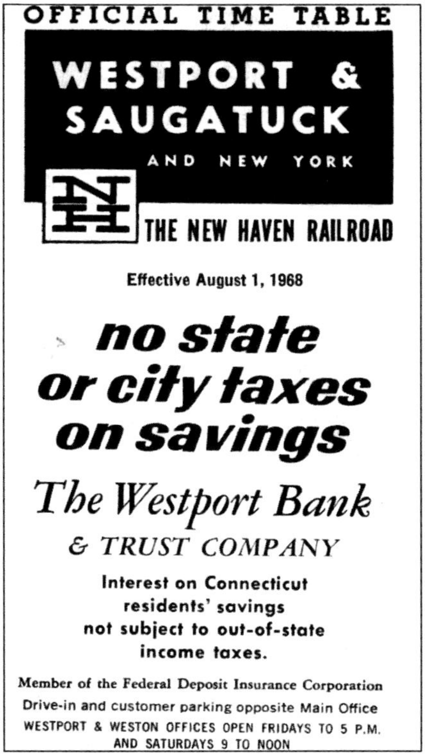

This interesting bank advertisement from the Westport & Saugatuck official timetable of August 1968, geared to commuters, states that there are "no state or city taxes on savings." Then, the small print reads, "Interest on Connecticut residents' savings not subject to out-of-state income taxes." (Courtesy Mark Frattasio collection.)

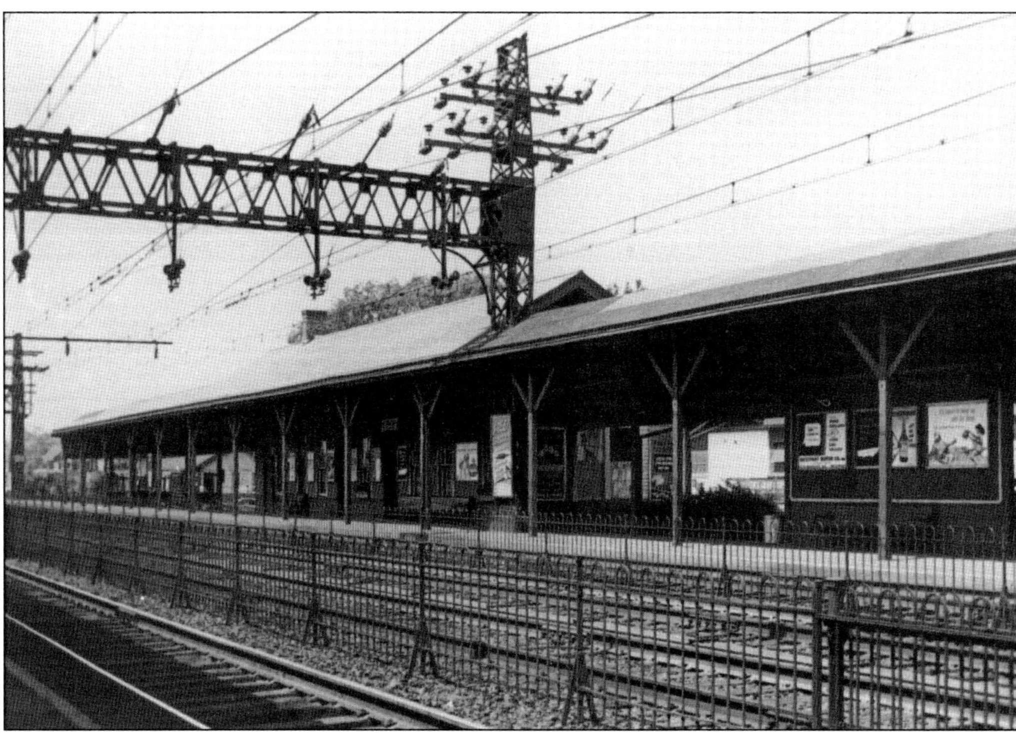

This 1954 view of the station shows an advertisement-filled ticket office in the background. (Courtesy Westport Historical Society.)

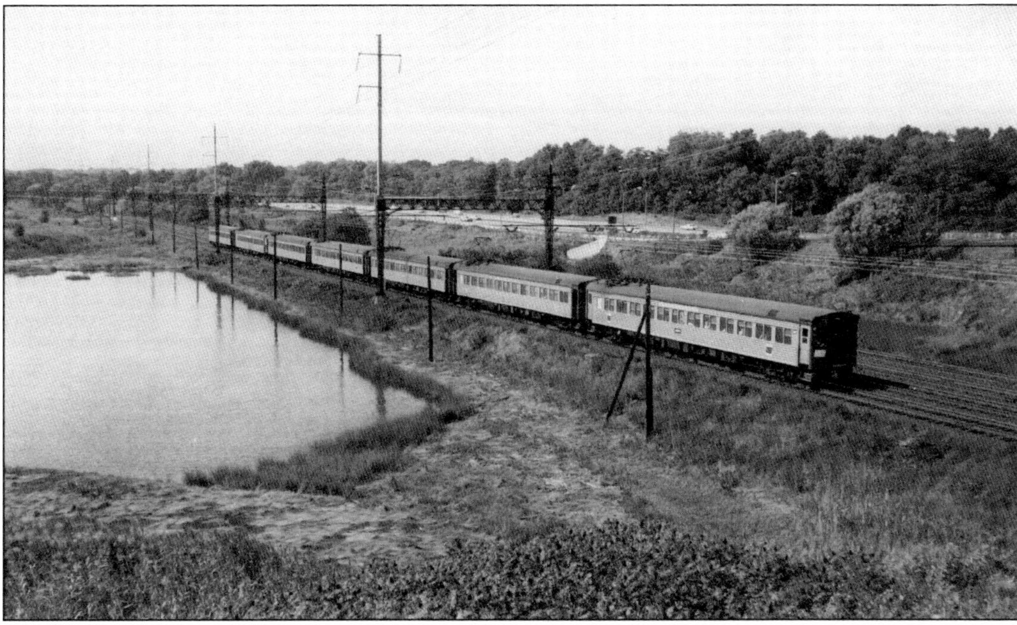

On September 19, 1970, rail historian Jack Swanberg took this photograph of Penn Central commuter cars traveling eastbound along Sherwood Island in Westport. (Courtesy J.W. Swanberg collection.)

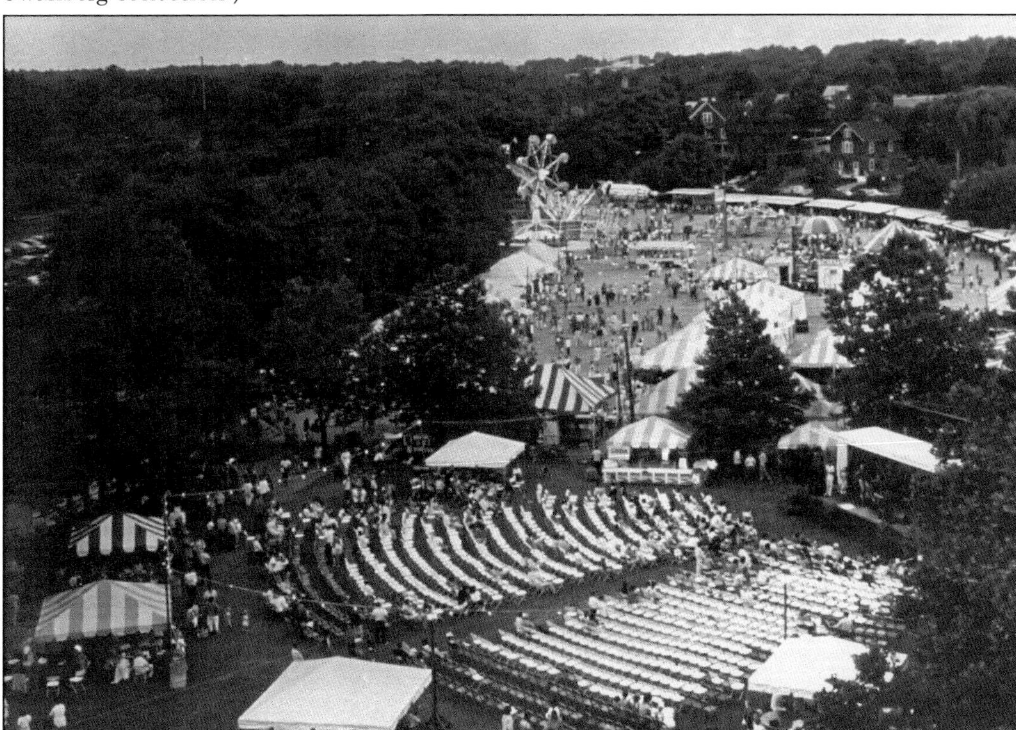

Luciano Park, just a short walk from the Westport Station in Saugatuck, hosts a variety of community events, including the annual Westport Sons of Italy Festival, shown here. Pass the sausage and peppers. (Courtesy Westport Historical Society.)

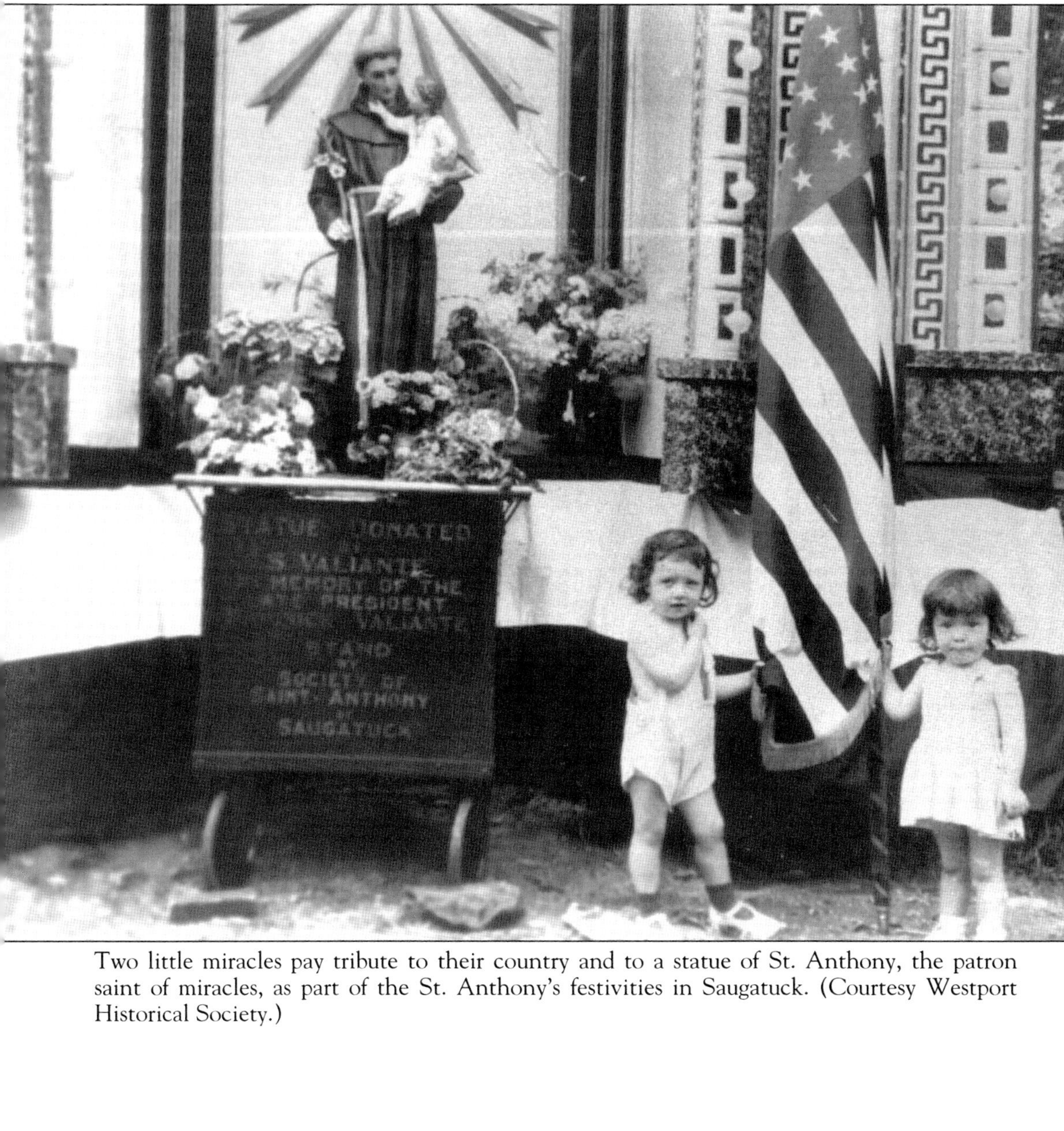

Two little miracles pay tribute to their country and to a statue of St. Anthony, the patron saint of miracles, as part of the St. Anthony's festivities in Saugatuck. (Courtesy Westport Historical Society.)

Seven

Fairfield Station

Fairfield Station is the center of life of the New Haven branch, one of the busiest and highly coveted locations for parking spaces. Commuters waiting for approval languish for years on an assigned parking-space list. The station's central location and bustle has led to vociferous calls to the Connecticut Department of Transportation for another Fairfield stop to ease the load. Its access to restaurants, shops, bookstores, and bars is unmatched anywhere along the line. A New York visitor departing the eastbound side in Fairfield is just a minute's walk away from dinner or a drink at one of the Post Road establishments, both casual and upscale.

Fairfield is best known for its books and festivals. The books come in the form of Borders Books, on the Post Road, and the Pequot Library, host every June to a huge weekend book sale that features more than 100,000 volumes and attracts bargain hunters from all over New England. The library showcases a rare collection on the Colonial era, the American Revolution, the Civil War, and original books by James Audubon. The library is a short walk from the limited-stop station in Southport, an exclusive section of Fairfield, loaded with elegant Colonial houses, historic churches, and yachts bobbing in the harbor. Across the harbor, cut out of the marsh, is the golf course of the Country Club of Fairfield, a sanctuary for the gentry, whose membership includes retired General Electric chief executive Jack Welch. General Electric is headquartered in Fairfield.

Festival season includes the blooming Dogwood Festival fair, held the first two weeks in May on the grounds of the Congregational Church in the upscale Greenfield Hill section of town, and the annual Irish Festival, held in the middle of June and featuring everything Irish, including music, books, food, and drink. Busloads of people depart from Fairfield Station to attend community festivals.

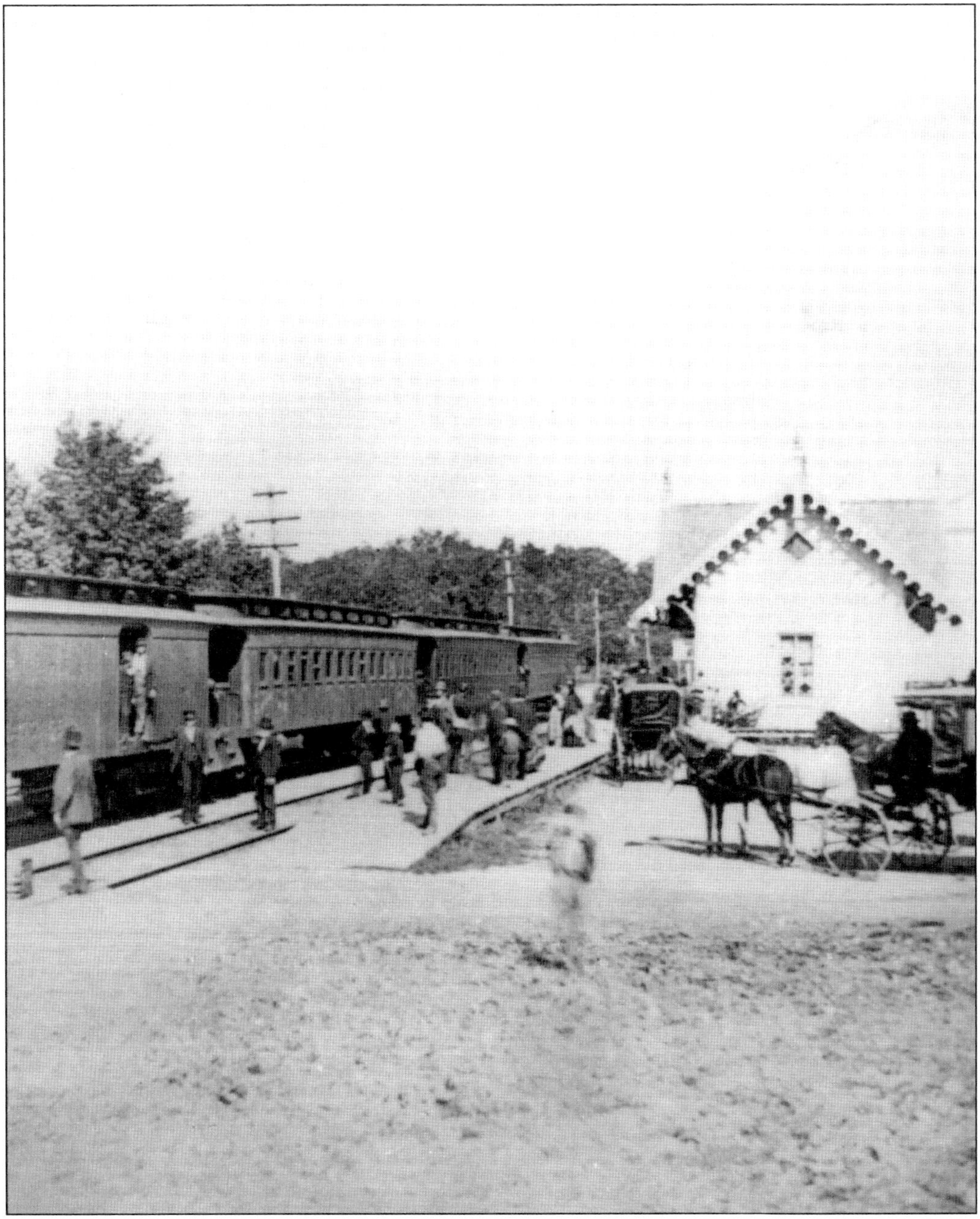

One of the earliest photographs from the Fairfield Historical Society's Southport collection shows the original Southport Station in 1873, the days of dirt roads and horse-drawn carriages. Southport remains a happening place for Fairfield's gentry. (Courtesy Fairfield Historical Society.)

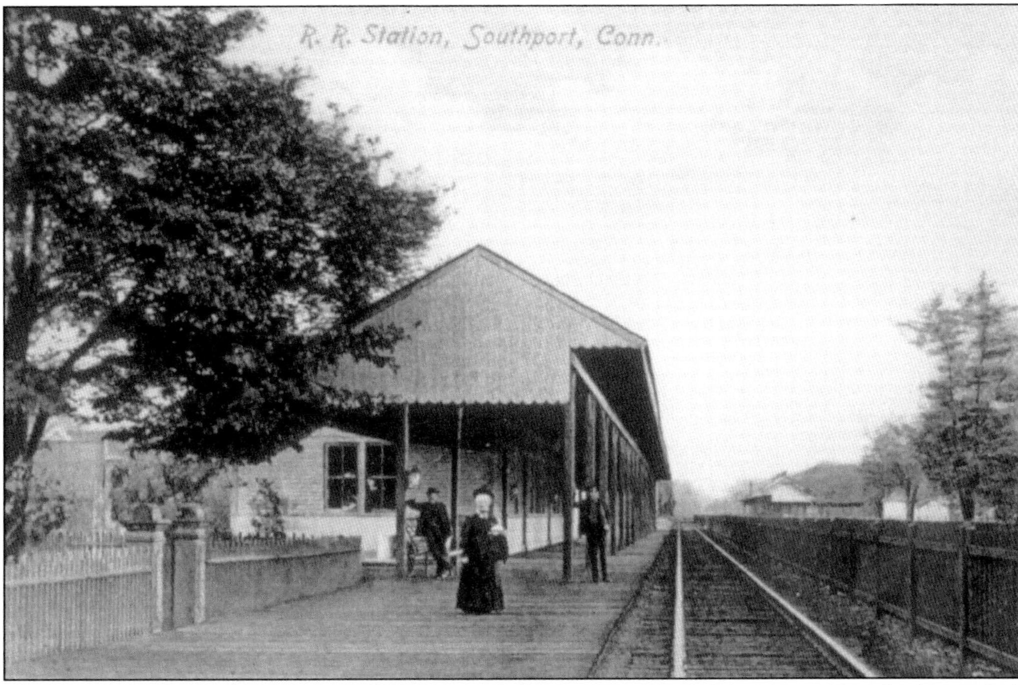

Another early photograph of Southport Station shows a woman waiting on the platform while two men lean against the station house support beams. (Courtesy Thomas J. Dodd Research Center, University of Connecticut.)

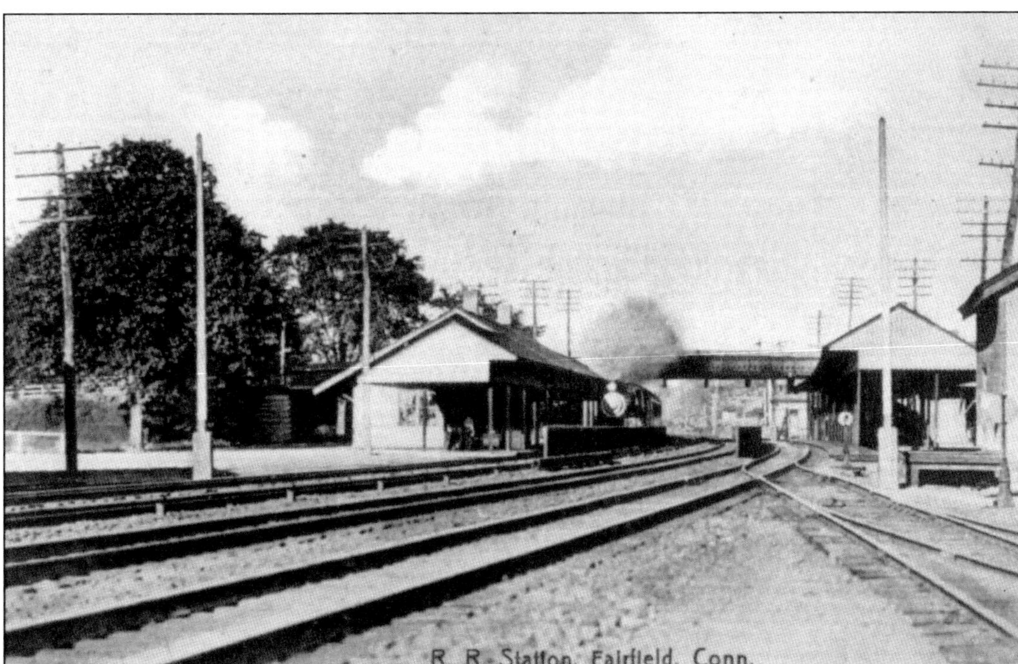

A steamer engine blows its top in Fairfield c. 1890. (Courtesy Thomas J. Dodd Research Center, University of Connecticut.)

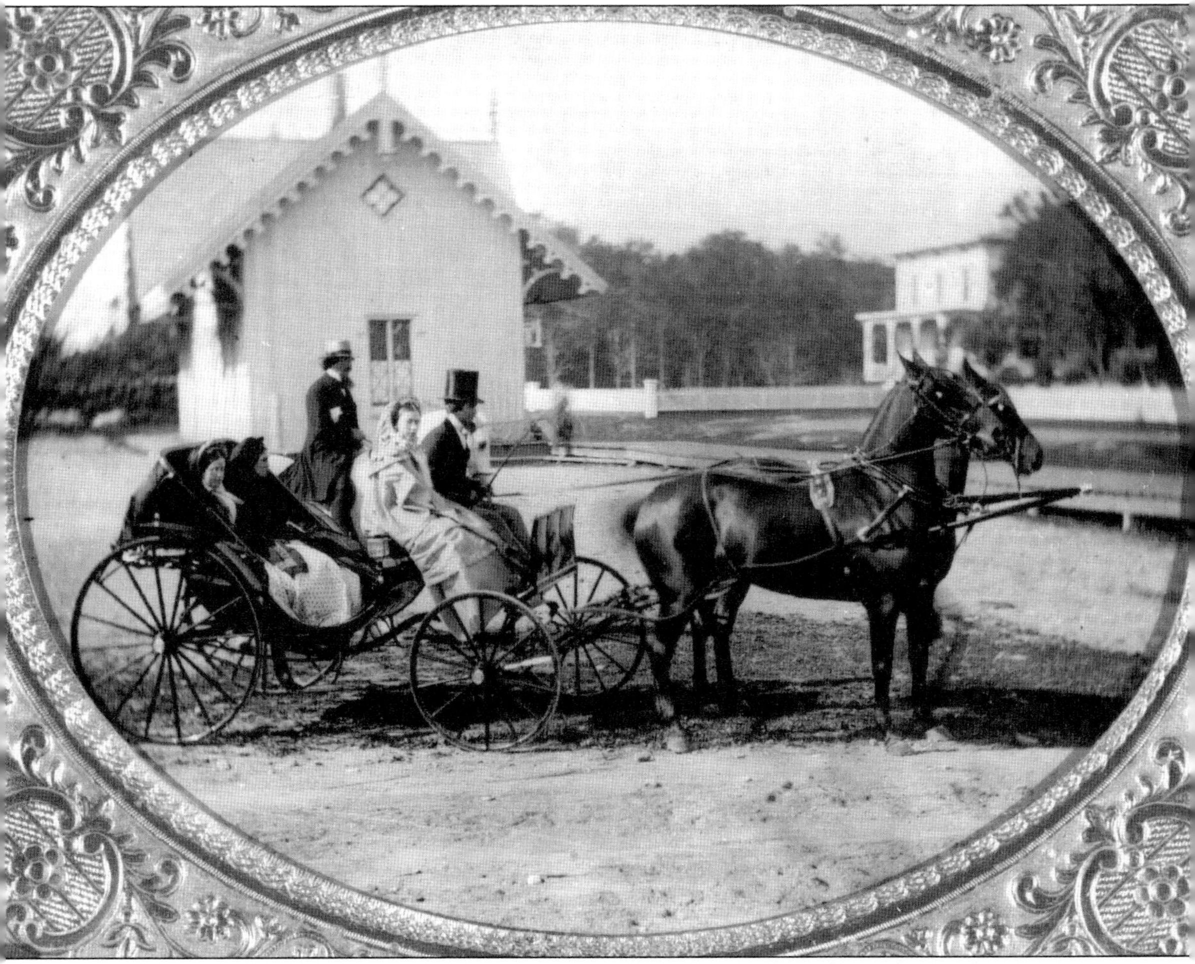

The station in elegant Southport *c.* 1890 shows a couple with friends in a horse-drawn carriage. Southport was (and still is) such an exclusive place that, from 1921 to 1975, this waterfront hamlet had its own Southport Club Car running to Grand Central Station. The 60-or-so members were from surrounding towns and paid a fee of roughly $200 per year for the privilege of riding in the car. (Courtesy Fairfield Historical Society.)

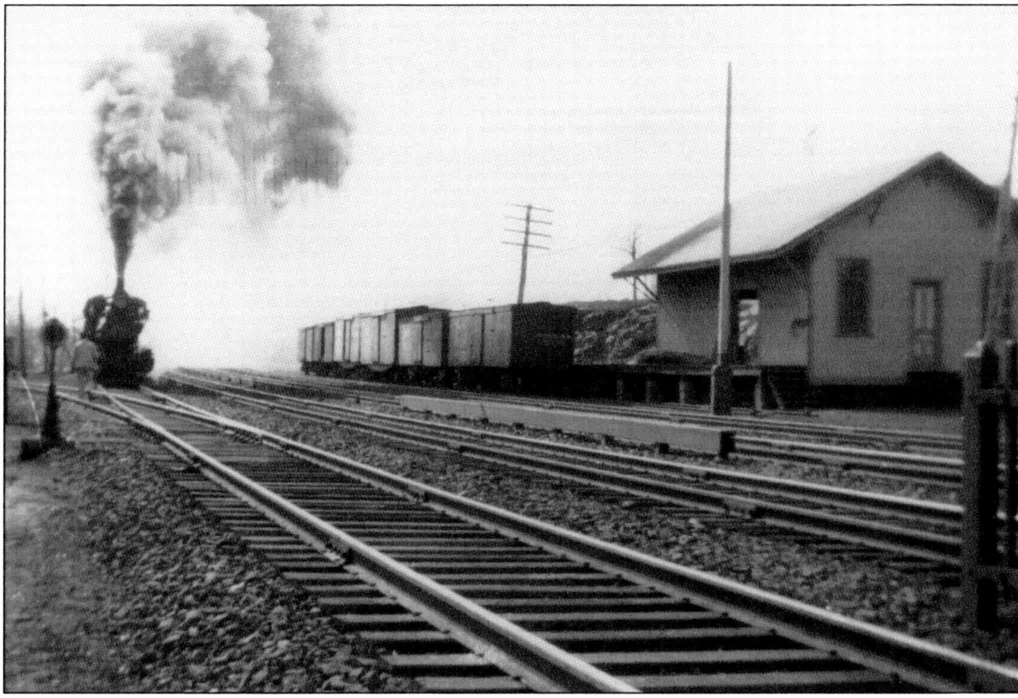

In this *c.* 1890 photograph, a classic early steamer roars into Fairfield Station. (Courtesy Fairfield Historical Society.)

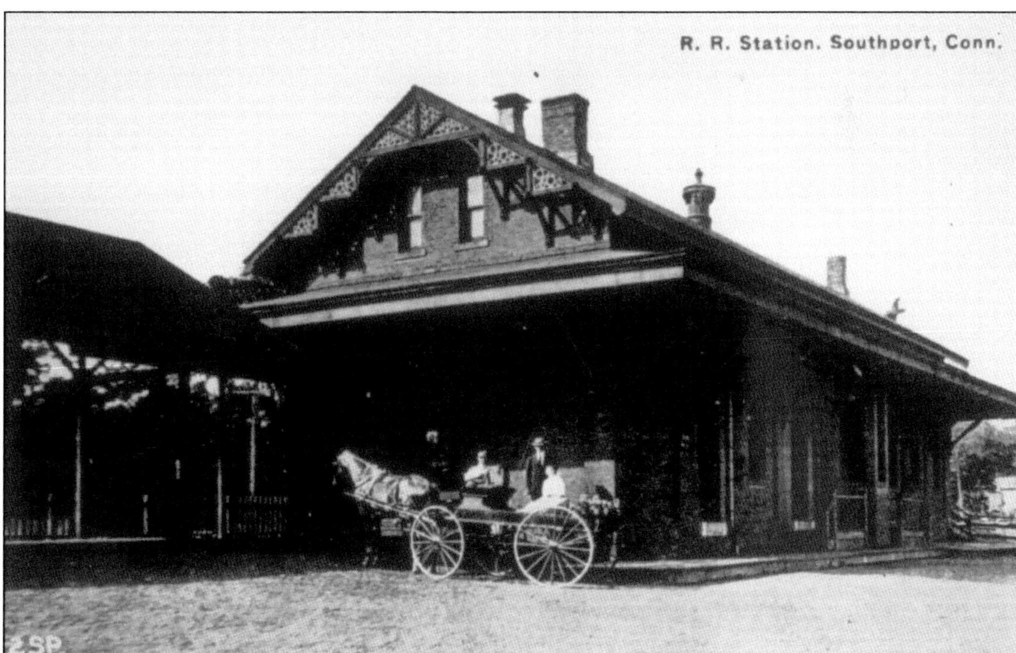

A trio in a horse and wagon pulls up to the covered platform connected to the station building in Southport. (Courtesy Thomas J. Dodd Research Center, University of Connecticut.)

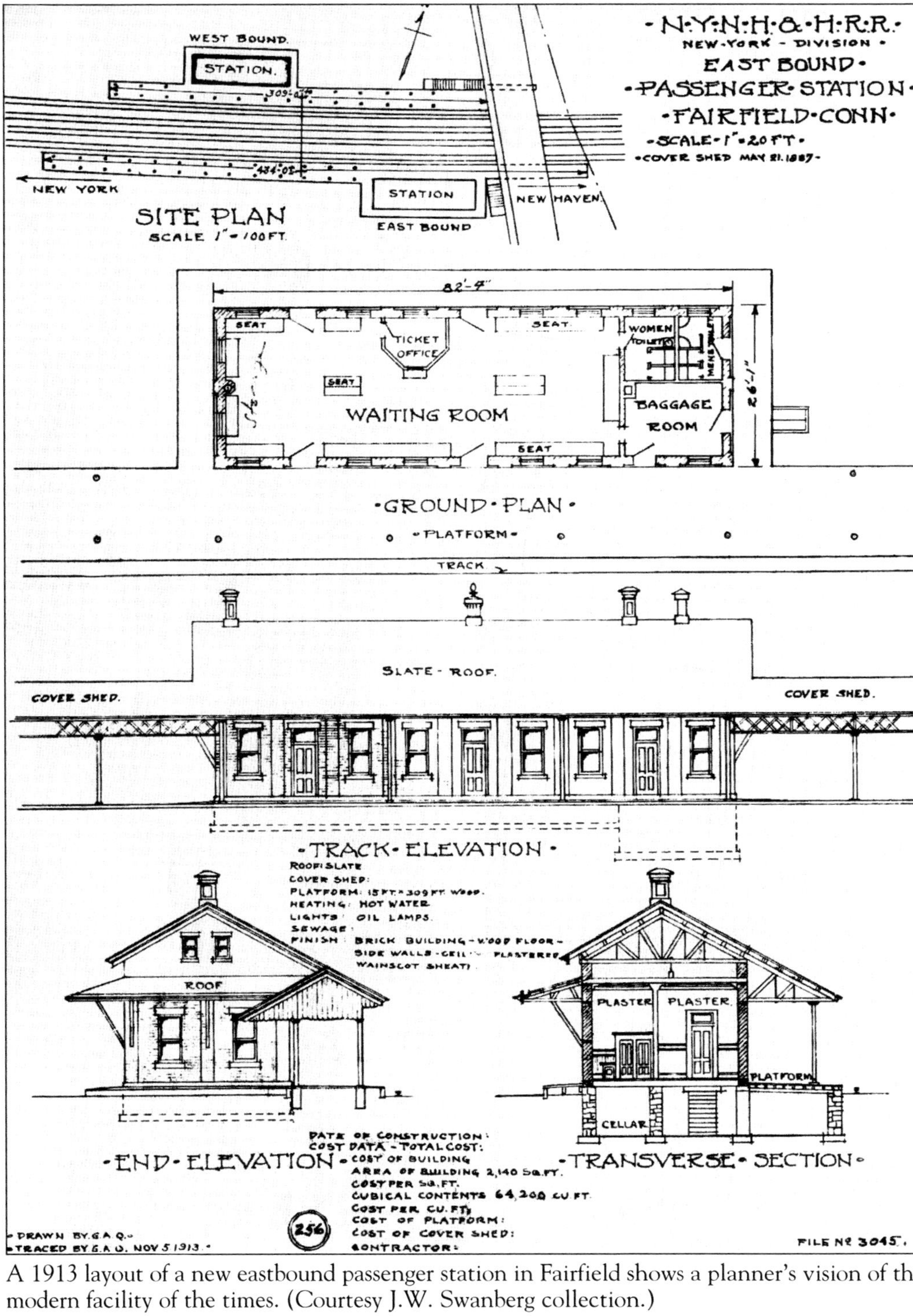

A 1913 layout of a new eastbound passenger station in Fairfield shows a planner's vision of the modern facility of the times. (Courtesy J.W. Swanberg collection.)

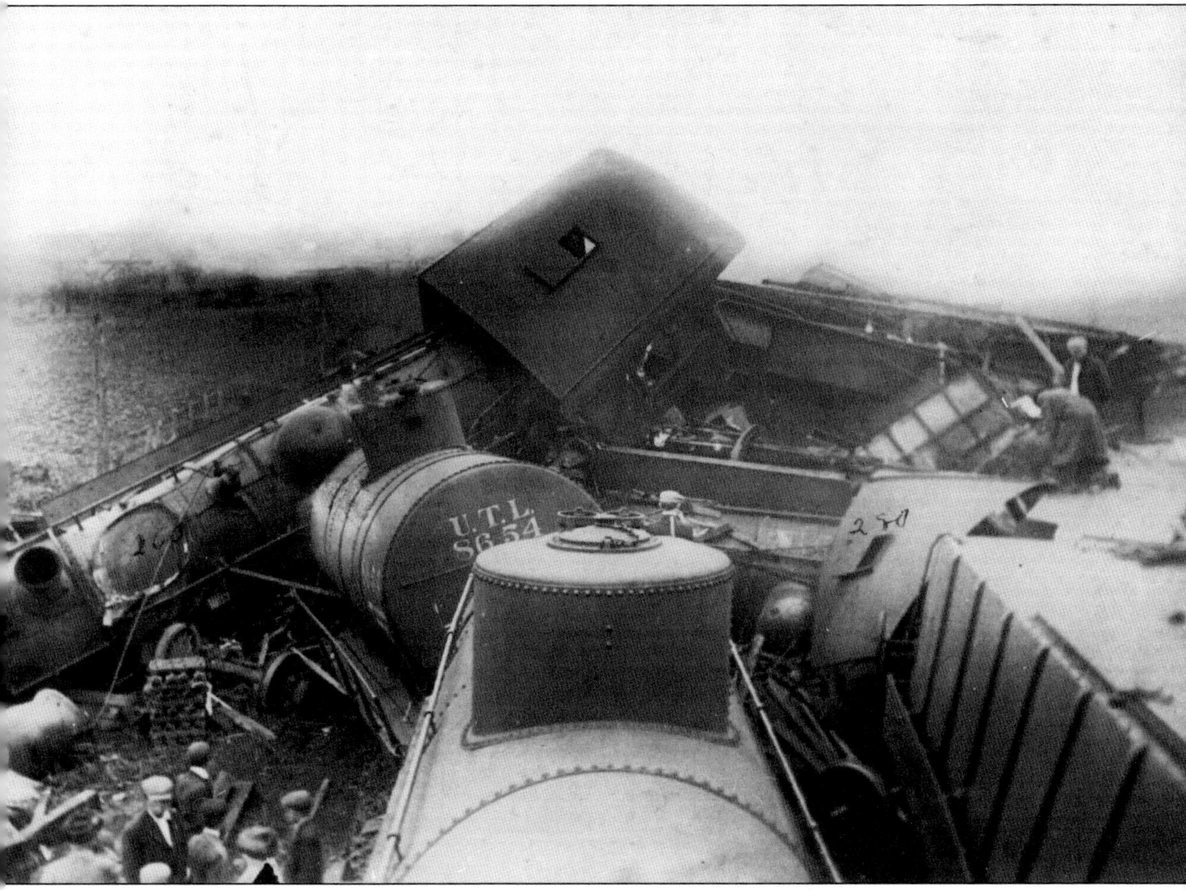

This is what happens when four freight trains collide. The New Haven Railroad wreck occurred on June 6, 1911, in Fairfield after a mechanical breakdown. At the lower left is a group of people trying to figure out what to do now. (Courtesy J.W. Swanberg collection.)

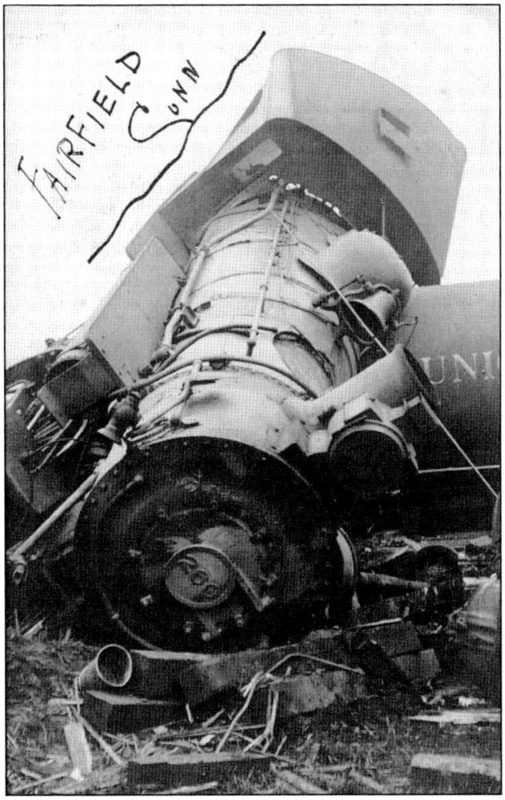

These two photographs show other views of the June 6, 1911 wreck of engines 260 and 280 of the New Haven Railroad. (Courtesy J.W. Swanberg collection.)

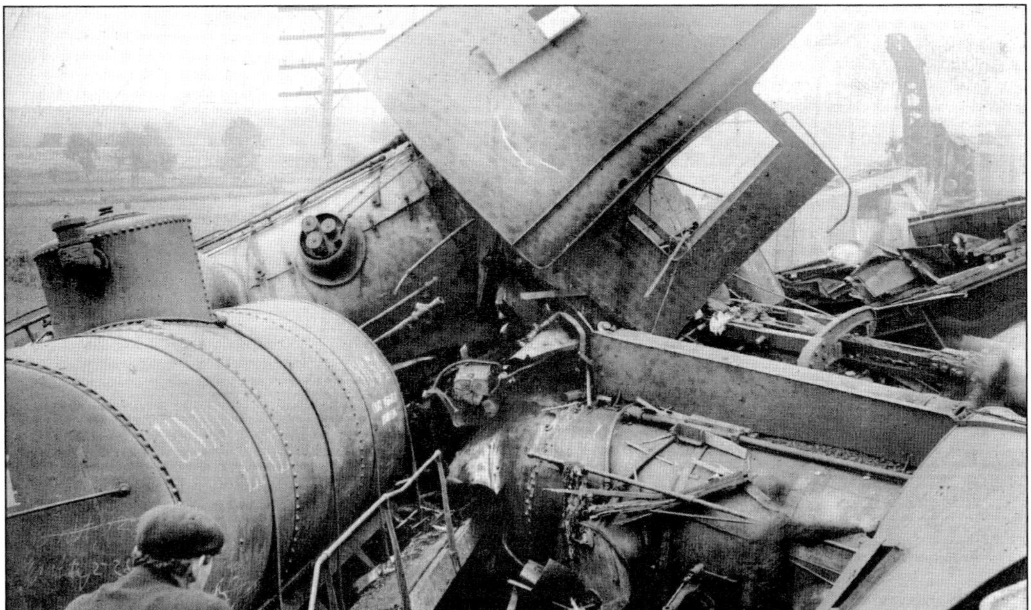

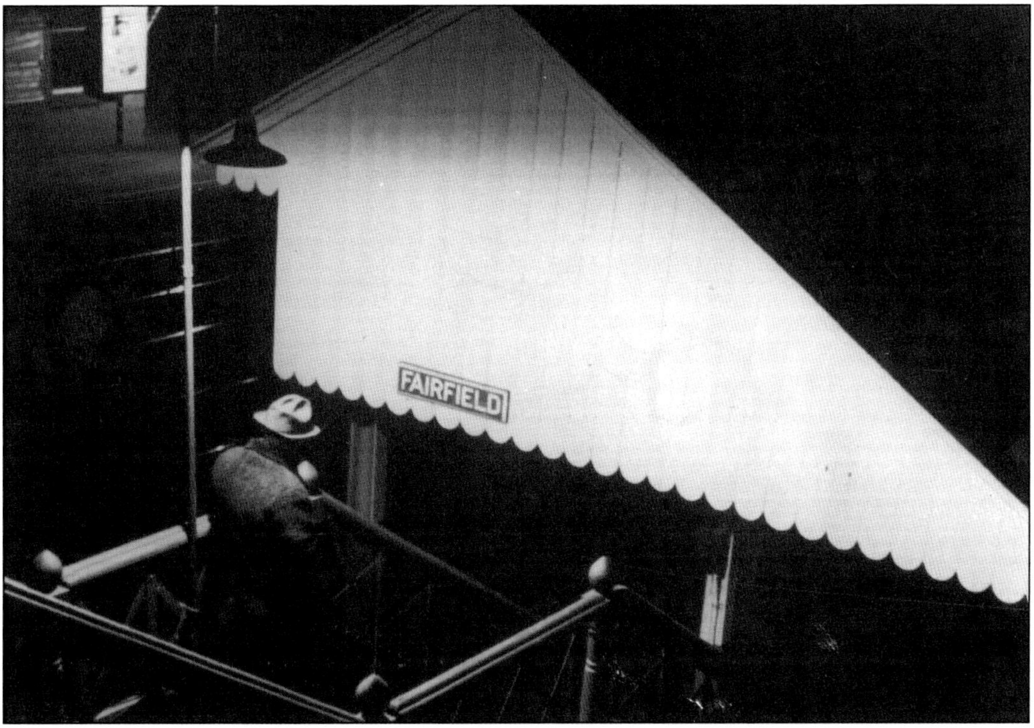

This photograph portrays the lonely life of a commuter, a man walking down the stairs near the Fairfield Station sign in 1939. (Courtesy Fairfield Historical Society.)

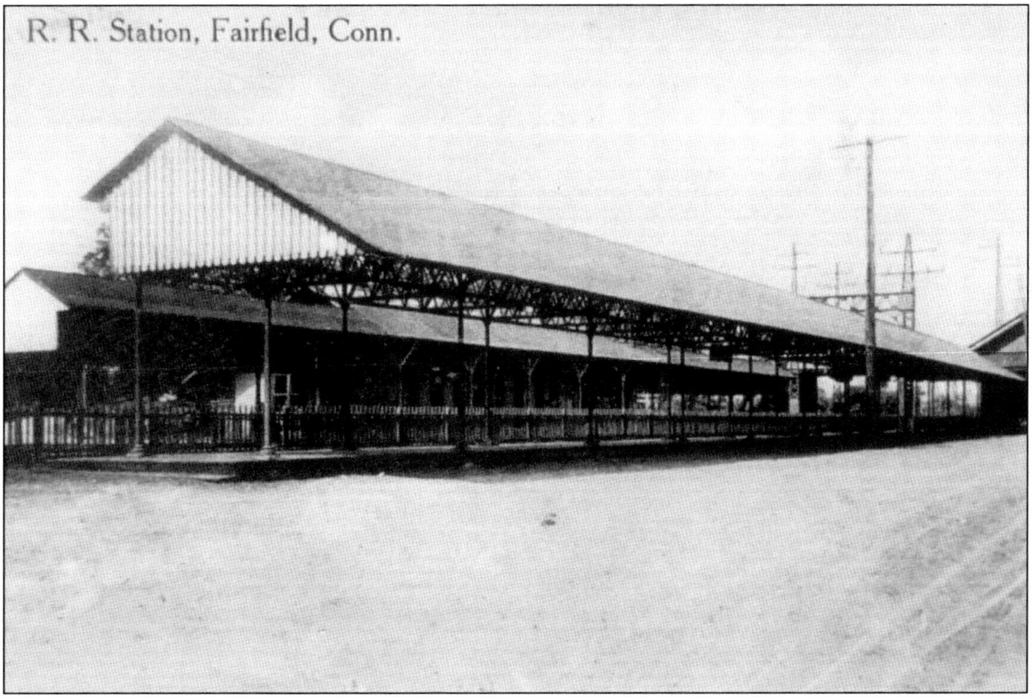

This view of the covered platform at Fairfield Station was taken *c.* 1940. (Courtesy Thomas J. Dodd Research Center, University of Connecticut.)

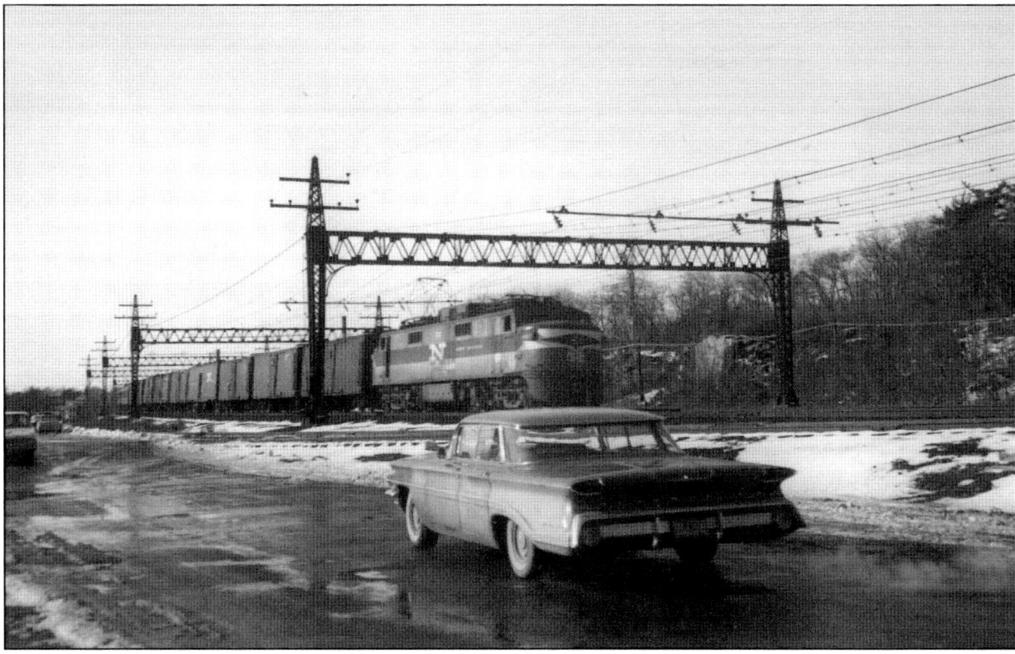

A New Haven Railroad passenger train with electric locomotive powers through Fairfield en route to Boston in 1962. (Courtesy J.W. Swanberg collection.)

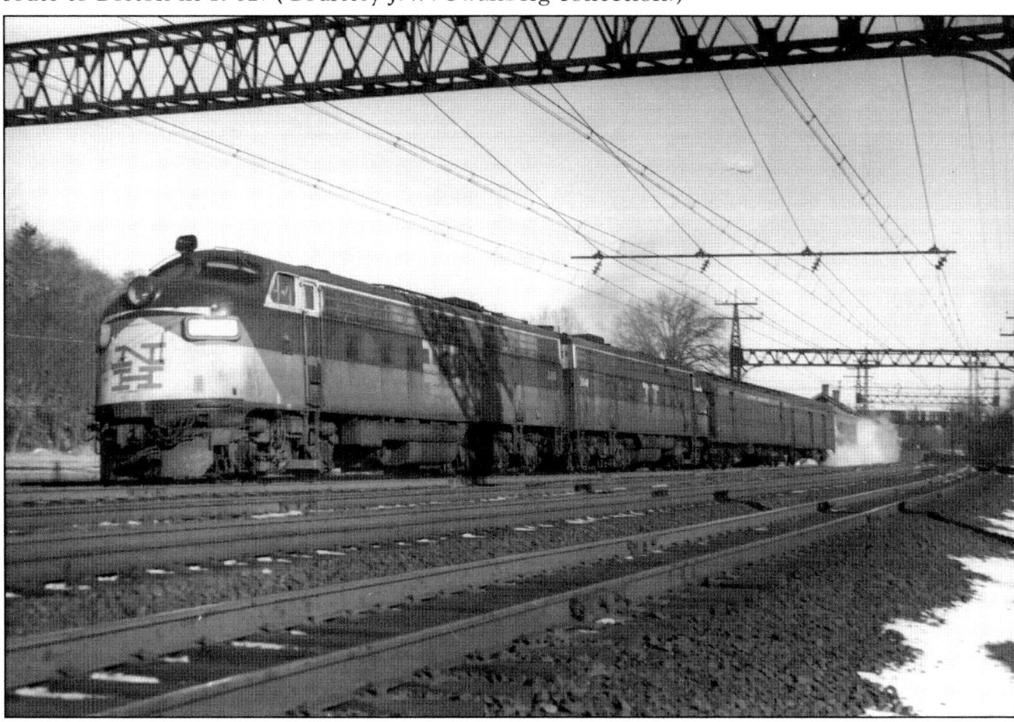

On Christmas Eve 1962, historian Jack Swanberg took this photograph of a New Haven Railroad passenger train with dual-powered FL-9 locomotives accelerating out of Fairfield Station for Grand Central. Note the steam for the train heat escaping at the rear. (Courtesy J.W. Swanberg collection.)

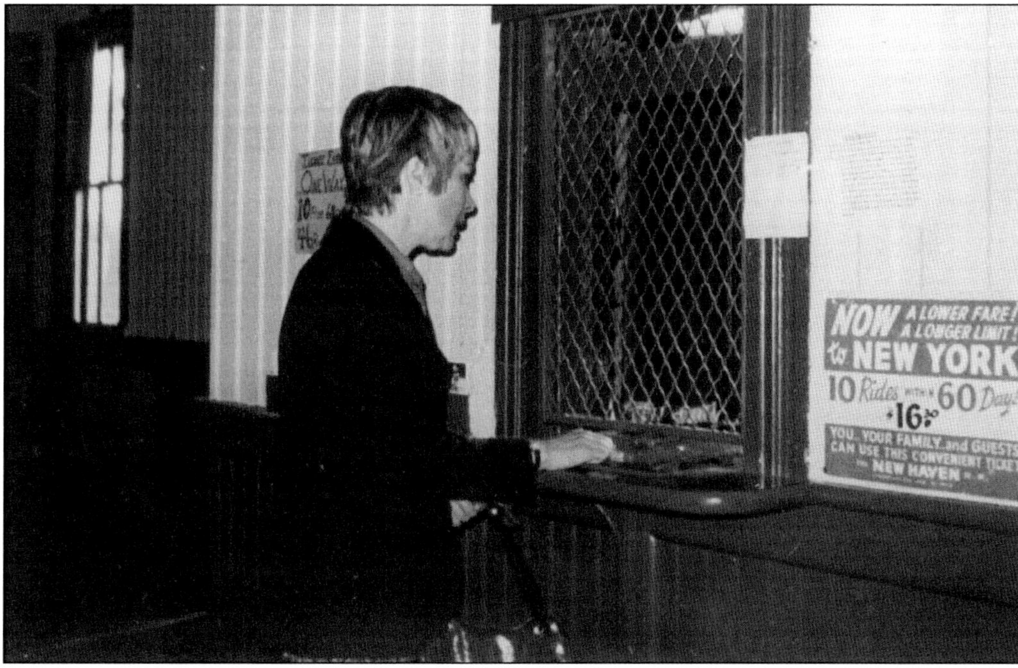

Talk about pushing a ticket special to Grand Central. Look at this offer from 1971, next to the woman at the ticket counter: "10 rides within 60 days for $16.30." (Courtesy Fairfield Historical Society.)

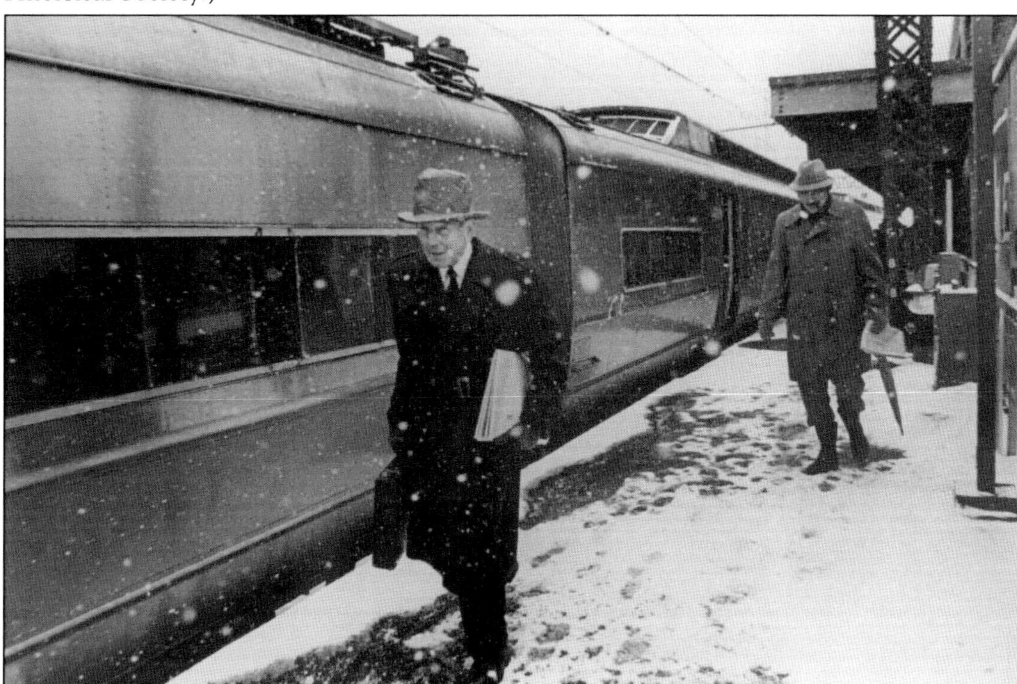

Look at it this way: the rails sure beat sloshing, sliding, and skidding through the snow on Interstate 95. Two men walk through the flakes of snow on the Fairfield Station platform in 1984. (Courtesy Fairfield Historical Society.)

FAIRFIELD HISTORICAL SOCIETY
636 Old Post Road
Fairfield, CT 06430
(203) 259-1598

LIBRARY

Manuscript No.: B39
Accession No.: (L90Sep9)

Date processed: September 1990
Processed by: Martha Rockwell

I. Title: Southport Club Car Collection 1958-1977

II. These papers were given to the Library on
by: Wm. Joshua Barney, Jr.

III. Linear feet of shelf space occupied: 1 1/2 feet
Approximate number of items: 1800

IV. Restrictions:

V. Literary property rights of all papers in the custody of the Fairfield Historical Society Library have been dedicated to the Fairfield Historical Society. Permission for copying and use must be obtained from the Fairfield Historical Society.

VI. Biographical and/or background notes: The Southport Club Car was started in 1921, and ran from Southport, Ct. to Grand Central Station. The 60 or 70 members were from surrounding towns and paid a membership fee of around $200. In 1975 due to change the Car was discontinued. Joshua Barney was the treasurer from 1962 to 1975.

VII. Analysis of collection: This collection consists of three boxes. Box I holds member correspondence, Box II financial papers and Box III miscellaneous papers. For more detail see table of contents.

From the collections of the Fairfield Historical Society, you can research just about anything you ever wanted to know about the Southport Club Car, an exclusive membership that had a dedicated car into Grand Central. The collection includes membership correspondence and financial papers. The club discontinued service in 1975. (Courtesy Fairfield Historical Society.)

Eight

Bridgeport Station

Connecticut's largest city is the domain of showman P.T. Barnum and a museum named for him. Traveler expert James G. Clark coined the illuminating line "Bridgeport, where the circus never left town." The line is apt because Phineas Taylor Barnum, who housed the winter headquarters for his circus in Bridgeport, left a political and social legacy that attracted admirers just as a circus parade draws visitors to the paid admission at the big top.

After a decades-long absence, the circus that retained his name, Ringling Brothers Barnum & Bailey Circus, returned in 2001 for a sold-out appearance at the city's spanking new arena at Harbor Yard, a 10,000-seat venue that has hosted the circus, professional hockey, college basketball, and rock concerts.

For day-trippers seeking entertainment action, the sports complex that connects the South End to Downtown includes the new arena and the baseball stadium, home to the Bridgeport Bluefish. Both are within easy walking distance from Bridgeport's train station, bus terminal, and Bridgeport–Port Jefferson Ferry. More than 500,000 people per year pass through the ferry terminal that transports visitors on the *P.T. Barnum* for a 60-minute, 13-mile run across Long Island Sound to Port Jefferson, New York.

You cannot visit Bridgeport without being aware that it is the home of Barnum, showman, philanthropist, and land developer, whose Yankee ingenuity attracted industrialists such as Elias Howe, the inventor of the sewing machine, to the city. No, Barnum never said, "There's a sucker born every minute"—not that the apocryphal expression would have bothered the man who did say, "I don't care what they say about me, as long as they say something." One thing is for sure, probably no person of his era used the New Haven Line more than Barnum, who made frequent visits to his Manhattan museum and other business enterprises in New York City. If you want to research the whole story of Barnum's life, the Historical Collections of the Bridgeport Public Library, the finest public library in the state, is a short walk from the train station.

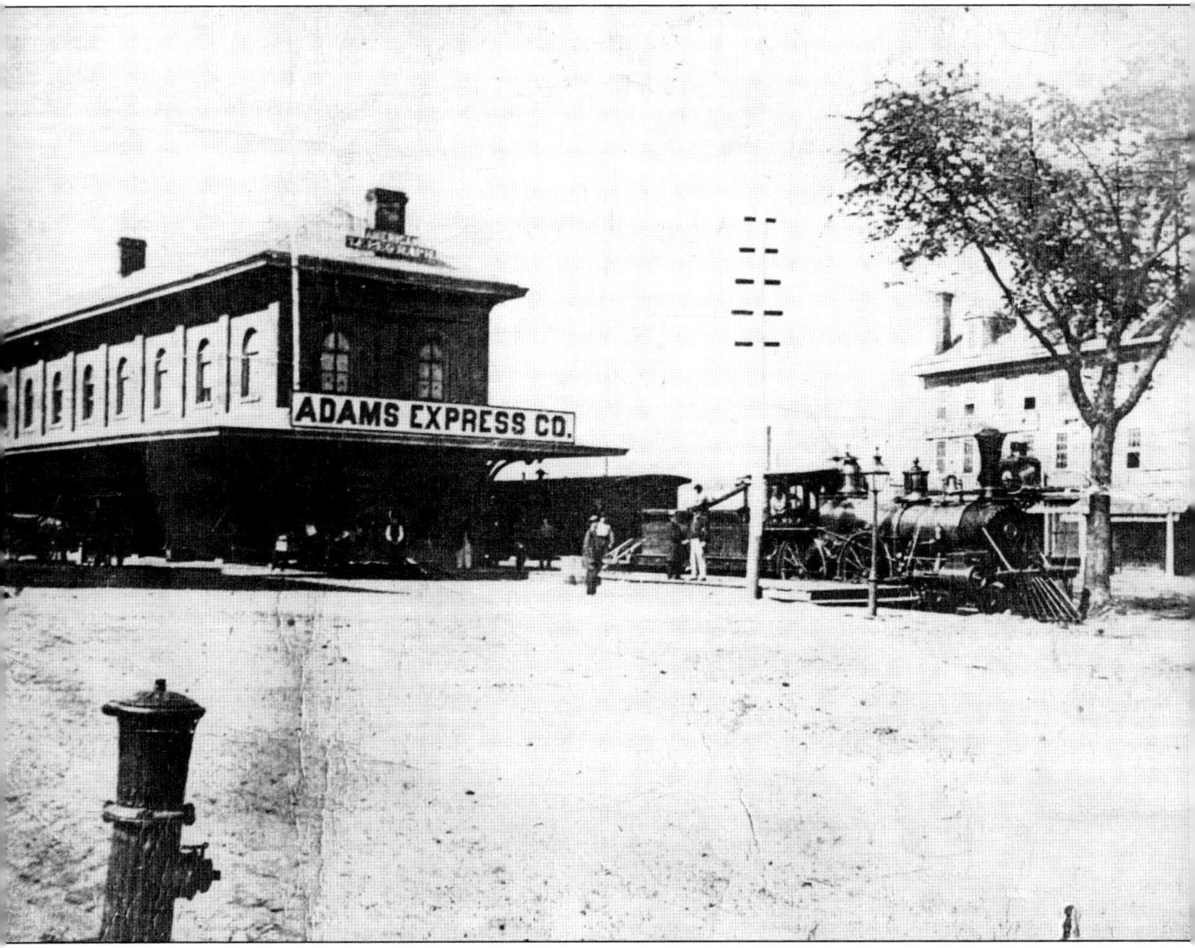

This 1868 photograph of Bridgeport Station shows a wood-burning engine at the right. Fireplace-sized logs were heaved to feed the steamers. Bridgeport's railroad terminal came from the Housatonic Railroad and was the chief reason for the city's incorporation in 1836. Led by the president of the Housatonic, Alfred Bishop, the line was built from the Massachusetts border just south of Sheffield and south through western Connecticut. The first steamer stopped in Bridgeport in 1840. It was not until years later that Bridgeport Station was consolidated into the New Haven Line. (Courtesy J.W. Swanberg collection.)

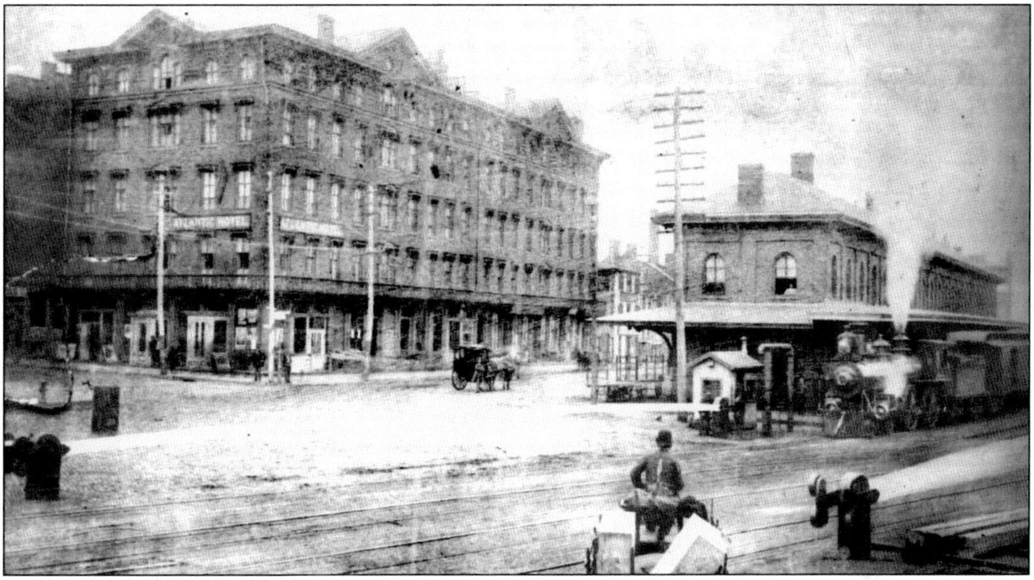

Shown here is the corner of Fairfield Avenue and Water Street *c.* 1890, with a steamer stationed at the right on the street-level tracks. Pedestrian fatalities were aplenty in those days, especially when the local watering-hole faithfuls consumed one too many. Some of those lucky enough to make it across the tracks crossed Water Street and fell into the harbor "never to be heard from again," according to Richard Howell, a Bridgeport newspaperman of the times. (Courtesy J.W. Swanberg collection.)

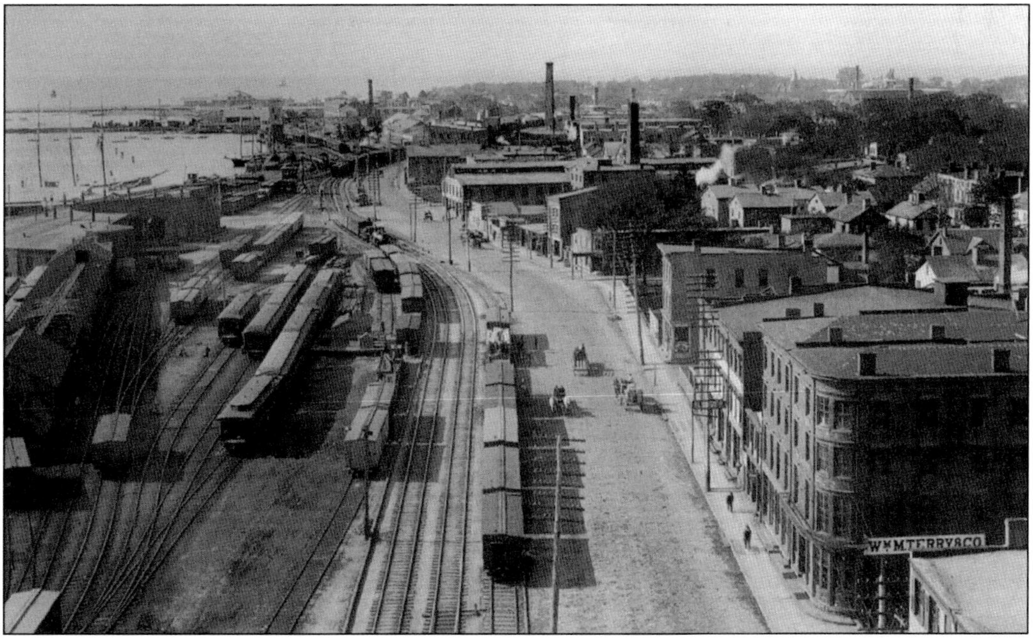

This 1888 view looking south over Bridgeport's downtown captures the city's link with the rails and harbor. Freighters are poised along Water Street, with the harbor at the left. This is an era in which Bridgeport produced sewing machines, electrical equipment, typewriters, corsets, and machines used in railroad repair shops. By rail and by sea, Bridgeport products were shipped throughout the world. (Courtesy Historical Collections, Bridgeport Public Library.)

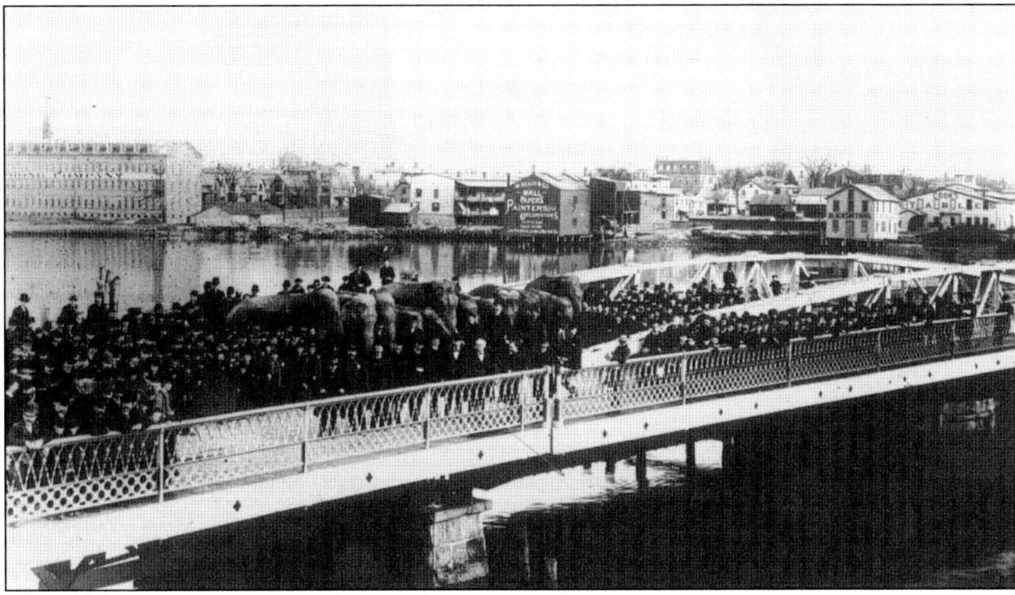

Shown here in 1888 is one of P.T. Barnum's classic publicity stunts. The Stratford Avenue Bridge was just replaced by a new iron structure. Of course, everyone wondered about its safety. Barnum paraded a dozen elephants, weighing roughly 36 tons, onto the bridge. Barnum always knew when the camera was on him. He is hatless and white-haired, standing in the middle of the photograph. No life jackets were necessary. More than 100 years later, the Barnum legend lives on and so does the Stratford Avenue Bridge. (Courtesy Historical Collections, Bridgeport Public Library.)

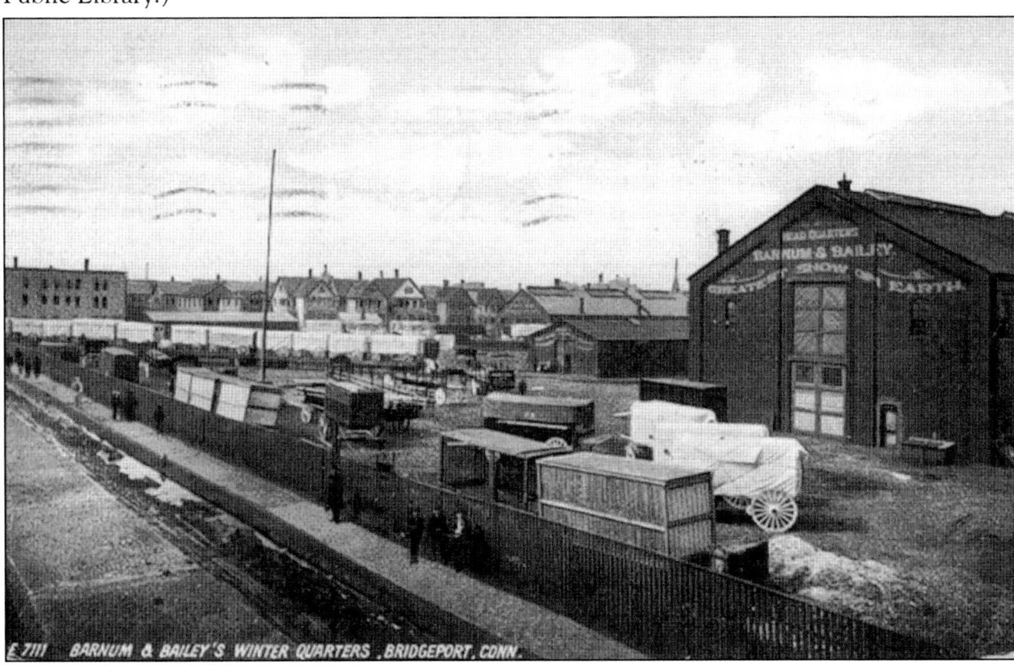

Barnum made Bridgeport the winter headquarters of his circus on a 10-acre lot in the West End. It was not uncommon for circus performers, such as Buffalo Bill Cody, to be strolling around town. (Courtesy Historical Collections, Bridgeport Public Library.)

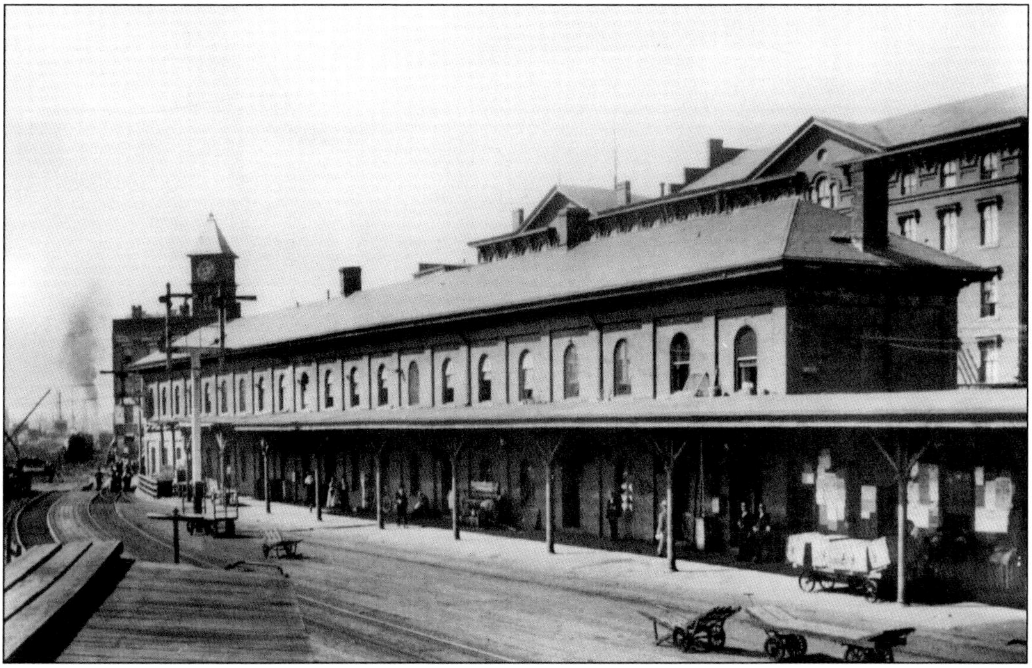

This view shows Bridgeport Station in the 1890s. Elevation of the tracks onto the present viaduct system occurred *c.* 1900. The viaduct is what many truck drivers call the "Great Wall" because they have to let air out of the tires in order to pass underneath. (Courtesy J.W. Swanberg collection.)

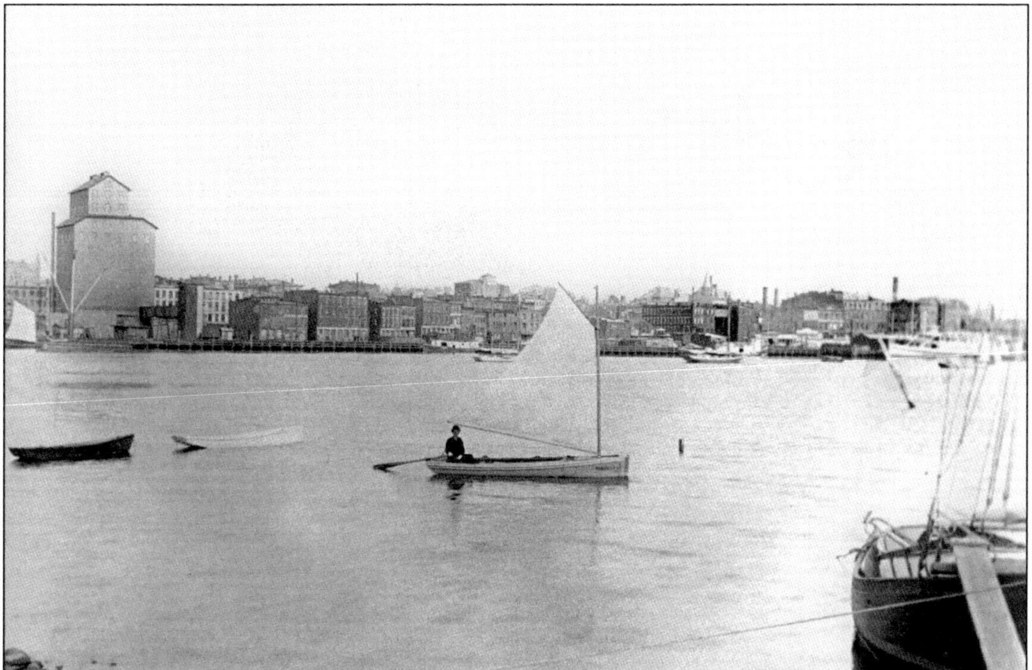

A man enjoys the tranquility of Bridgeport Harbor in 1888, with Bridgeport's legendary factory buildings in the background. (Courtesy Historical Collections, Bridgeport Public Library.)

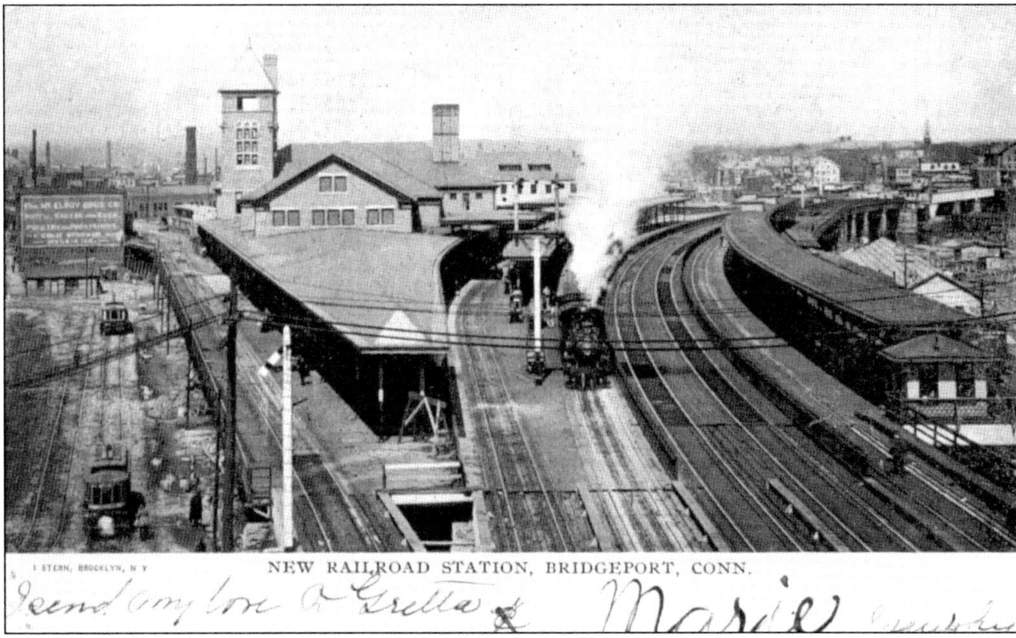

A steamer (center) whistles past the new Bridgeport Station shortly after 1900, following the track elevation. (Courtesy J.W. Swanberg collection.)

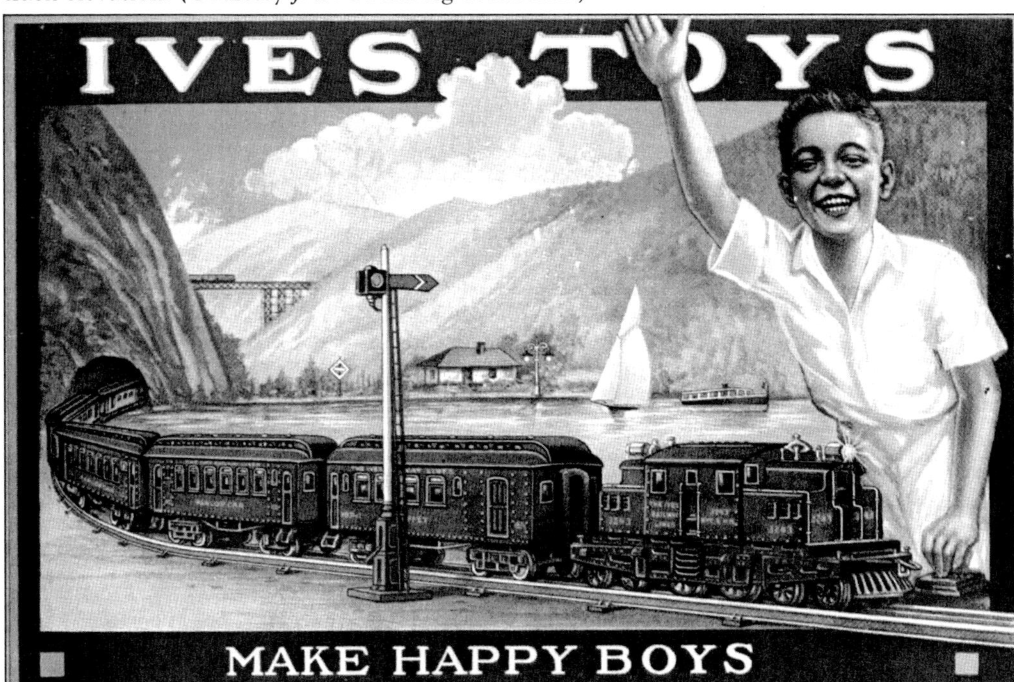

In 1901, the Ives Manufacturing Company produced the first mechanical trains to run on tracks. The company slogan was "Unhampered by the Interstate Commerce Commission, immune from freight rate regulation, and undetected as yet by the Government." Ives and then Lionel trains inspired the windup toy craze that makes them precious collector's items. Shown here is an advertisement from 1923. (Courtesy Historical Collections, Bridgeport Public Library.)

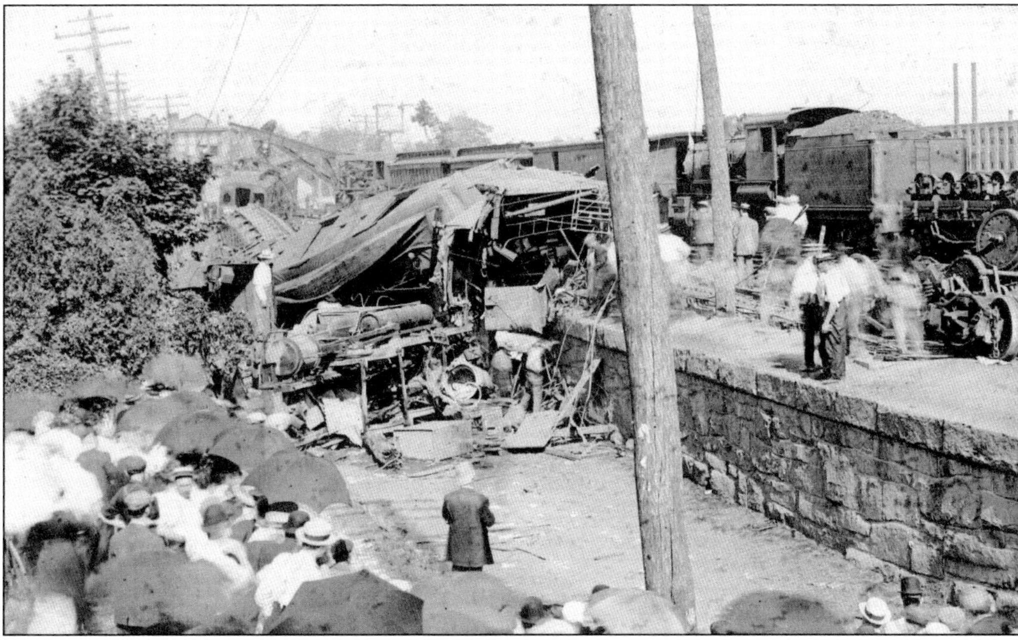

These are two views of what is arguably the most famous crash in the history of the New York, New Haven & Hartford Railroad Company: the July 11, 1911 wreck of the *Federal Express*. The crash killed 14 people and injured 47. It occurred when the train ran across a switch point at the Fairfield Avenue overpass, in the city's West End, at 60 miles per hour. The train jumped the tracks and plunged 20 feet into a roadway, destroying the locomotive and five cars. Above is the aftermath of the crash. Note the people holding umbrellas to shade the blazing sun. Below is the car of the St. Louis Cardinals baseball team, whose players were among the passengers. No player was hurt, and the manager of the team, Roger Bresnahan, rescued many people in the crash. (Courtesy J.W. Swanberg collection.)

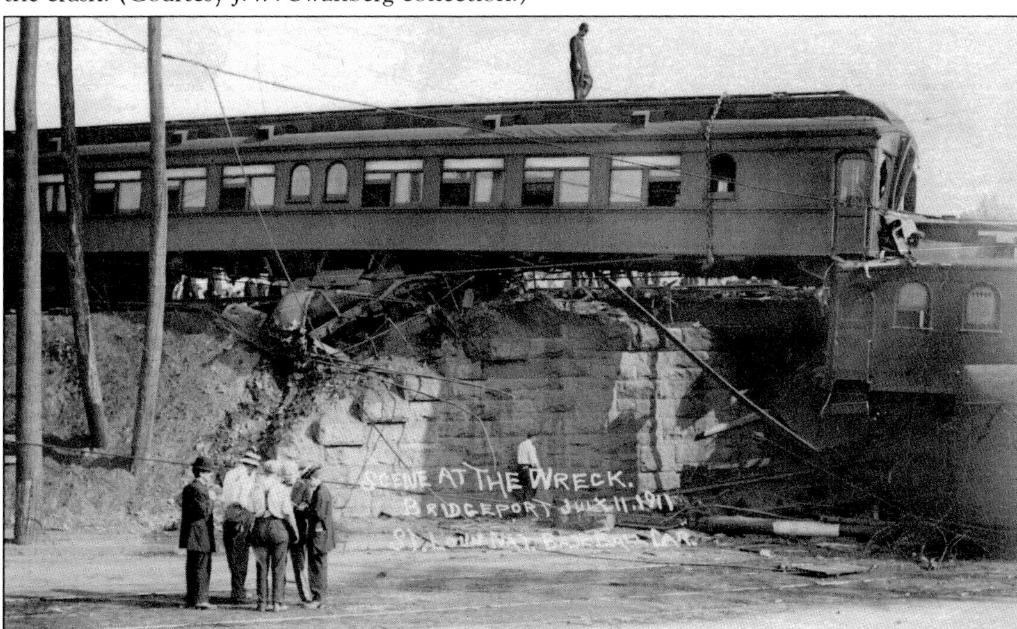

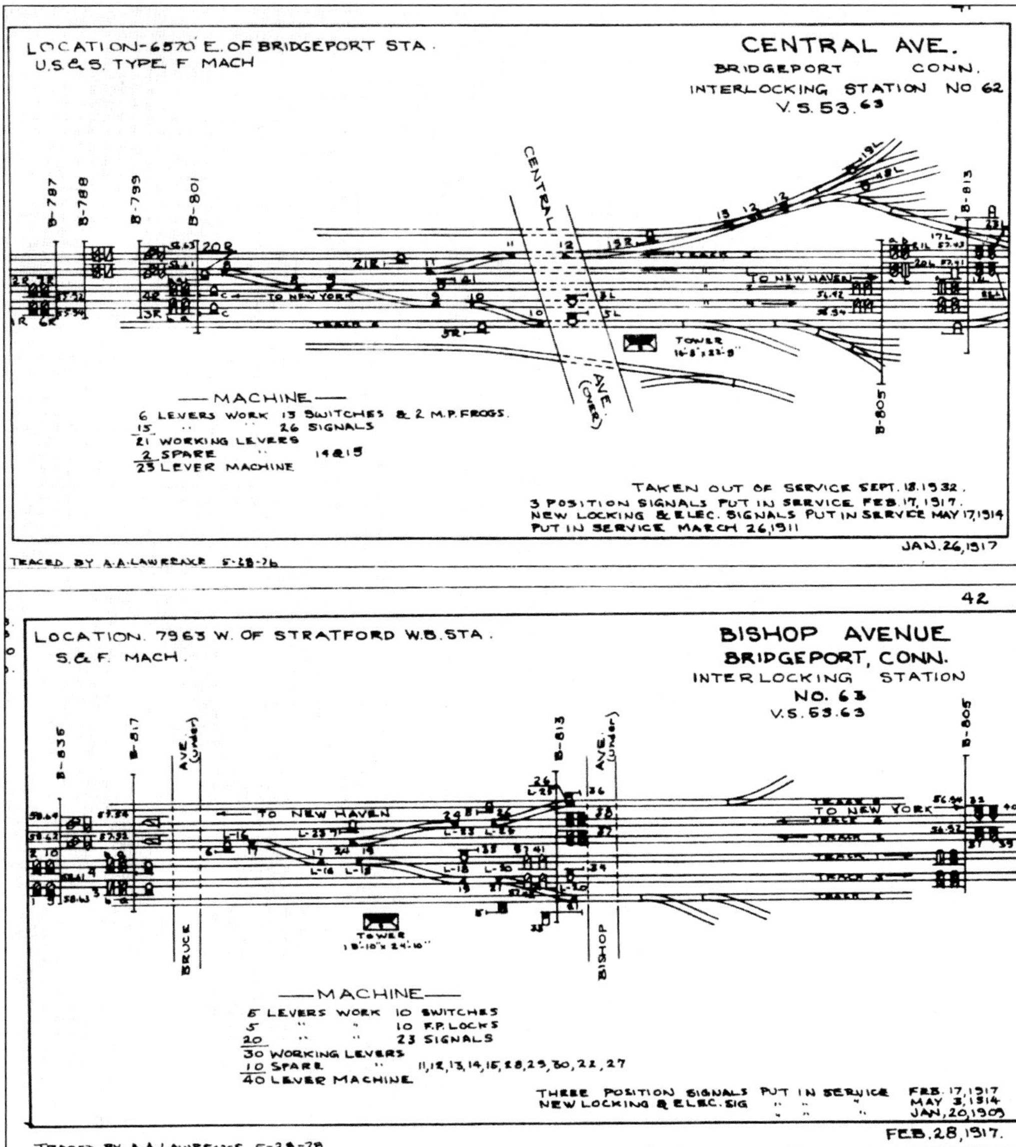

Perhaps confusing at first glance, this has been identified by historian and engineer Jack Swanberg as the east side of the Bridgeport interlocking station. In the early days, if a train required crossover flexibility, a New Haven Line operator manually powered levers from a tower that switched the direction of the rails. Now you know the genesis of "falling asleep at the switch." (Courtesy J.W. Swanberg collection.)

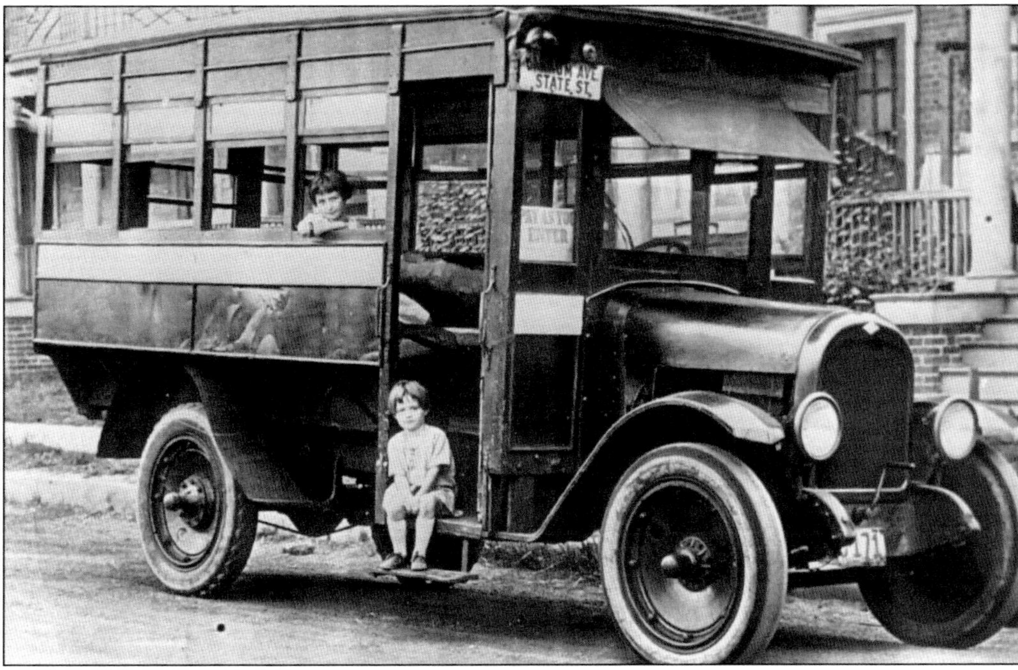

A sister-and-brother act take over this operation on Bridgeport's East Side *c.* 1925. The sign next to the vacant driver's seat reads, "Pay as you enter." Anything to earn a few pennies. (Courtesy Historical Collections, Bridgeport Public Library.)

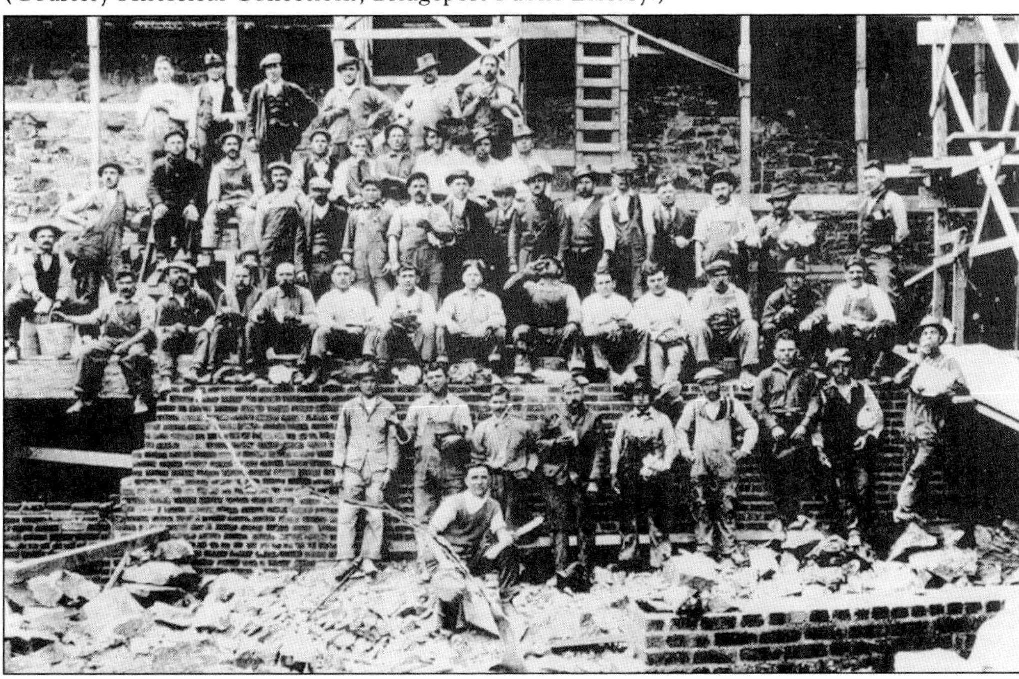

Bridgeport's Yankee ingenuity and immigrant muscle spawned all kinds of innovations and entertainment, including show houses that attracted top-line Broadway performers. These workers for the T.J. Pardy Construction Company take time out in 1920 from building the twin theaters designed by Sylvester Poli. (Courtesy Historical Collections, Bridgeport Public Library.)

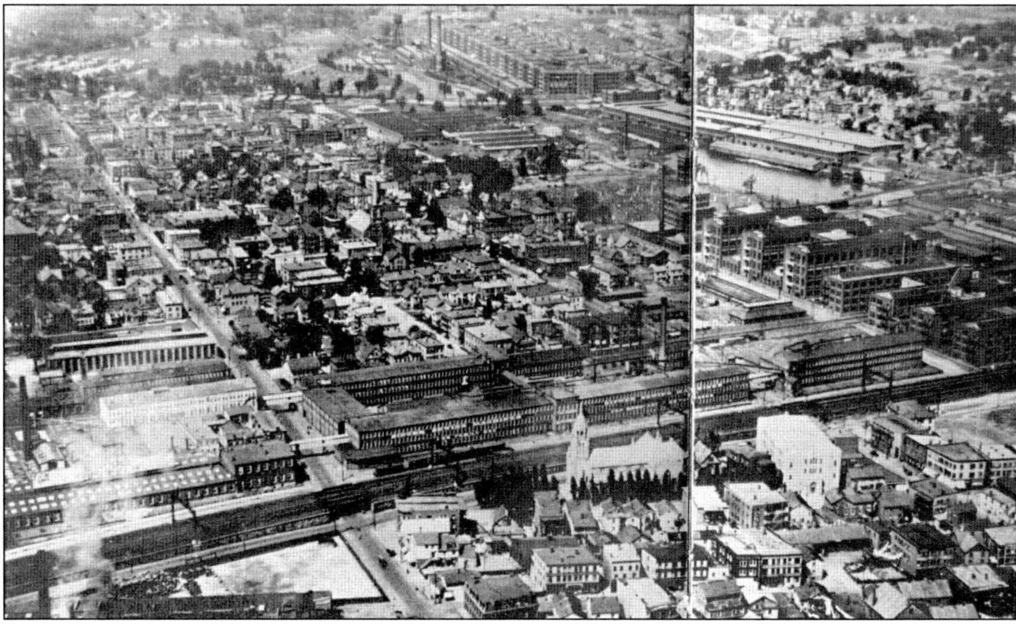

This aerial view shows the East Side of Bridgeport c. 1930. The raised rails of the New Haven Line are sandwiched by buildings that housed the Singer Sewing Machine Company (center) and the white building of SS. Cyril and Methodius Roman Catholic Church. (Courtesy Historical Collections, Bridgeport Public Library.)

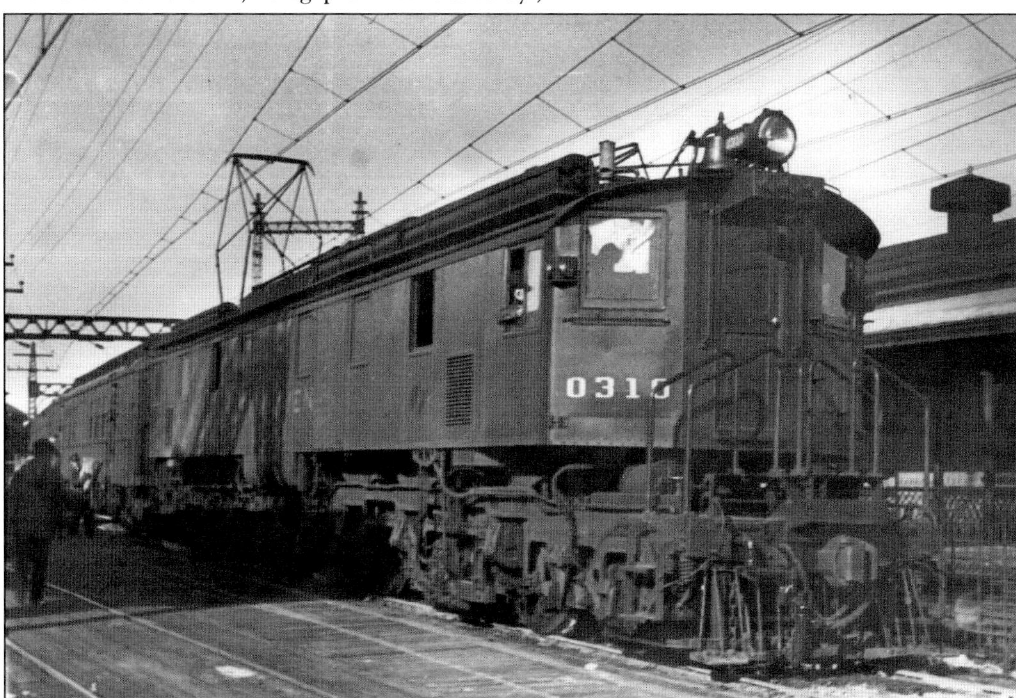

This photograph was taken in the electrification era in Bridgeport c. 1936. The rail buffs call this engine an NH EP-2 0310, a New York–bound passenger train. (Courtesy J.W. Swanberg collection.)

NEW YORK TO BRIDGEPORT

EASTERN STANDARD TIME

Schedule symbols should be checked carefully against "REFERENCES" at bottom of tables

MONDAY THRU FRIDAY		SATURDAY		SUNDAY	
Leave G. C. T.	Due Bridgeport	Leave G. C. T.	Due Bridgeport	Leave G. C. T.	Due Bridgeport
12:10AM	1:34AM	12:10AM	1:34AM	12:10AM	1:34AM
x12:45	2:11	x12:45	2:11	x1:10	2:28
PS2:20	3:28	PS2:20	3:28	PS2:20	3:28
x3:00	6:40	x3:00	6:40	.....	.....
A4:45	6:25	.....	.....	.....	.....
B5:55	7:38	5:55	7:38	5:55	7:38
A6:10	7:38	.....	.....	.....	.....
7:00	8:23	7:00	8:23	.....	.....
8:00	9:13	8:00	9:13	8:00	9:13
.....	.....	.....	.....	8:35	9:56
8:35	9:55	8:35	9:55	.....	.....
10:00	11:07	10:00	11:07	10:00	11:07
10:30	11:50	10:30	11:50	10:30	11:50
PS11:00	12:14PM	PS11:00	12:14PM	PS11:00	12:14PM
11:35	1:06	11:35	1:06	x11:30	12:52
12:30PM	1:37	12:30PM	1:37	12:30PM	1:37
.....	.....	12:50	2:16	.....	.....
1:50	3:19	1:50	3:19	1:50	3:19
PS2:00	3:14	PS2:00	3:14	PS2:00	3:14
2:30	4:02	2:30	4:02	2:43	4:02
3:00	4:07	3:00	4:07	3:00	4:07
A3:30	4:56	3:30	4:56	.....	.....
PS4:00	5:12	PS4:00	5:12	PS4:00	5:12
4:10	5:20	4:10	5:20	4:10	5:20
A4:30	5:54	.....	.....	.....	.....
C5:00	6:24	5:05	6:45	.....	.....
A5:05	6:45	5:10	6:19	5:10	6:28
5:10	6:19	.....	.....	.....	.....
5:32	7:05	6:00	7:12	6:00	7:12
6:00	7:12	6:02	7:40	.....	.....
A6:02	7:30	.....	.....	.....	.....
.....	.....	PS7:00	8:10	PS7:00	8:10
PS7:00	8:10	7:02	8:35	7:02	8:35
7:02	8:35	.....	.....	D7:28	8:40
E7:28	8:40	8:00	9:16	8:00	9:12
F8:00	9:12	.....	.....	8:02	9:26
G8:00	9:16	.....	.....	.....	.....
E8:02	9:26	PS8:25	9:41	PS8:25	9:41
Ax8:09	9:55	9:00	10:24	9:00	10:22
PS8:25	9:41	10:00	11:22	10:00	11:26
9:00	10:22	.....	.....	11:00	12:20AM
10:00	11:26	11:35	1:00AM	.....	.....
11:35	1:00AM	.....	.....	.....	.....

REFERENCES

–Runs Monday mornings only.
–Does not run Monday mornings.
–All Grand Central Terminal trains except those marked "x" stop at 125th St. Station approximately 10 minutes after leaving G. C. T.
–All Grand Central Terminal trains except those marked "y" stop at 125th St. Station approximately 10 minutes before arrival at G. C. T.

BRIDGEPORT TO NEW YORK

EASTERN STANDARD TIME

Schedule symbols should be checked carefully against "REFERENCES" at bottom of tables

MONDAY THRU FRIDAY		SATURDAY		SUNDAY	
Leave Bridgeport	Due G. C. T.	Leave Bridgeport	Due G. C. T.	Leave Bridgeport	Due G. C.
a2:19AM	y4:05AM	.....	.....	.....	.....
b2:56	y4:53	2:56AM	y4:53AM	2:56AM	y4:5
3:47	PS5:15	3:47	PS5:15	3:47	PS5:1
A5:05	6:38	5:05	6:38	.....	.....
A6:01	7:55	.....	.....	.....	.....
6:14	7:30	6:14	7:30	6:14	7:3
6:41	PS7:55	6:26	8:24	6:41	PS7:5
A6:49	8:12	6:41	PS7:55	.....	.....
H7:04	8:42	.....	.....	.....	.....
C7:12	8:40	7:04	8:42	.....	.....
C7:24	8:44	7:51	9:14	.....	.....
A7:51	9:14	.....	.....	8:08	9:3
B8:17	y9:25	8:29	10:04	.....	.....
8:29	10:04	8:55	10:00	8:55	10:0
8:55	10:00	.....	.....	.....	.....
A8:59	10:20	9:28	10:53	9:22	10:3
9:28	10:53	.....	.....	10:43	12:0
.....	.....	10:26	11:57	.....	.....
10:26	11:57	12:03PM	PS1:15PM	12:03PM	PS1:1
12:03PM	PS1:15PM	12:15	1:40	12:15	1:4
12:15	1:40	1:09	2:15	1:09	2:1
1:09	2:15	.....	.....	2:05	3:2
.....	.....	2:08	PS3:20	2:08	PS3:2
2:08	PS3:20	2:15	3:35	.....	.....
2:15	3:35	3:50	5:17	3:50	5:1
3:50	5:17	4:29	5:49	4:29	5:4
4:29	5:49	5:22	6:30	5:22	6:3
5:22	6:30	5:33	6:48	.....	.....
5:33	6:48	6:14	PS7:20	6:14	PS7:2
6:14	PS7:20	6:32	8:00	6:32	8:0
6:32	8:00	.....	.....	7:20	8:2
J7:20	8:25	7:31	8:45	7:31	8:4
7:31	8:45	8:13	9:19	8:13	9:1
8:13	9:19	9:15	PS10:25	8:53	10:2
K8:53	10:25	9:26	10:38	9:15	PS10:2
9:15	PS10:25	9:48	PS11:00	9:28	10:3
9:26	10:38	.....	.....	D9:40	10:5
E9:40	10:52	.....	.....	9:56	11:1
9:48	PS11:00	.....	.....	10:23	11:3
J9:56	11:15	.....	.....	D11:08	12:2
L10:23	11:35	11:28	12:45AM	11:29	12:4
E11:08	12:20AM	1:01AM	2:10	1:01AM	2:1
11:28	12:45	.....	.....	.....	.....
1:01AM	2:10				
.....	.....				

REFERENCES

A—Will not run Nov. 27, Dec. 25, Jan. 1 and Feb. 23.
B—Will run only on Nov. 27, Dec. 25, Jan. 1 and Feb. 23.
C—Will not run on Oct. 13, Nov. 4, 11 and 27, Dec. 25, Jan. 1, Feb. and 23.
D—Will not run Feb. 22.
E—Will run only on Monday, Feb. 23.
F—Will run only on Oct. 13, Dec. 24 and Feb. 23.
G—Will not run Feb. 23.
H—Will run only on Oct. 13, Nov. 4, 11 and 27, Dec. 25, Jan. Feb. 12 and 23.
J—Will run only on Nov. 27 and Feb. 23.
K—Will run only on Oct. 13, Nov. 27, Dec. 25, Jan. 1 and Feb. 23.
L—Will run only on Oct. 13 and Feb. 23.
PS—Trains so referenced leave from or arrive in Pennsylvania Station and do not stop at 125th St. Station.

Auth. & Distr. by the New Haven R. R. Publ. by Page Transportation Displays, Inc., Grand Central Terminal, N. Y. Not responsible for errors. Subj. to change without notice.

The official Bridgeport timetable from January 1953 includes advertisements for the Broadway shows *Pal Joey* and *The King and I.* Note how the Hotel Barnum has a place called the Pink Elephant Lounge. P.T. Barnum showcased a white elephant, but we are not so sure about a pink one. (Courtesy Marc Frattasio collection.)

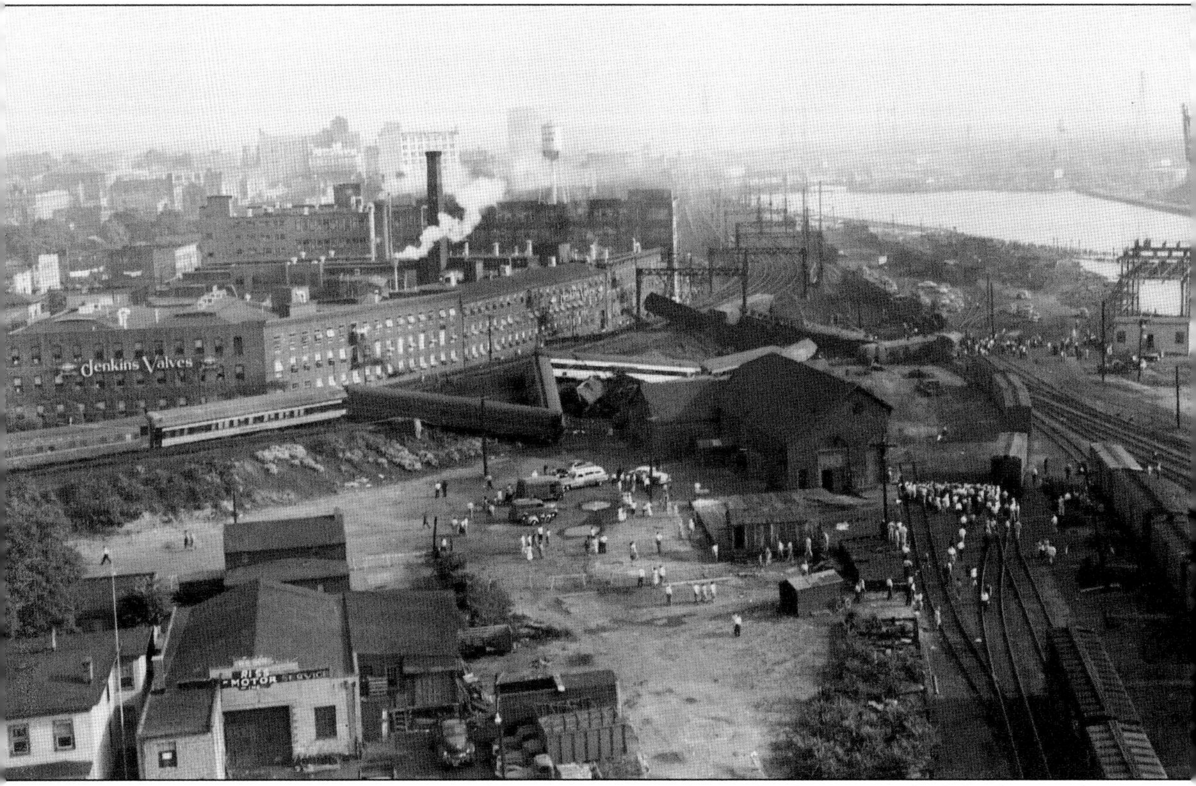

Just when you thought the legendary night train, the *Federal Express*, had had enough, it happened again. This crash occurred on July 14, 1955, the same month as the first one 44 years earlier. The train was en route to Boston from Washington, D.C., when it accelerated too fast around a curve. (Courtesy J.W. Swanberg collection.)

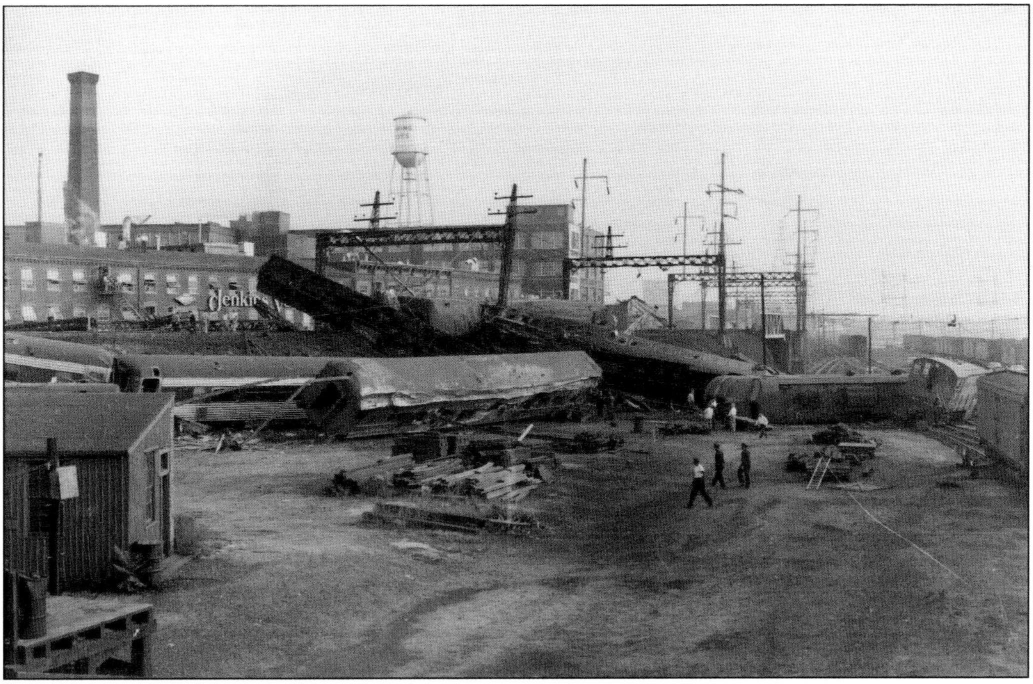

These two photographs give a closer view of the 1955 *Federal Express* wreckage. Above are the elevated tracks with the Jenkins Valve building in the background. Today, the Jenkins Valve site is home to a minor league baseball stadium and sports arena. Below, an undertaker waits for the remains of the engineer killed in the wreck. Note the U462 license plate at the right, the U of which stands for undertaker. (Courtesy J.W. Swanberg collection.)

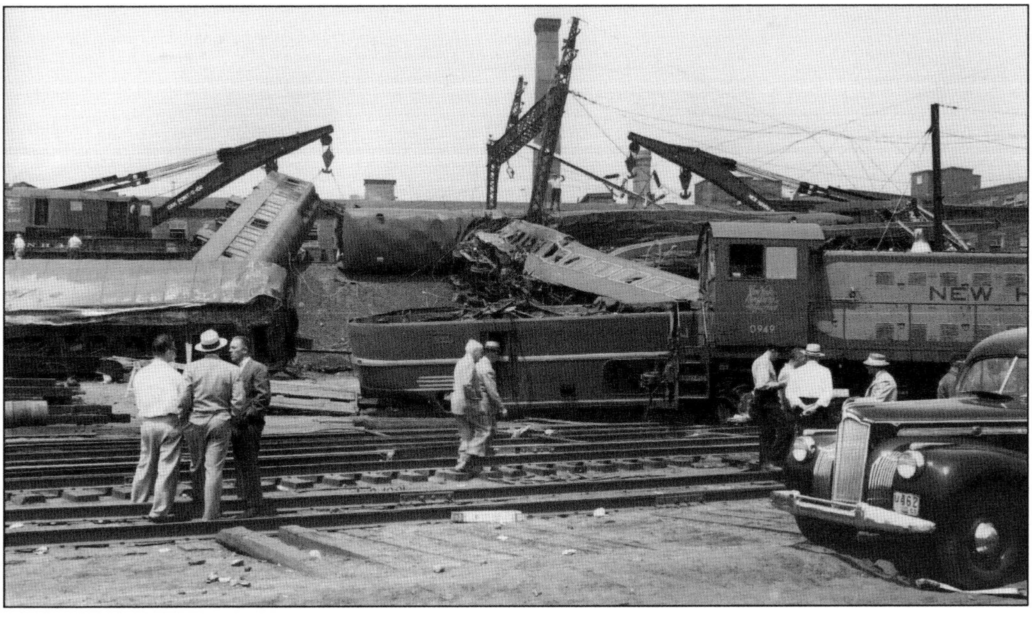

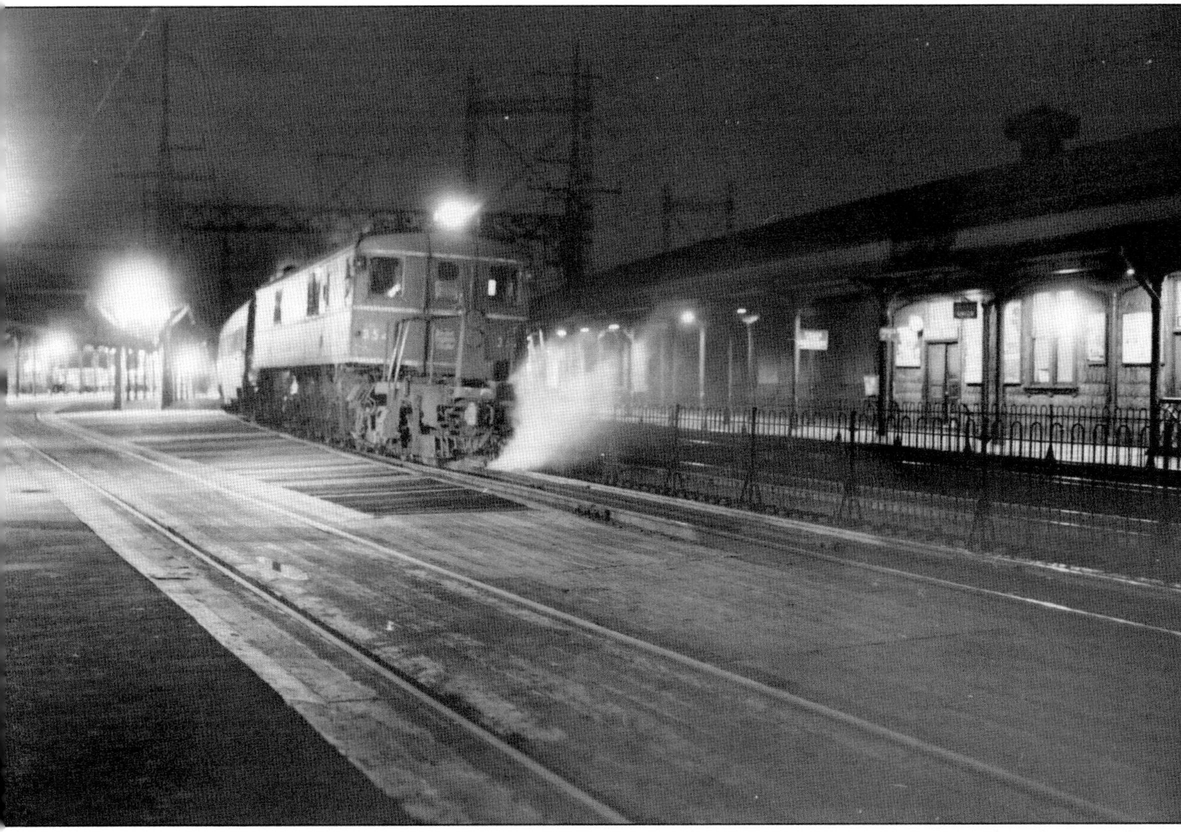

On January 1, 1958, a New Haven Railroad electric locomotive passenger train heads out of Bridgeport Station, spewing steam that heats the train. The buffs call this an NH 354 on train 385. The train ran on Sundays and holidays only. (Courtesy J.W. Swanberg collection.)

High-tension wires tower above a Bridgeport drawbridge on January 21, 1968, as New Haven Railroad locomotive 374 pulls the train known as the *Senator*. (Courtesy J.W. Swanberg collection.)

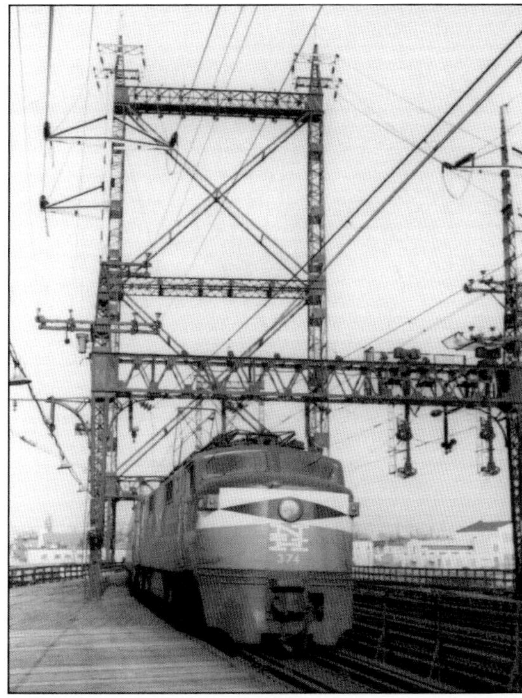

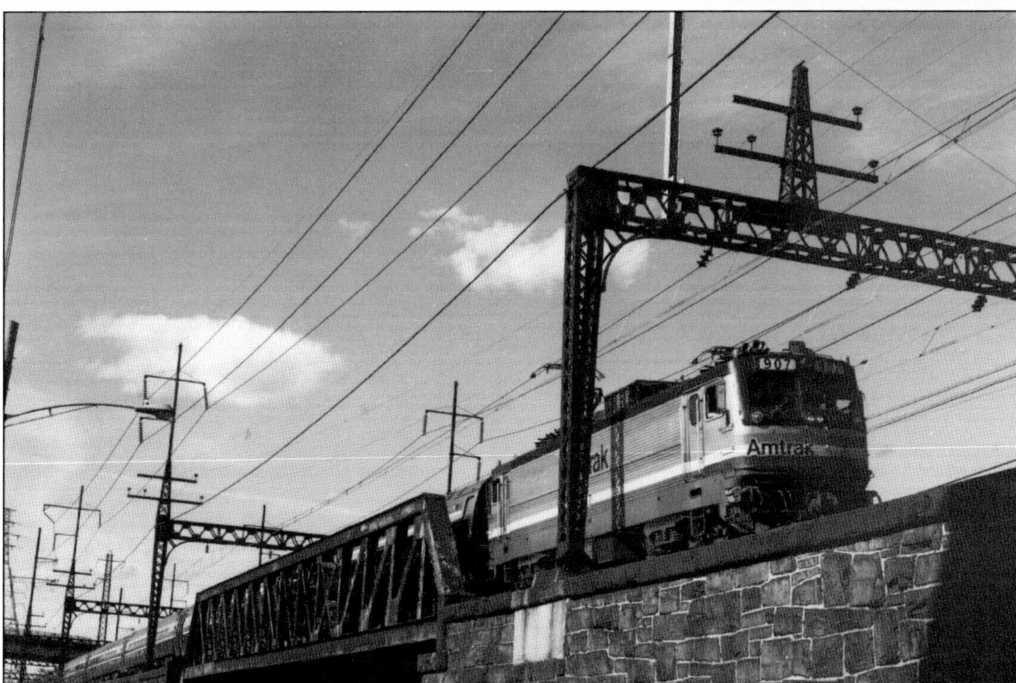

An Amtrak 907 electric locomotive heads for Washington, D.C., on August 29, 1982, pulling the *Minute Man* just before Jenkins Curve, which got its name from the Jenkins Valve factory nearby. This is the curve that now wraps around the outfield fence of Bluefish Stadium at Harbor Yard. The vacant Jenkins Building was demolished to make way for the ballpark in 1998. (Courtesy J.W. Swanberg collection.)

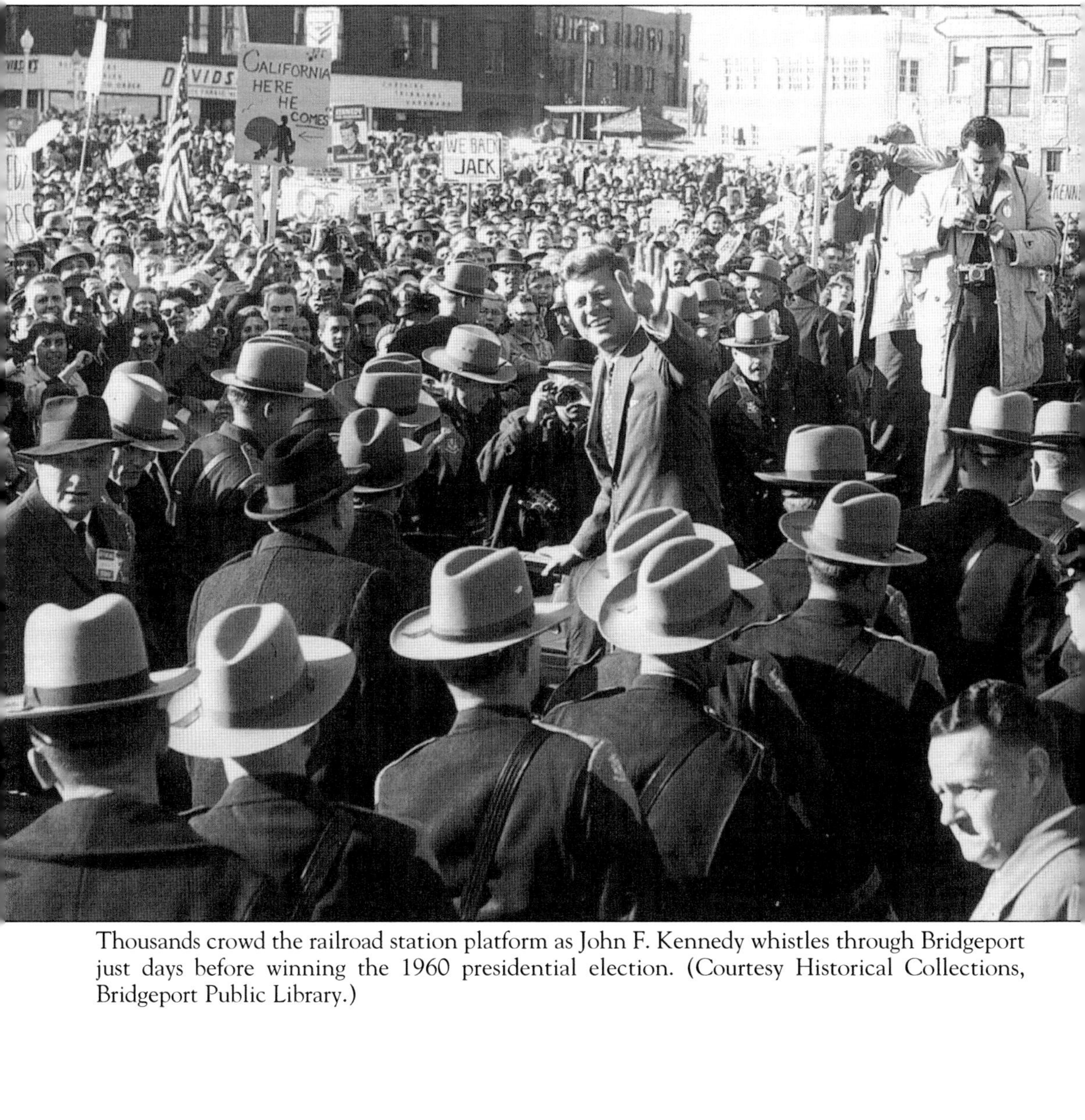

Thousands crowd the railroad station platform as John F. Kennedy whistles through Bridgeport just days before winning the 1960 presidential election. (Courtesy Historical Collections, Bridgeport Public Library.)

Nine

Stratford and Milford Stations

Stratford and Milford are separate stops along the New Haven branch, although New Haven Railroad timetables in the early days combined the two communities. Stratford has a rail line and a Sikorsky line. The legacy of Igor Sikorsky's helicopter is preserved with the company that carries his name and an assembly line of workers paying tribute to his vertical aerodynamics. The National Helicopter Museum, located just steps from the Metro-North platform, features photographs of rotary wing development, highlighting its contributions to rescue efforts and to the economy of the region.

If you are dining in the Shell Station restaurant for the first time, the thunderous jolt is not a volcanic eruption but rather the shakes and screams of Metro-North and Amtrak trains racing by. Railroad parking, as at many stops along the western tip, is a challenge. There is a two-year waiting list to secure a permit. A station garage is in the planning stages. Be patient.

Stratford offers an interesting blend of blue-collar worker and Colonial history. The center of town, just south of the railroad tracks, is a walker's delight. The Congregational church is a classic, white 18th-century building, representative of many greens in Connecticut towns. Next door is the Sterling House, a community center in Victorian design. The Judson House, on Academy Hill, is home to the Stratford Historical Society.

Milford is the first stop along Metro-North in New Haven County and the next-to-last stop along the New Haven branch. Milford is a favorite spot for beach-house renters, boaters, and sun worshippers.

The area around the station and the Milford Green, located a short block from the station, are the town's pride and joy. Many older homes, now funeral parlors and insurance offices, line the green. Various monuments to the fallen in every war are scattered along the green, which runs for about a half mile. There is also a monument to fallen volunteer firemen. A plaque highlighting a brief history of the town explains Milford's past.

The Milford Green is used for numerous public events, such as arts-and-crafts shows and the annual Oyster Festival in August on Flower Field, a short distance away. Bands, food, and oyster-eating contests provide the entertainment.

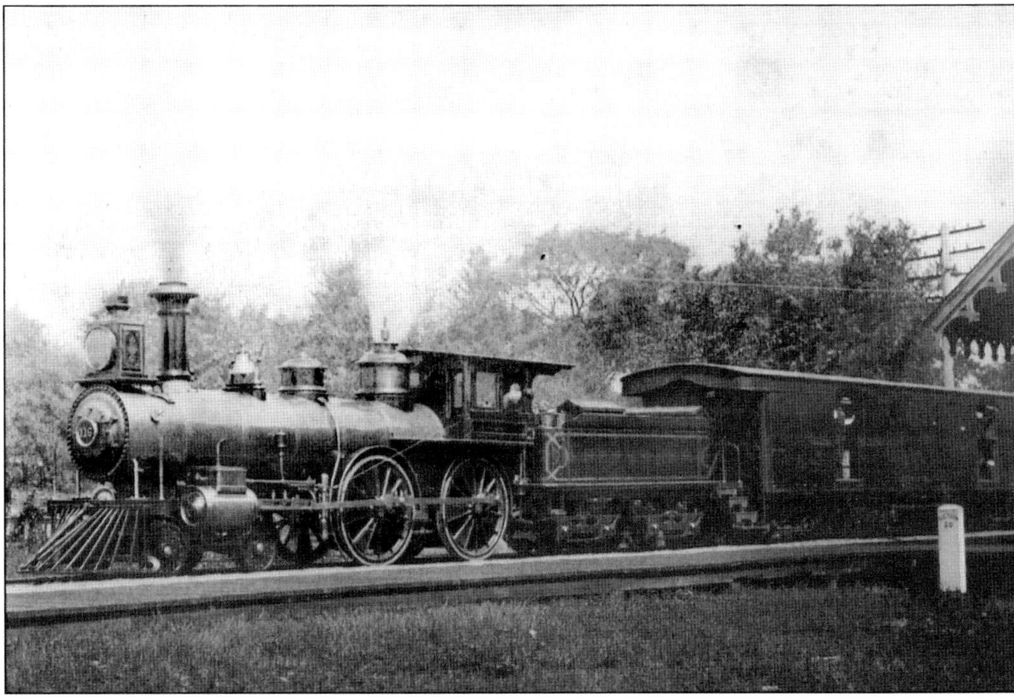

Shown is an early steamer in Stratford, No. 116, shortly after the 1872 consolidation of the New Haven Railroad. (Courtesy Stratford Historical Society.)

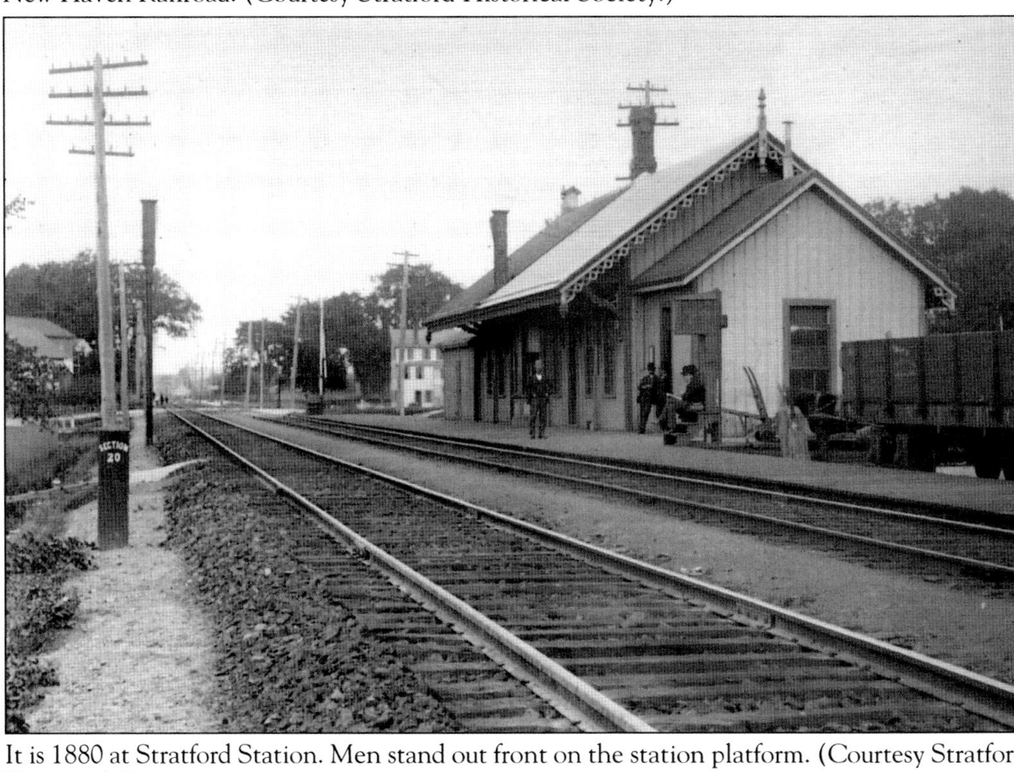

It is 1880 at Stratford Station. Men stand out front on the station platform. (Courtesy Stratford Historical Society.)

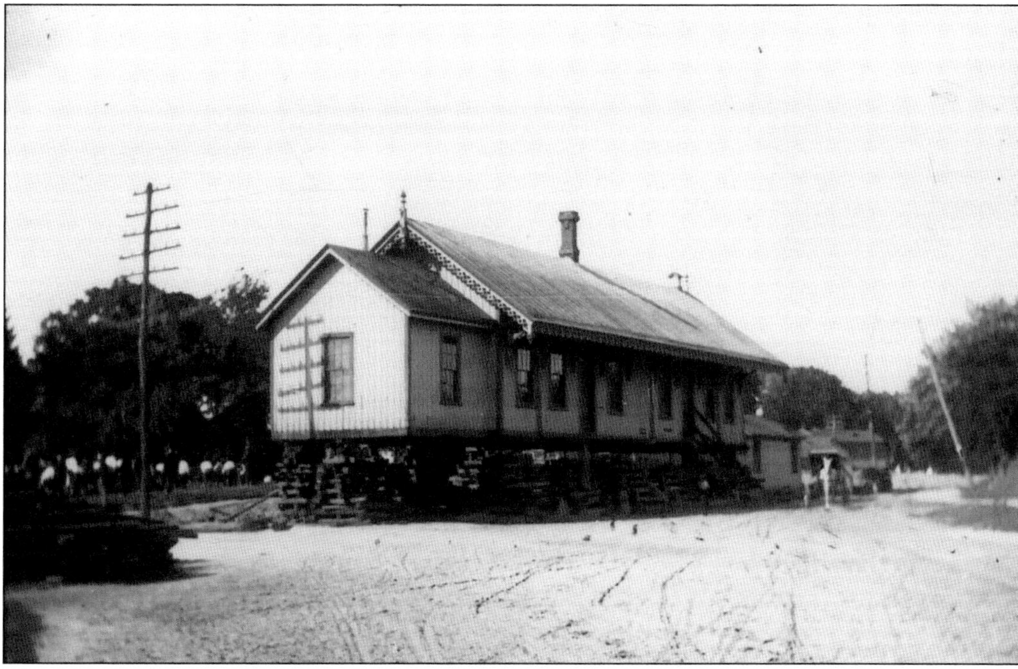

The Stratford Station building in 1894 is being prepared for its relocation to the station's present-day site in Stratford Center. The station building was lifted onto a flatcar and transported along the tracks. (Courtesy Stratford Historical Society.)

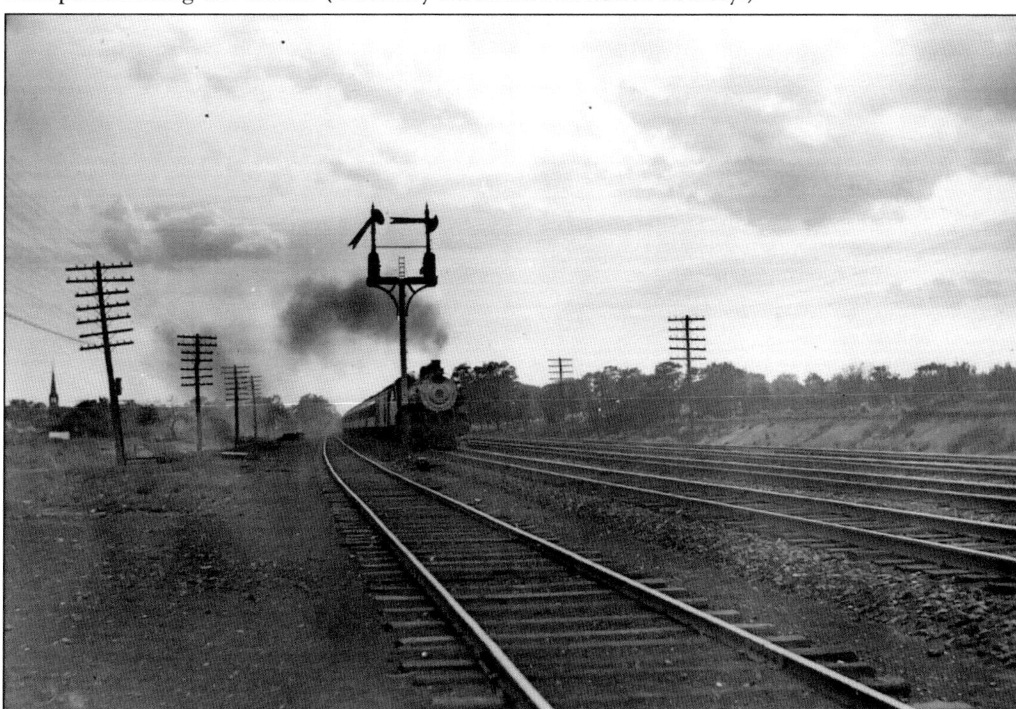

A steamer heads east for New Haven through Stratford on a four-track mainline. This photograph was taken before electrification. (Courtesy Stratford Historical Society.)

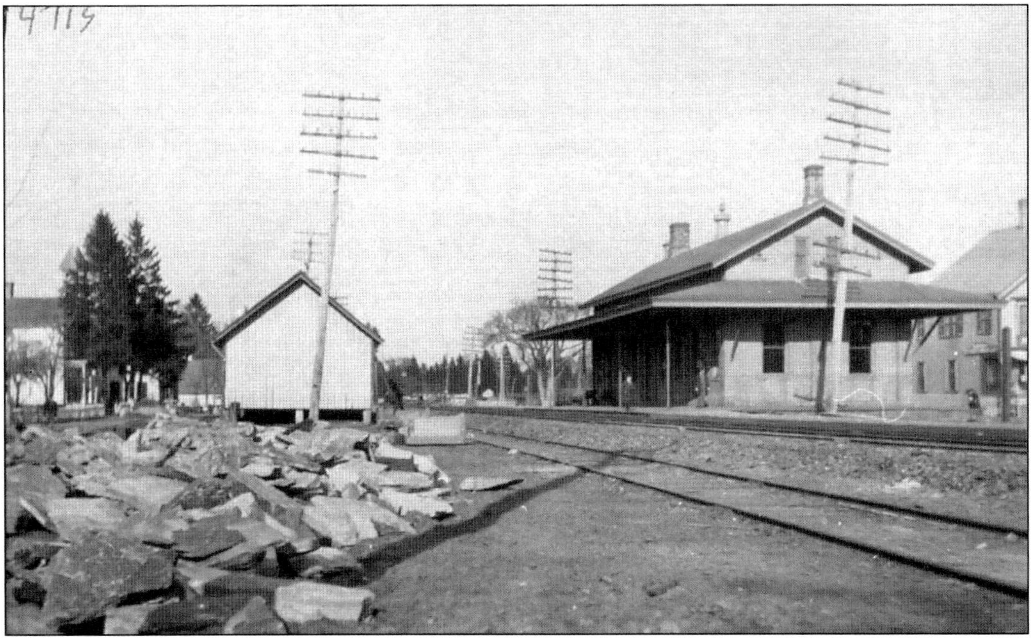

Here are two views of Milford Station. The pre-electrification one, above, shows a pile of rocks left of the tracks, with the station building across tracks at the right c. 1900. The view below shows the station with steel towers for electrified tracks. (Courtesy Thomas J. Dodd Research Center, University of Connecticut.)

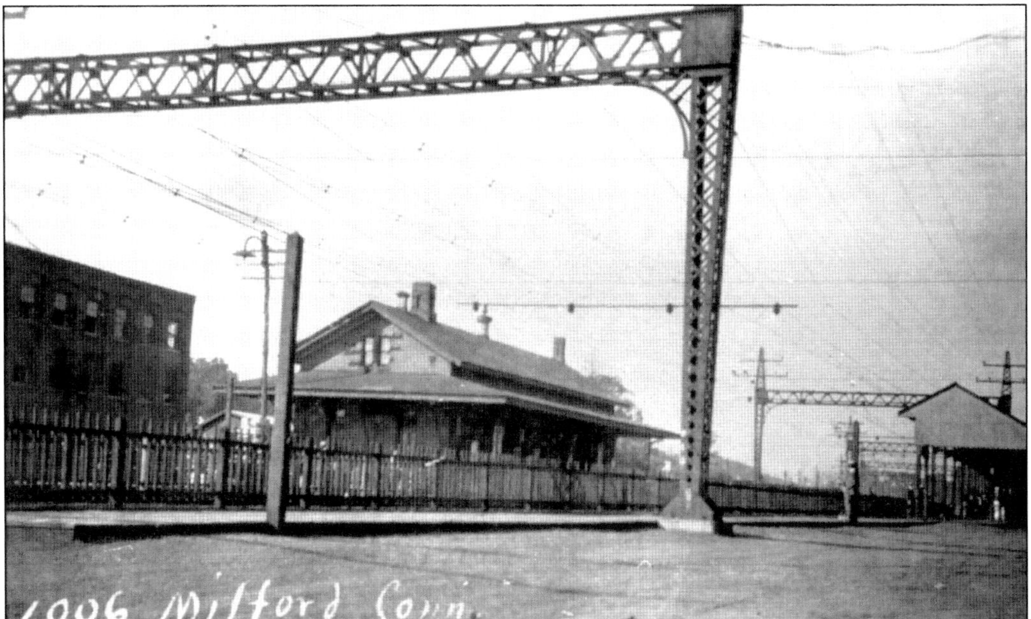

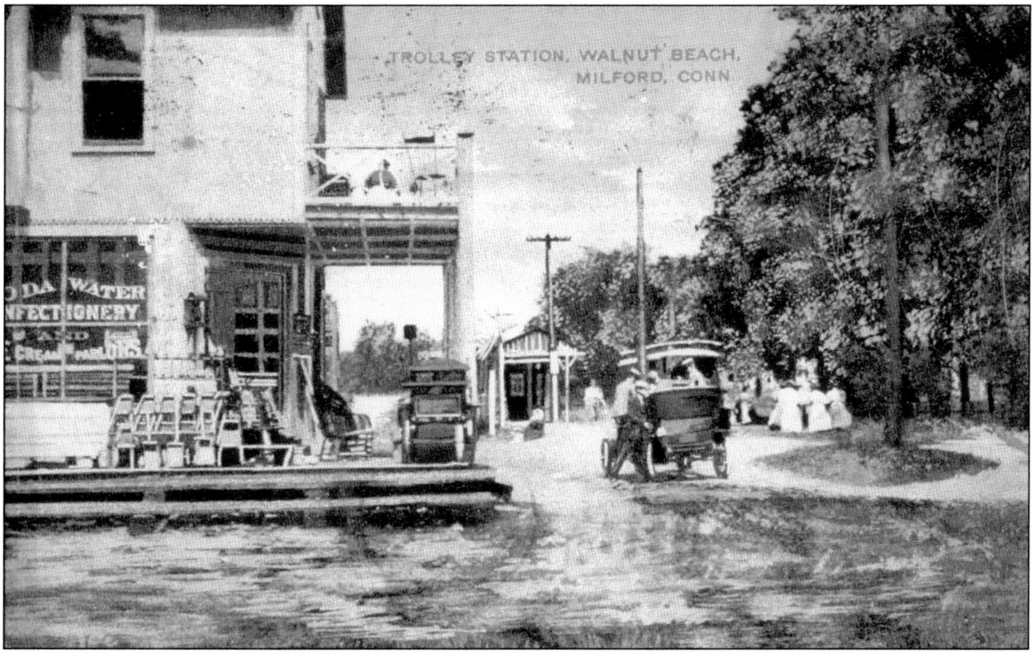

A *c.* 1908 postcard shows the leisurely life around the trolley station at Walnut Beach in Milford. At the left is a confectionery and ice-cream parlor. At the right are an early automobile and a group of women walking to the trolley station. (Courtesy Thomas J. Dodd Research Center, University of Connecticut.)

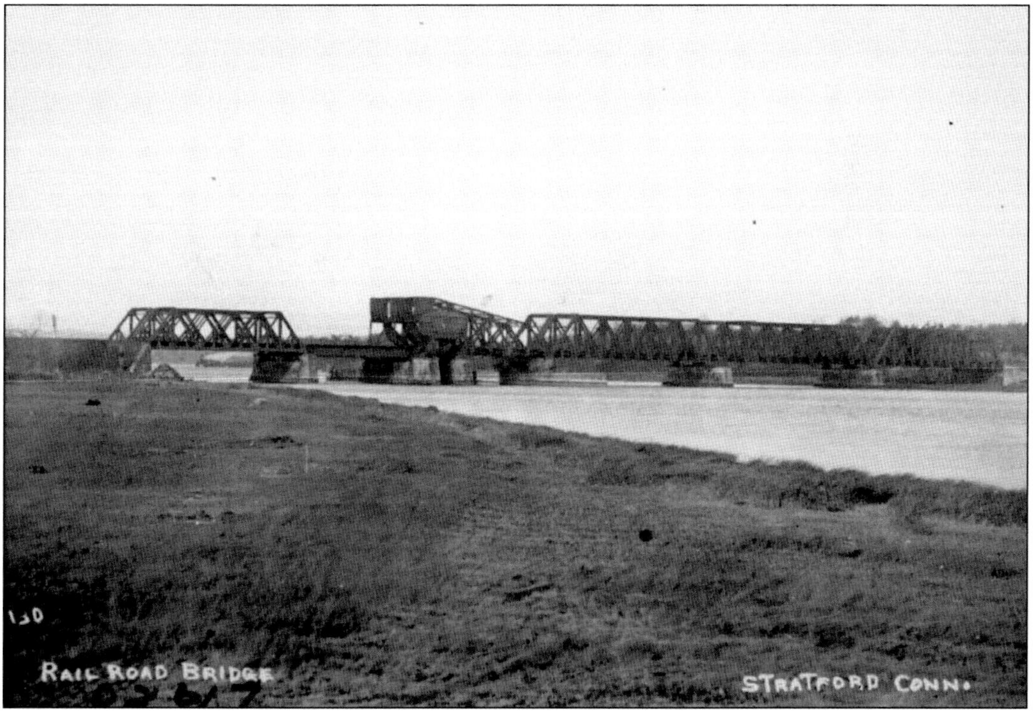

Shown here *c.* 1910 is the railroad bridge over the Housatonic River in Stratford before it was electrified. (Courtesy Thomas J. Dodd Research Center, University of Connecticut.)

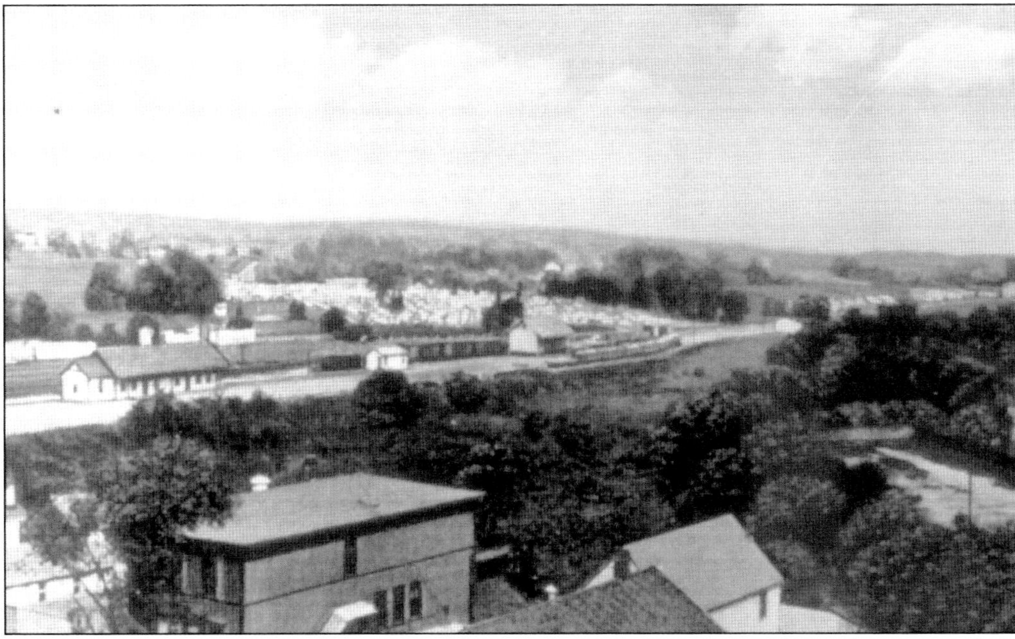

This overview shows the town of Stratford *c.* 1910, with town buildings, houses, and the railroad station in the background. The white area at the rear of the photograph is the Union Cemetery. (Courtesy Thomas J. Dodd Research Center, University of Connecticut.)

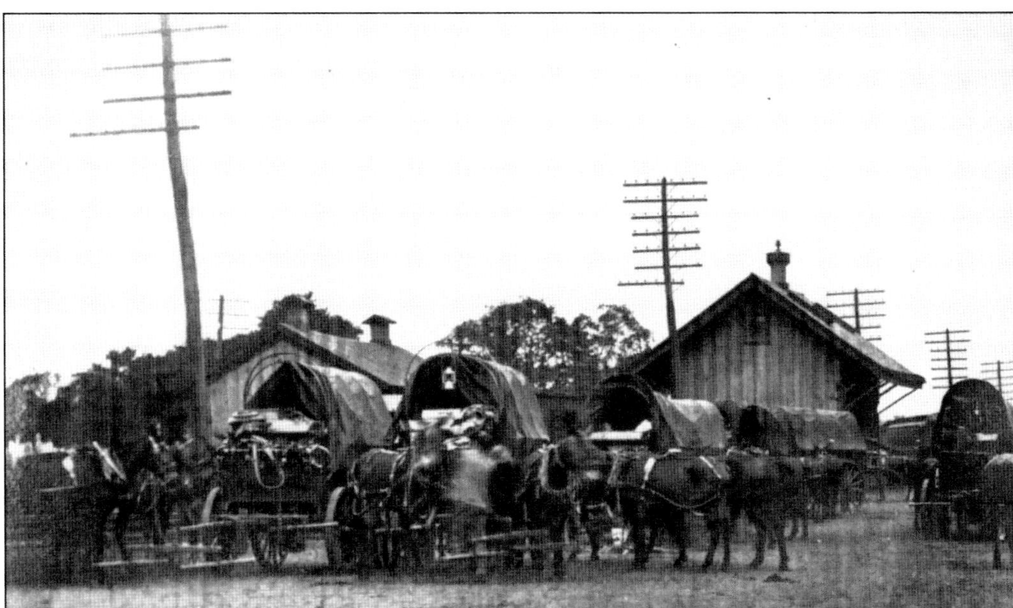

Talk about circling the wagons. Teams of horses are hitched to covered wagons surrounding the Stratford Station building in 1912. We do not know where this wagon train is headed. Actually, this is part of a U.S. military exercise preparing for war maneuvers. America's involvement in World War I is still several years away, but why wait for the last minute? (Courtesy Thomas J. Dodd Research Center, University of Connecticut.)

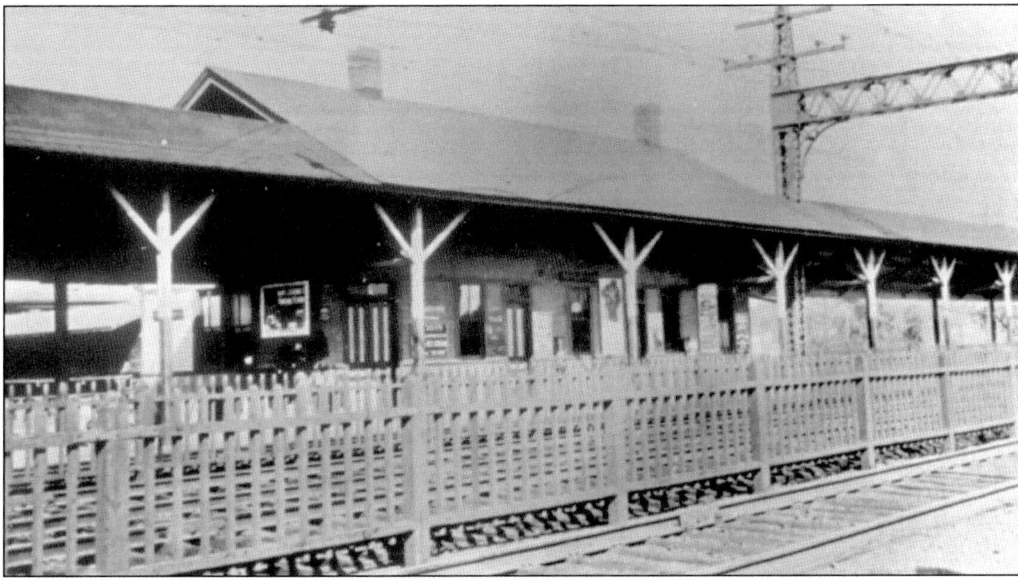

Shown is the westbound railroad station in Milford in 1916. A fence separates tracks in front of a covered platform attached to the station building. Advertising posters are mounted on the exterior wall of the building, with an electrified tower above. (Courtesy Thomas J. Dodd Research Center, University of Connecticut.)

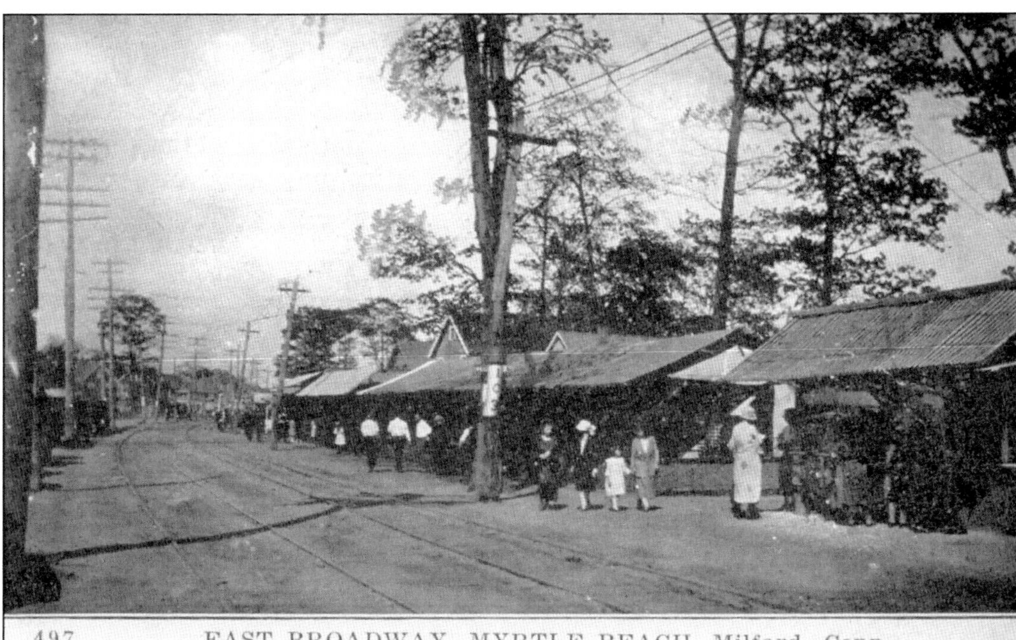

This *c.* 1915 postcard of East Broadway at Myrtle Beach in Milford shows men, women, and children walking along a dirt way, with trolley tracks in front of street vendor stands. (Courtesy Thomas J. Dodd Research Center, University of Connecticut.)

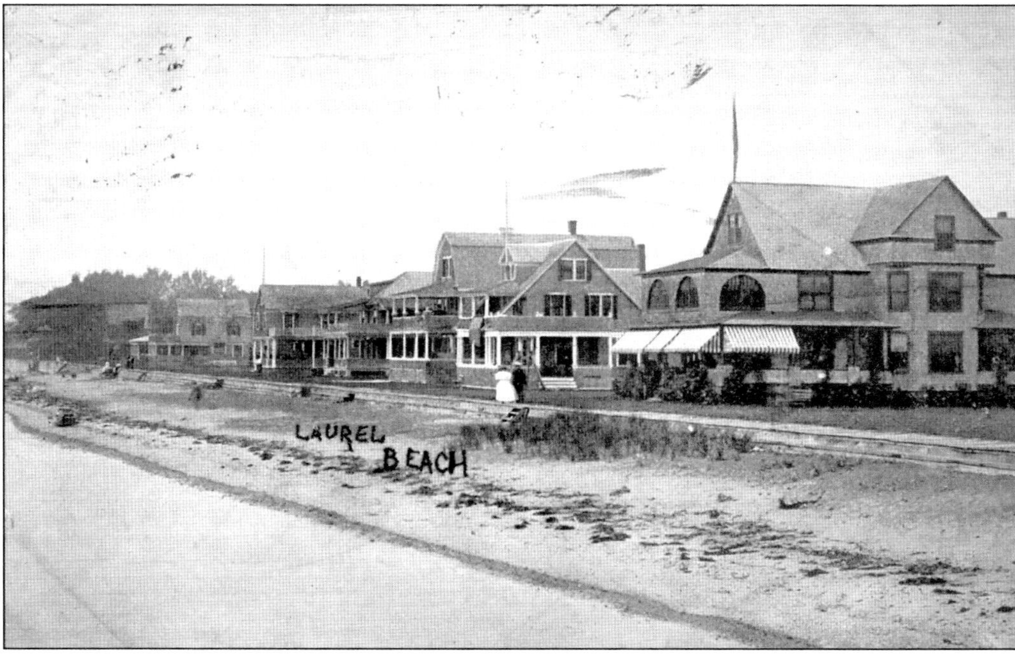

At Laurel Beach in Milford *c.* 1911, two people walk along the boardwalk near the shore in front of the famously large Milford beach houses. (Courtesy Thomas J. Dodd Research Center, University of Connecticut.)

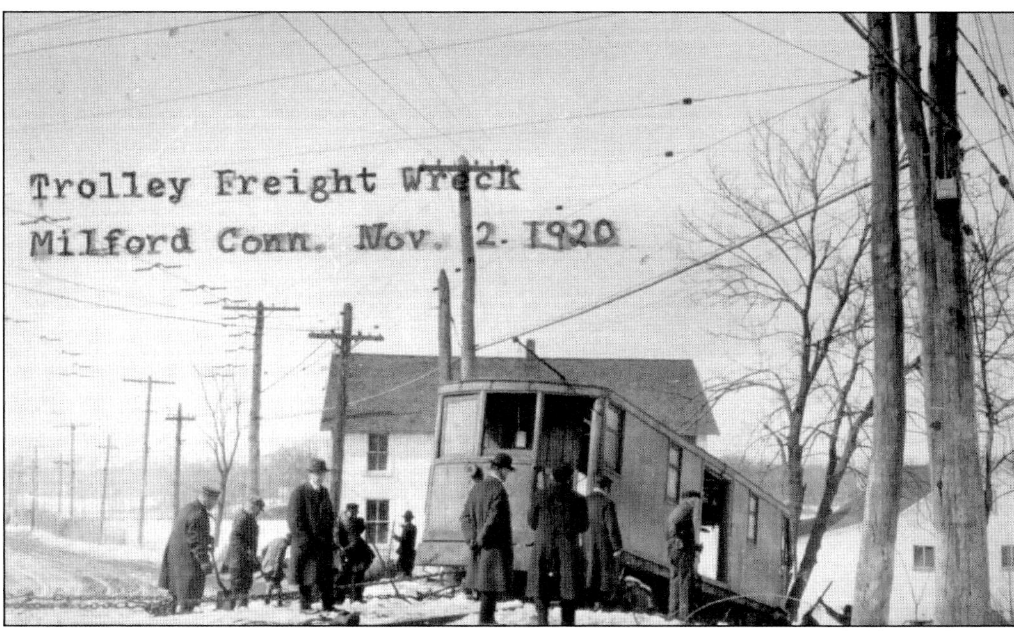

A trolley freight wreck occurred in Milford on November 2, 1920. The photograph shows a group of men standing in the snow, looking at the ruined trolley car while others work to free the car. See, winter did arrive much earlier in those days. (Courtesy Thomas J. Dodd Research Center, University of Connecticut.).

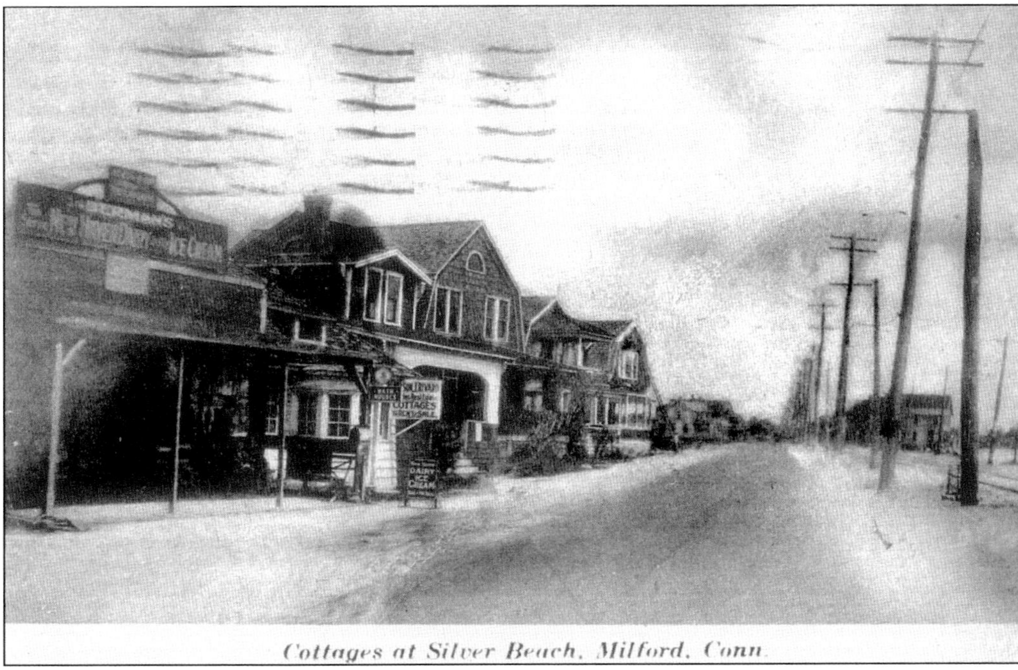

A postcard shows cottages along Silver Beach in Milford *c.* 1925, with advertising signs in front of the store. The lines at the top come from the postmark bleeding through the card. (Courtesy Thomas J. Dodd Research Center, University of Connecticut.)

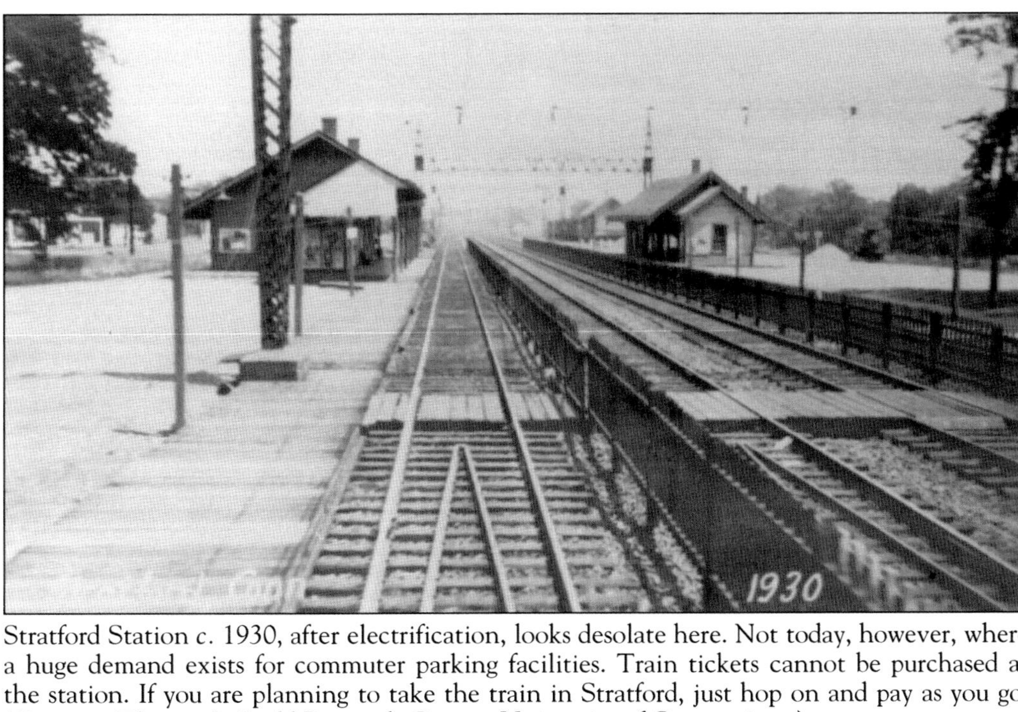

Stratford Station *c.* 1930, after electrification, looks desolate here. Not today, however, where a huge demand exists for commuter parking facilities. Train tickets cannot be purchased at the station. If you are planning to take the train in Stratford, just hop on and pay as you go. (Courtesy Thomas J. Dodd Research Center, University of Connecticut.)

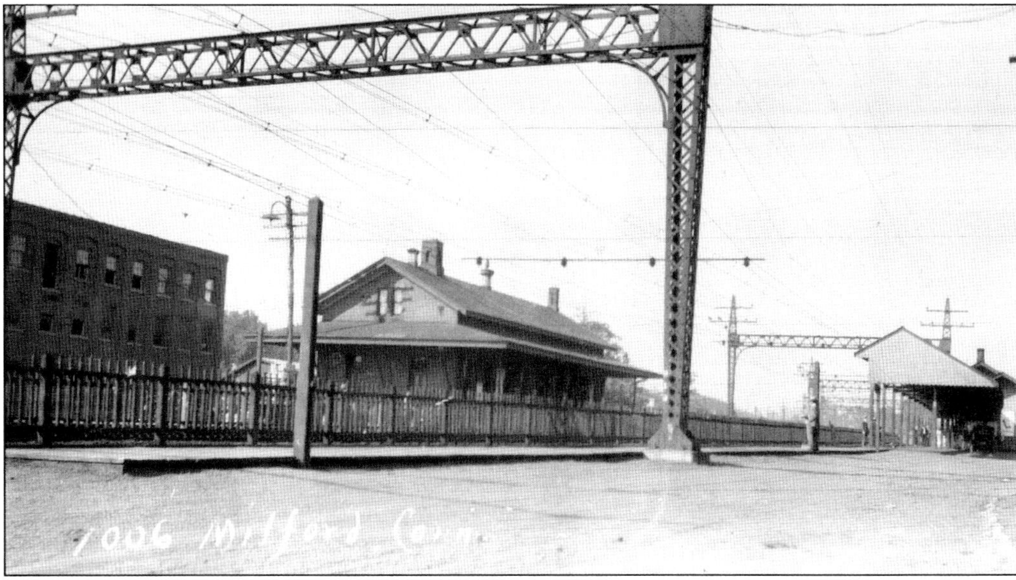

These two views show Milford Station in the 1930s. (Above courtesy J.W. Swanberg collection; below courtesy Thomas J. Dodd Research Center, University of Connecticut.)

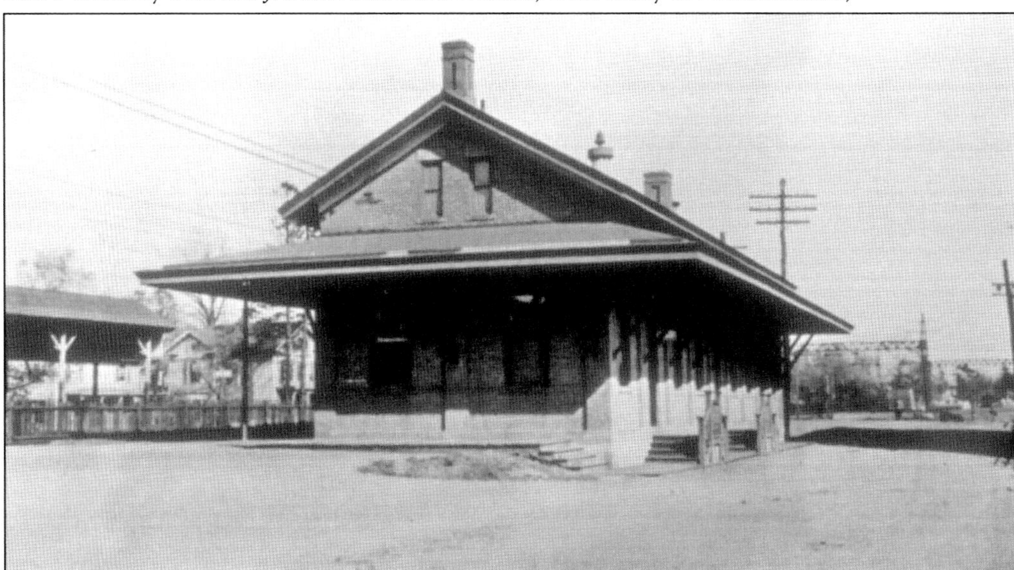

The brilliant Igor Sikorsky views a model of his invention that has saved thousands of lives during war and peace. He first tested his VS-300 helicopter in a flight over Stratford Meadows in 1939. This led to the world's first helicopter assembly line in Bridgeport. Sikorsky's legacy lives today at the Stratford plant, which has created hundreds of thousands of jobs. (Courtesy Historical Collections, Bridgeport Public Library.)

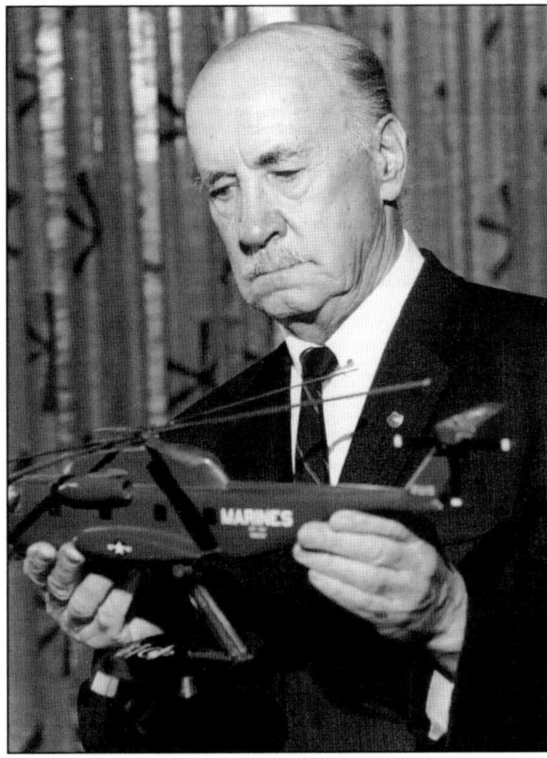

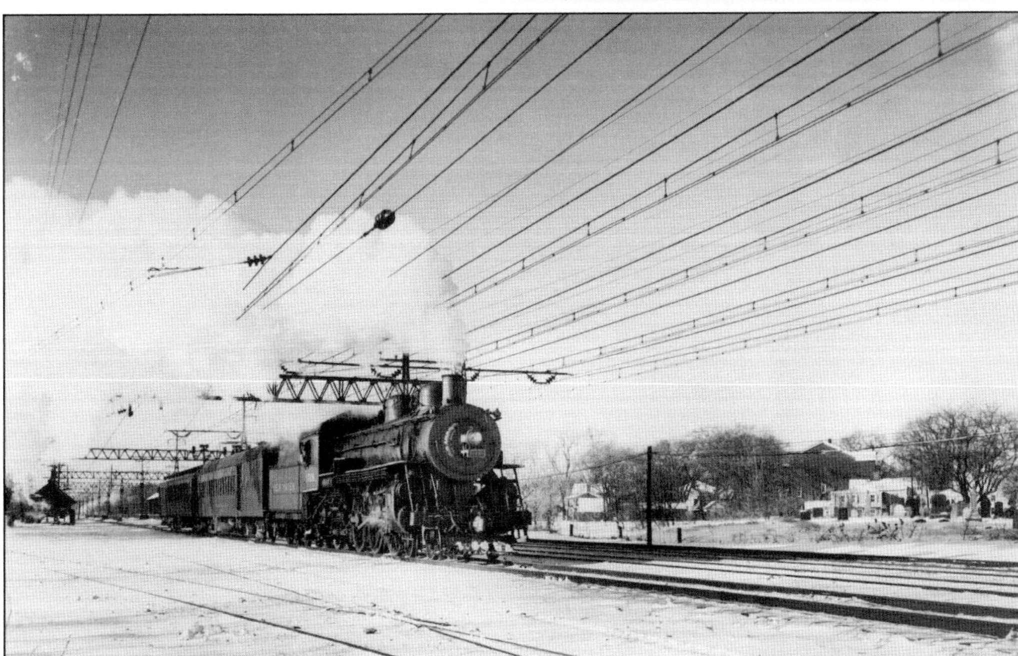

The New Haven Railroad steam age still exists *c.* 1945, as a coal-fired engine rushes through Stratford. The tender on this train holds 6,000 gallons of water and 14 tons of coal—an awful lot of shoveling for the fireman. If you look carefully enough at the far right above the tracks, you will see headstones from the Union Cemetery. (Courtesy J.W. Swanberg collection.)

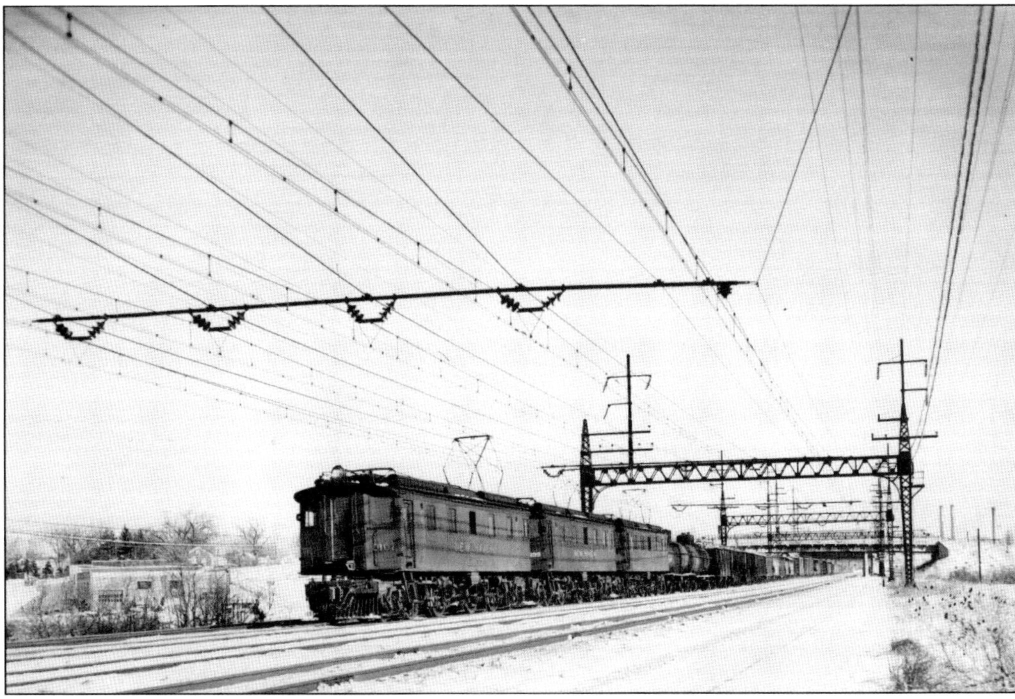

A New Haven Railroad freight train, with electric locomotives, heads to New York from Stratford in the mid-1940s. (Courtesy J.W. Swanberg collection.)

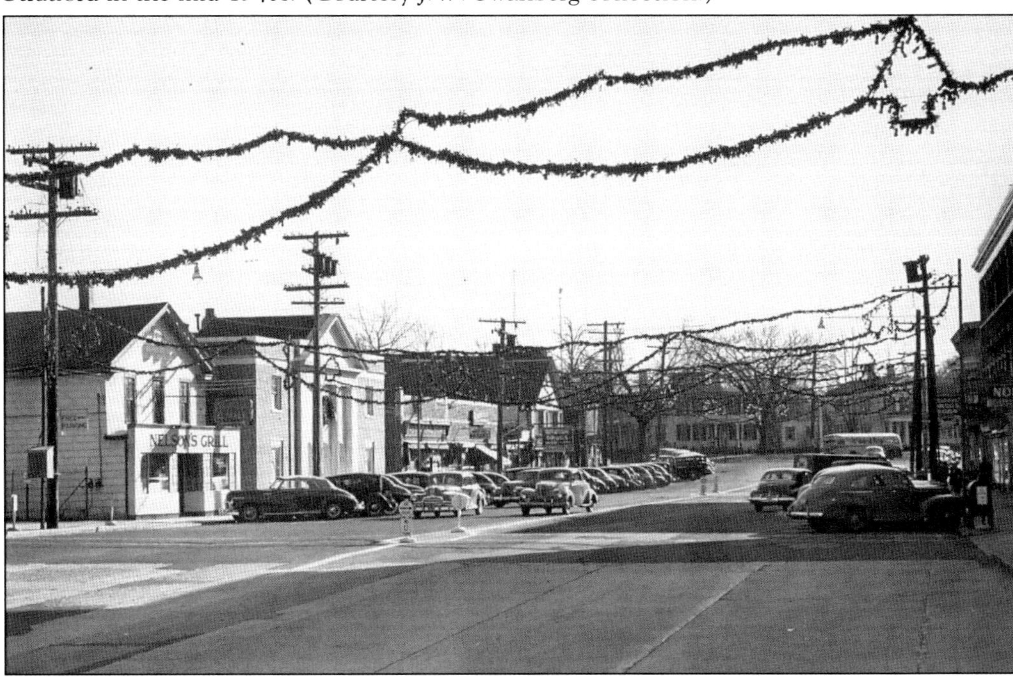

Main Street in Stratford during the 1949 Christmas season shows automobiles parked on both sides of the street, near businesses such as Nelson's Grill and First National. This location is Stratford Center, near the railroad station. (Courtesy Thomas J. Dodd Research Center, University of Connecticut.)

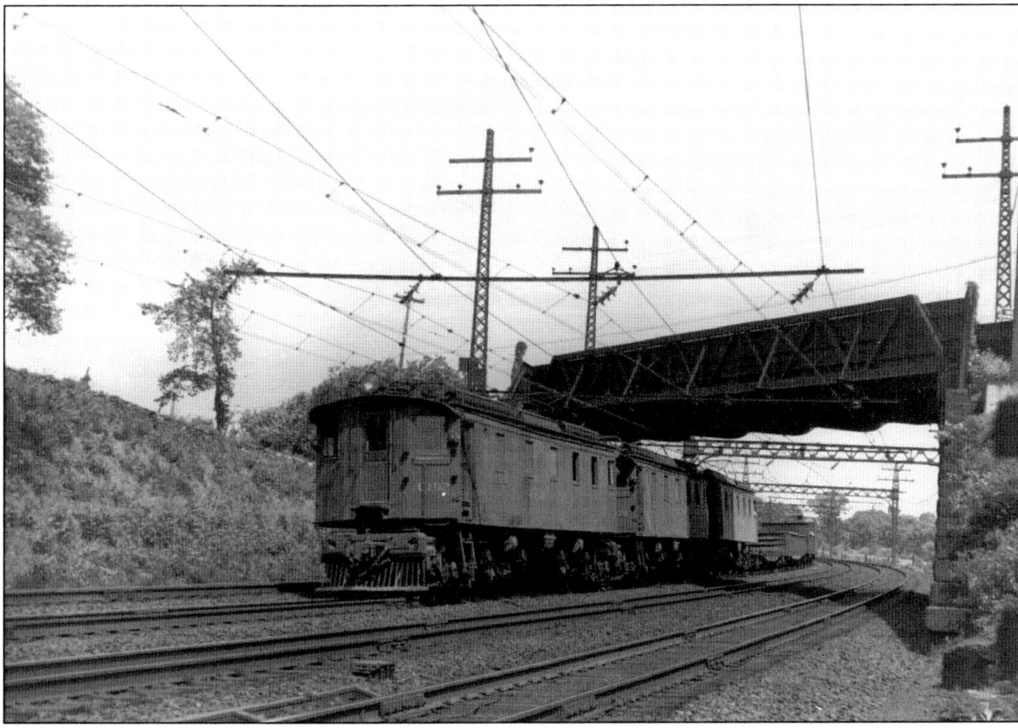

Electric locomotives lead a New Haven Railroad freight train through Milford, heading for New York in 1949. (Courtesy J.W. Swanberg collection.)

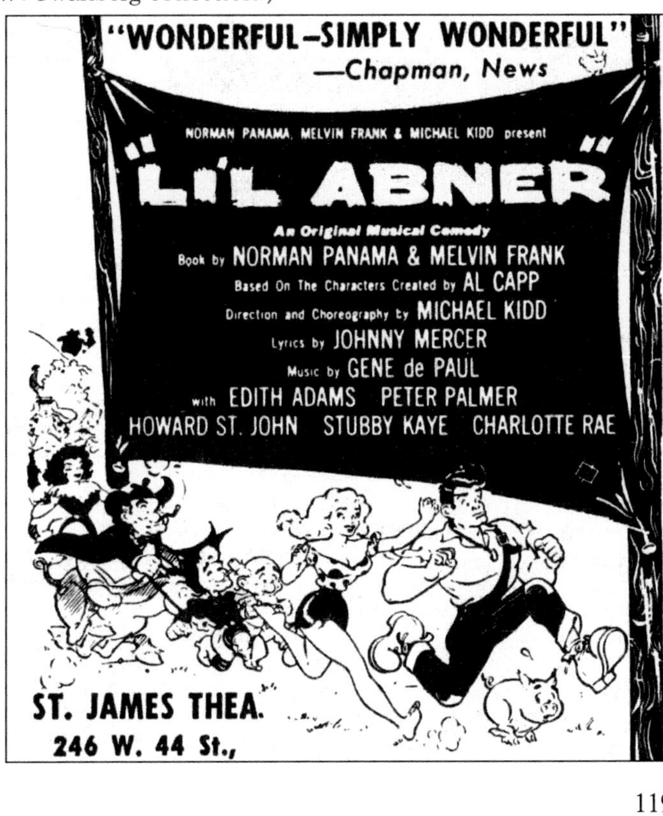

The Milford-Stratford to Bridgeport and New York timetable from 1957 features an advertisement with a local connection: *Li'l Abner*, which was created by Bridgeport's own Al Capp. A hitchhiking trip through the South following Capp's high school days inspired him to sketch the cartoon strip. (Courtesy Marc Frattasio collection.)

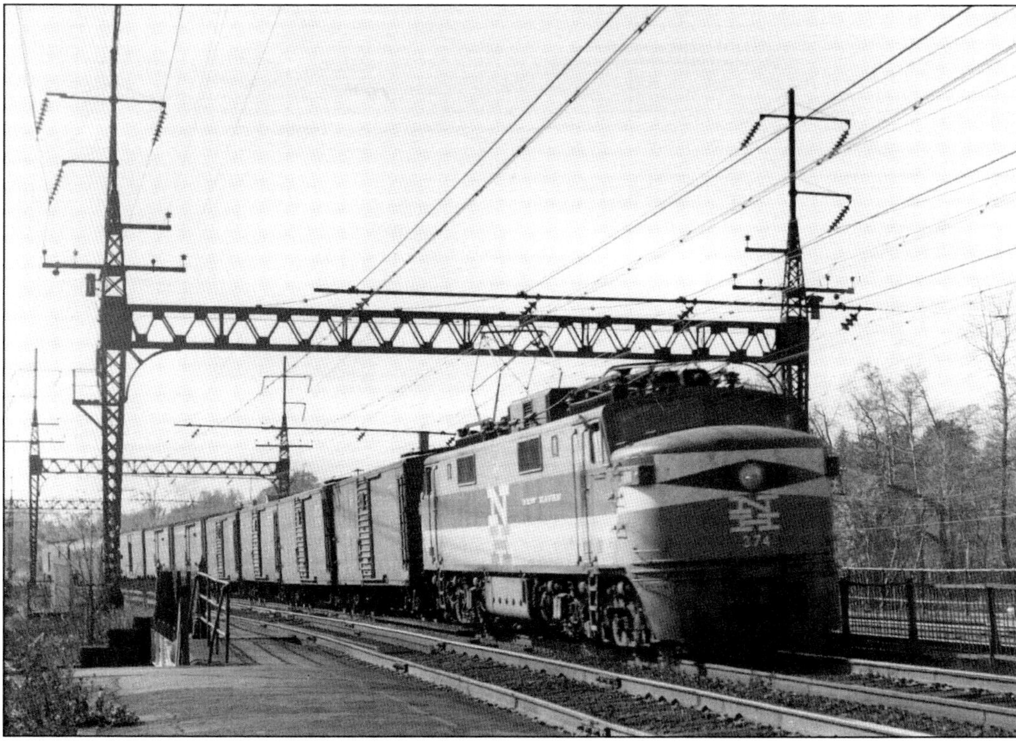

A New Haven Railroad mail and express train, what the rail buffs call an electric locomotive EP-5 rectifier 374 and train 182, storms through Milford en route to Boston on November 1, 1969. The train originated from Penn Station. (Courtesy J.W. Swanberg collection.)

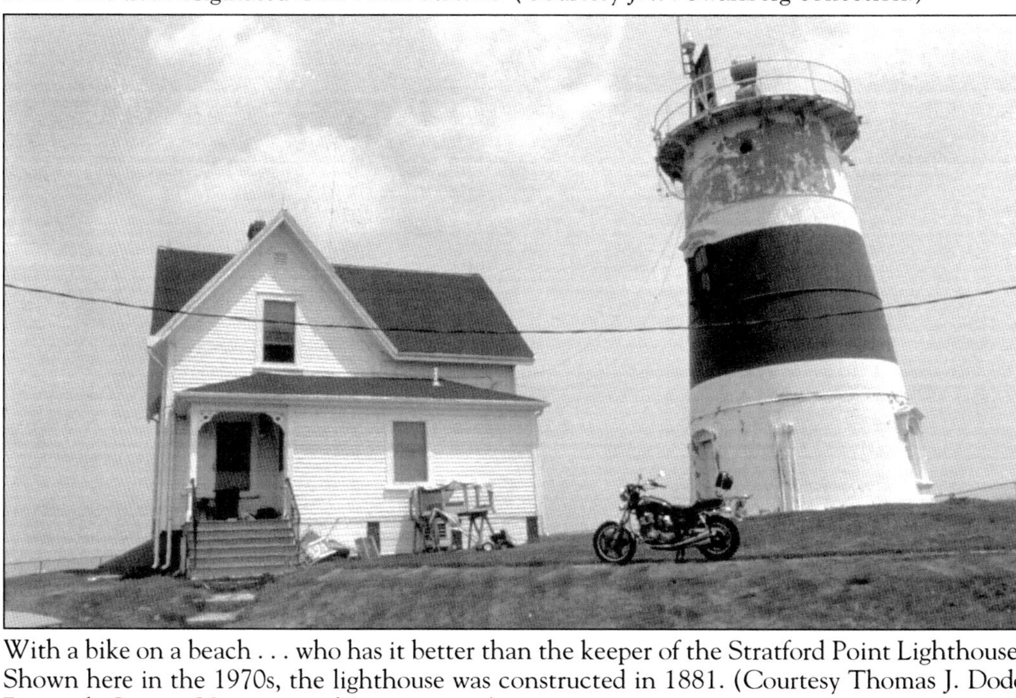

With a bike on a beach . . . who has it better than the keeper of the Stratford Point Lighthouse? Shown here in the 1970s, the lighthouse was constructed in 1881. (Courtesy Thomas J. Dodd Research Center, University of Connecticut.)

Ten

New Haven Station

We have reached the final stop on what the buffs call the West End of the New Haven Line. New Haven is the cultural capital of Connecticut. To enter New Haven by rail is to have arrived, public transportation expert James G. Clark noted. Union Station is a majestic stop along the Metro-North Line. Completed in 1920, it was designed by Cass Gilbert, who also designed the Woolworth Building in Manhattan.

You enter the station through tunnels that evoke the spirit of travel and adventure. Ascending up the escalators, you arrive in the 35-foot-high waiting room. The ceiling is gilded, and huge globes hang over the waiting room. It is a nice appetizer to a city filled with fun and excitement both day and night, thanks in large part to Yale University.

The campus of Yale and the green dominate the downtown. Around it are museums, theaters, and restaurants, with people bustling from one to the other. For theater, there is the Shubert and the Palace, the Yale Repertory, Yale Drama School and Yale Cabaret, and the Long Wharf Theater. Also in the area, thanks to the generosity of some Yale graduates, are the Yale Art Museum and Yale Center for British Art, and for dinosaur fans there is the Peabody Museum.

On theater nights, one is hard-pressed to find a seat in the many restaurants that ring the downtown area. The choices are outstanding. However, many people who want to eat out in New Haven head for Wooster Street, a three-block area known for the finest pizza eateries in the country: Pepe's, the Spot, and Sally's. Which one makes the best pizza is a matter of contentious debate. All are made in coal-fired brick ovens. The crust is extra thin, and you cannot claim to have lived until you order a white clam pie at one of these places.

Beware, James G. Clark warned us, others have the same idea. The lines begin to form before the pizza restaurants are even open. It is not uncommon for 30 people to be standing outside, waiting for the door to open. This requires dedication but, if you are a pizza lover, the wait is worth it.

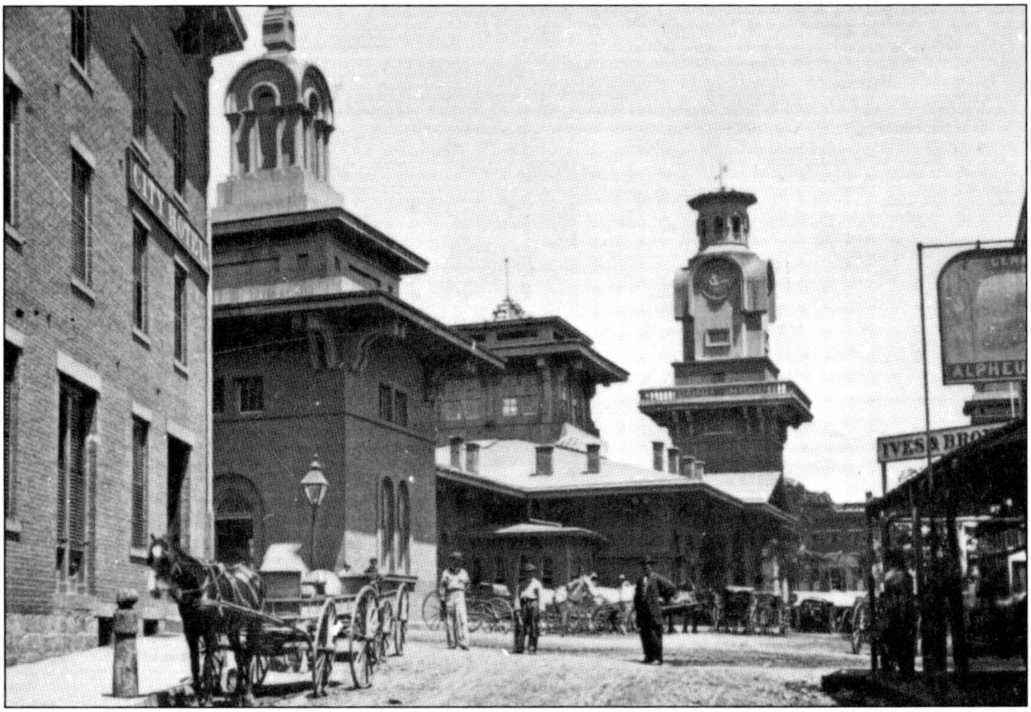

The original New Haven Station on Chapel Street was built in 1848 and closed in 1871. The former station (center) is shown *c.* 1880, during its use as a market. The horse and carriage at the left is parked in front of a city hotel, with shops on the right side. The market that replaced the station burned in 1894. (Courtesy J.W. Swanberg collection.)

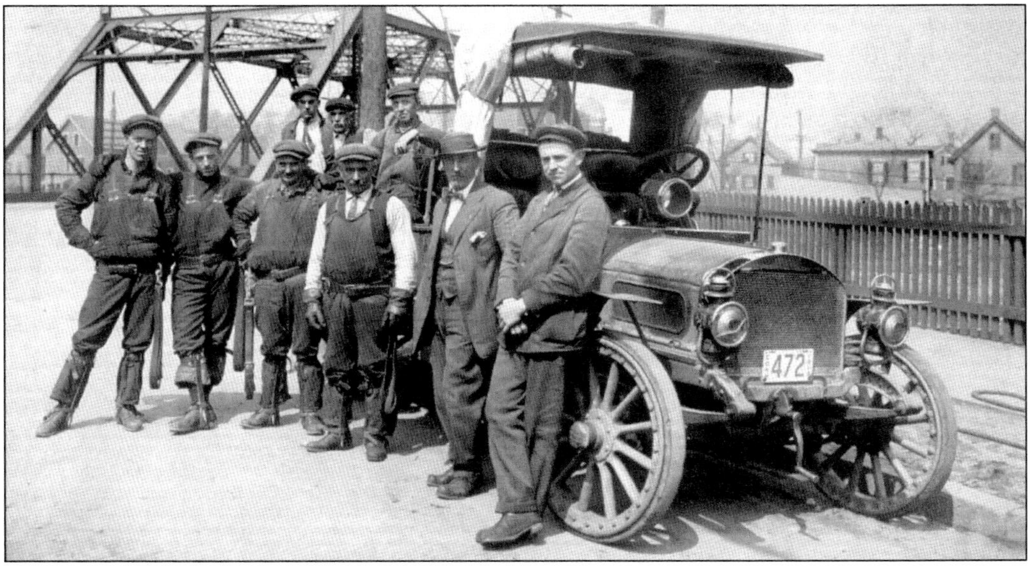

New Haven receives credit for being the first city in the world to open a commercial telephone switchboard, in 1878. These telephone workers pose *c.* 1915 near Middletown Avenue and Ferry Street. Pictured, from left to right, are the following: (front row) Jim Moran, Jim Gordon, David Jackson, Andy Wilson, John Coller, and Dick Shaler; (back row) Mike Foster, Ed Reynolds, and George Hampton. (Courtesy Thomas J. Dodd Research collection, University of Connecticut.)

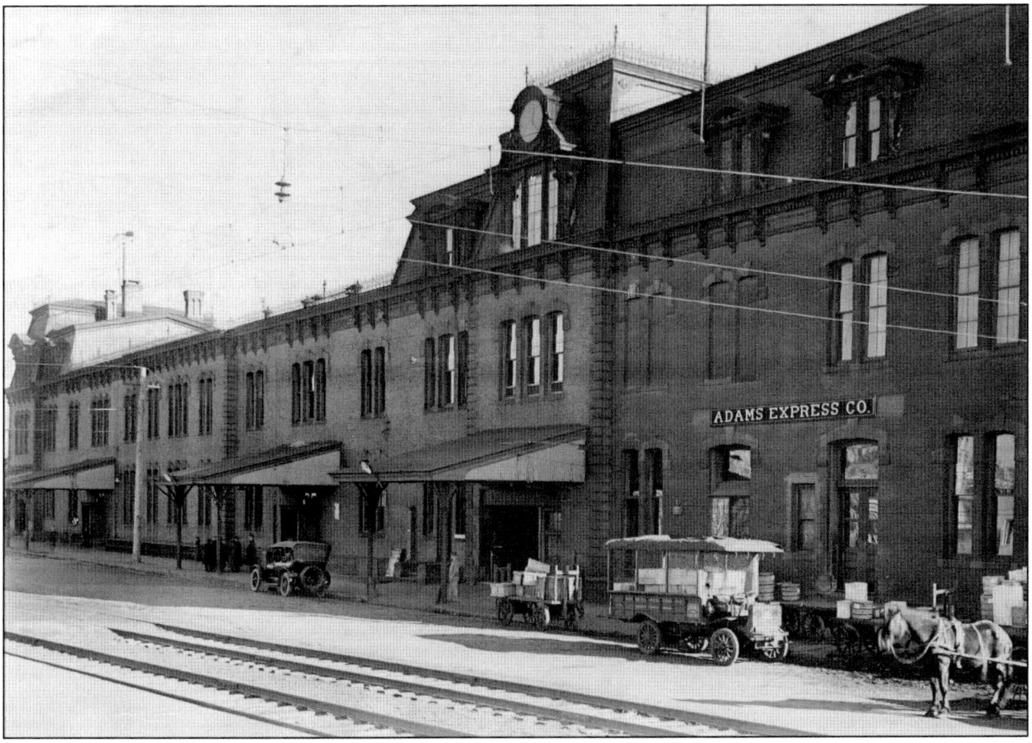

These are two views of the second station in New Haven. The upper one shows the building fronted by automobiles, a baggage cart, a horse and carriage, and tracks. The lower one shows the station on fire being hosed by city firemen. The covered platform is in the foreground. The burning of this building led to the construction of Union Station in 1920. (Courtesy J.W. Swanberg collection.)

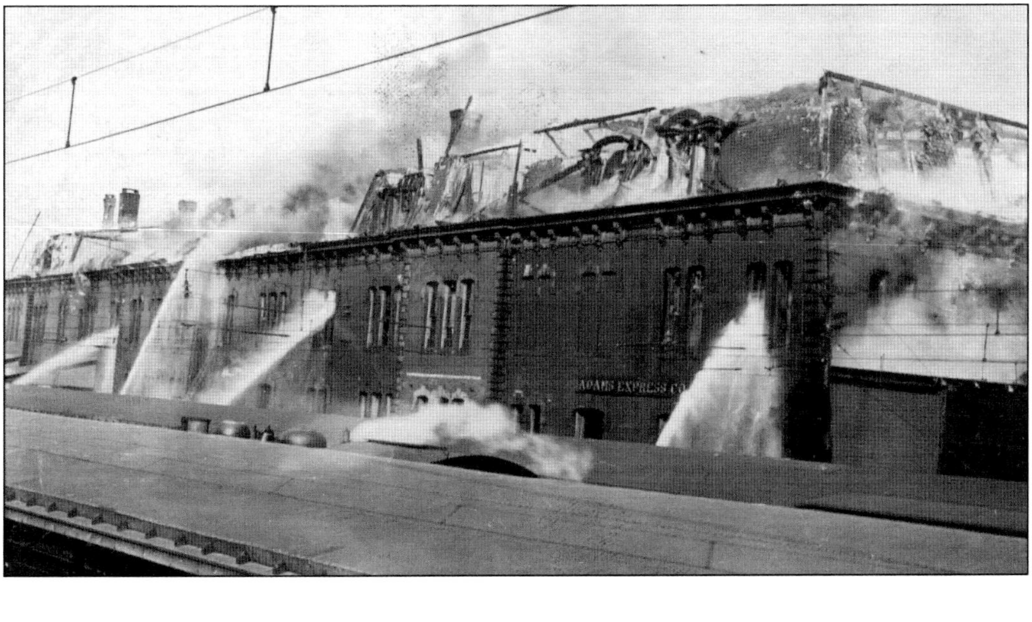

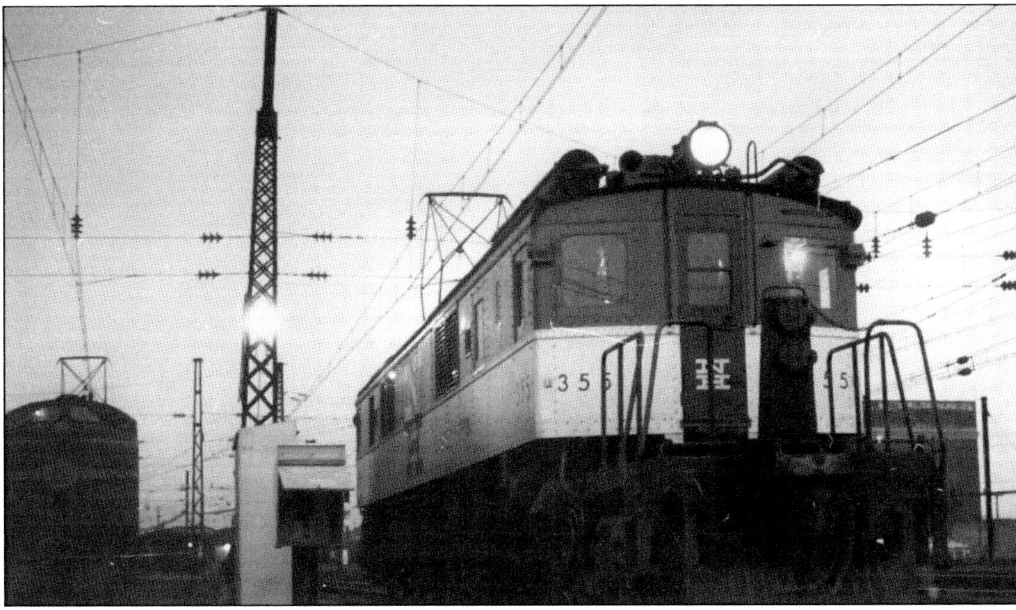

New Haven Line historian Jack Swanberg has dedicated his life to chronicling the steel and cable of the railroad in words and pictures. Here, we see another Swanberg photograph, from March 2, 1958. At the left, a New Haven Railroad locomotive waits in the servicing area of New Haven Station. At the right, a New Haven locomotive prepares for an evening jaunt to New York. (Courtesy J.W. Swanberg collection.)

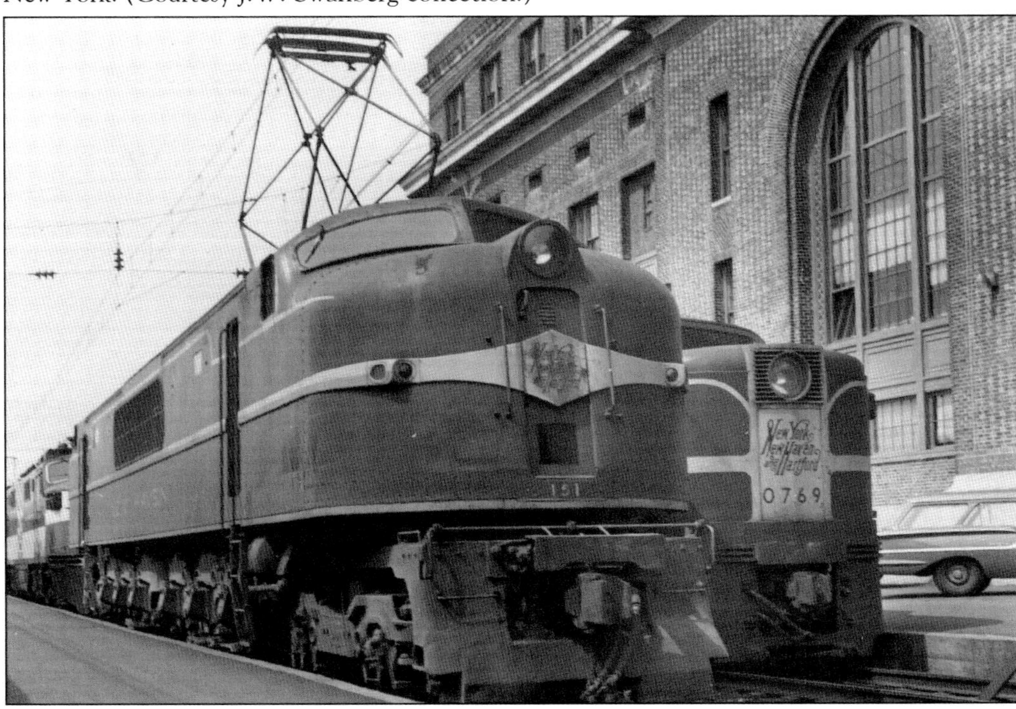

Two trains line up at Union Station in New Haven in 1958. The train at the right, No. 0769, is a diesel heading to Boston. The locomotive at the left, No. 151, is an electric on its way to New York. (Courtesy J.W. Swanberg collection.)

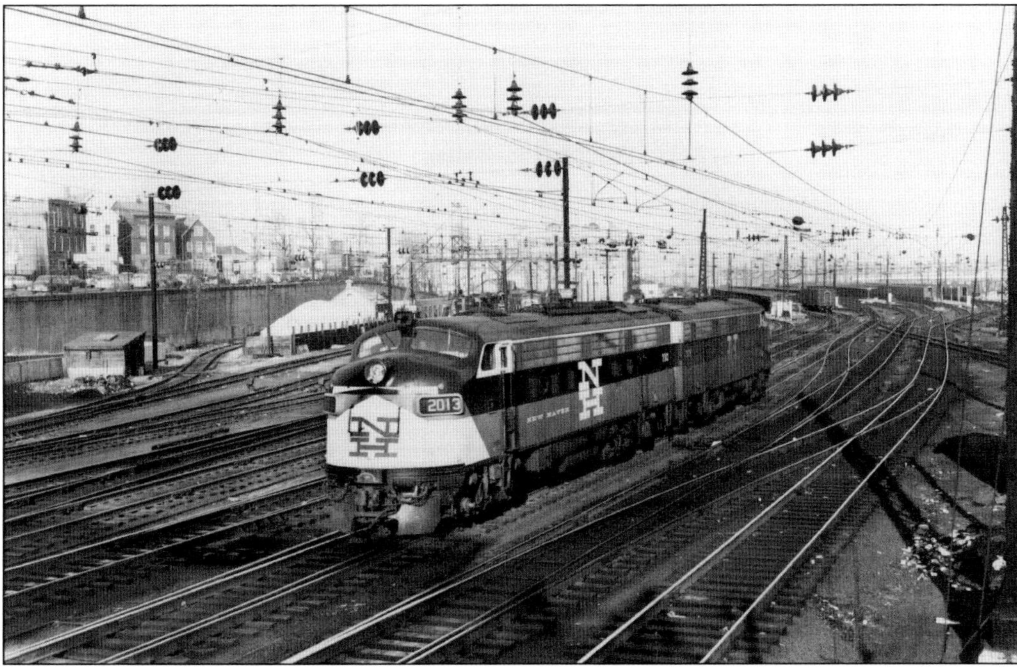

A dual-powered engine (operational on both diesel and electric) roars through New Haven on December 27, 1958. (Courtesy J.W. Swanberg collection.)

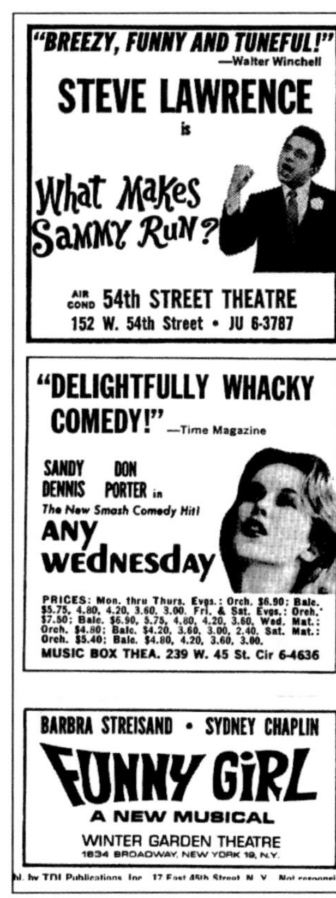

Okay, we have some serious Broadway choices from the New Haven timetable of February 1, 1965. Do you want to see Steve Lawrence, Sandy Dennis, or Barbara Streisand? Note that *Funny Girl* is a new musical. (Courtesy Marc Frattasio collection.)

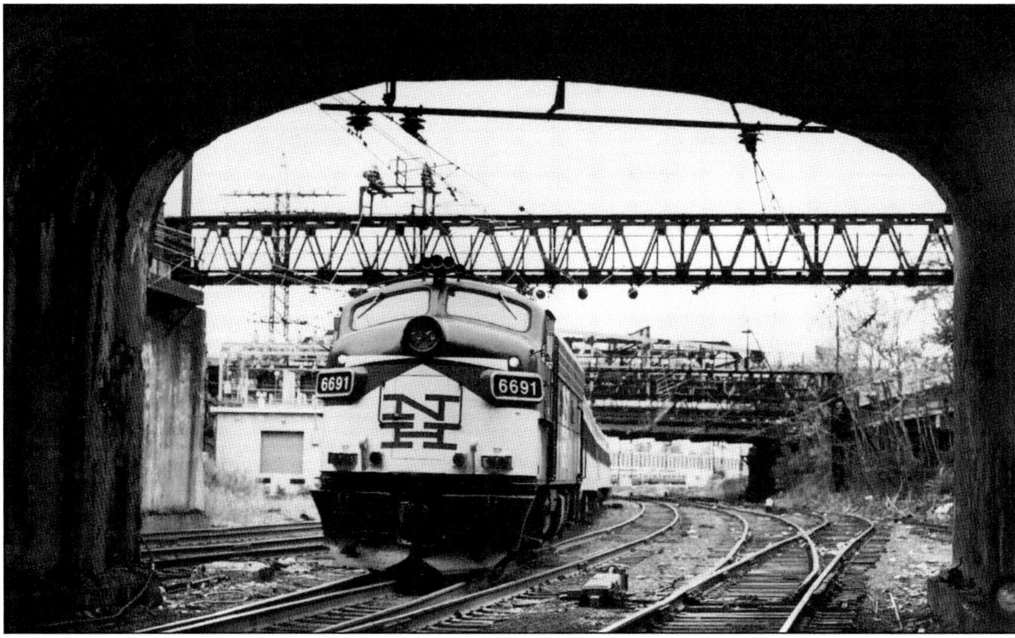

On July 24, 1990, a Shore Line East train from Old Saybrook arrives in New Haven. The Shore Line East covers several communities east of New Haven, such as Branford, Guilford, and Madison, and into New London. The rail buffs refer to this train as a push-pull operation, meaning it can go in either direction. In this photograph, the train is heading west, away from us. (Courtesy J.W. Swanberg collection.)

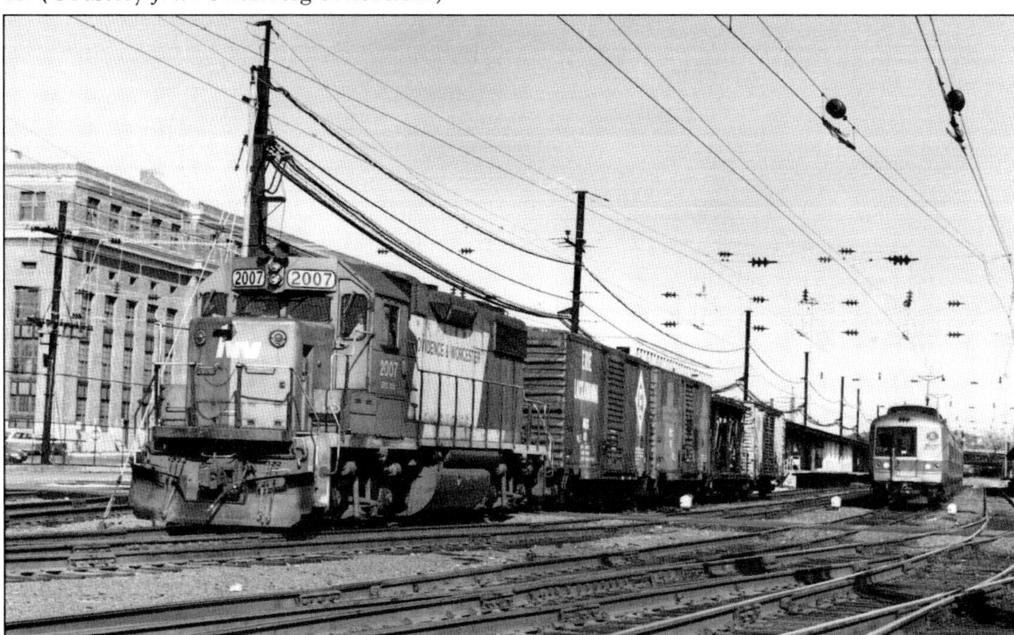

Rail historian Jack Swanberg captures both a freighter and a commuter train in this image dating from February 6, 1992. At the left is a Providence-Worcester freighter in New Haven. At the right is a Metro-North passenger train. (Courtesy J.W. Swanberg collection.)

An Amtrak 902 locomotive on 173, the *Yankee Clipper* passenger train, departs New Haven for Washington, D.C., on March 19, 1992. Do you think an automobile would make it through this squall? (Courtesy J.W. Swanberg collection.)

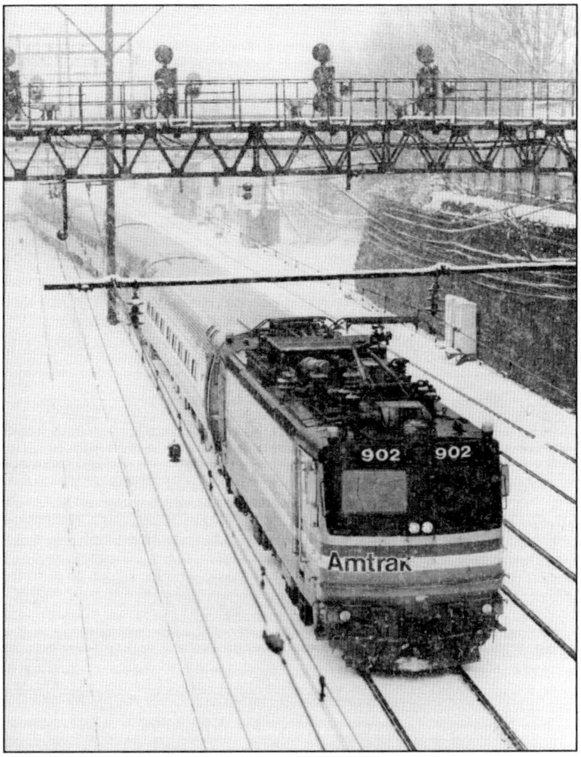

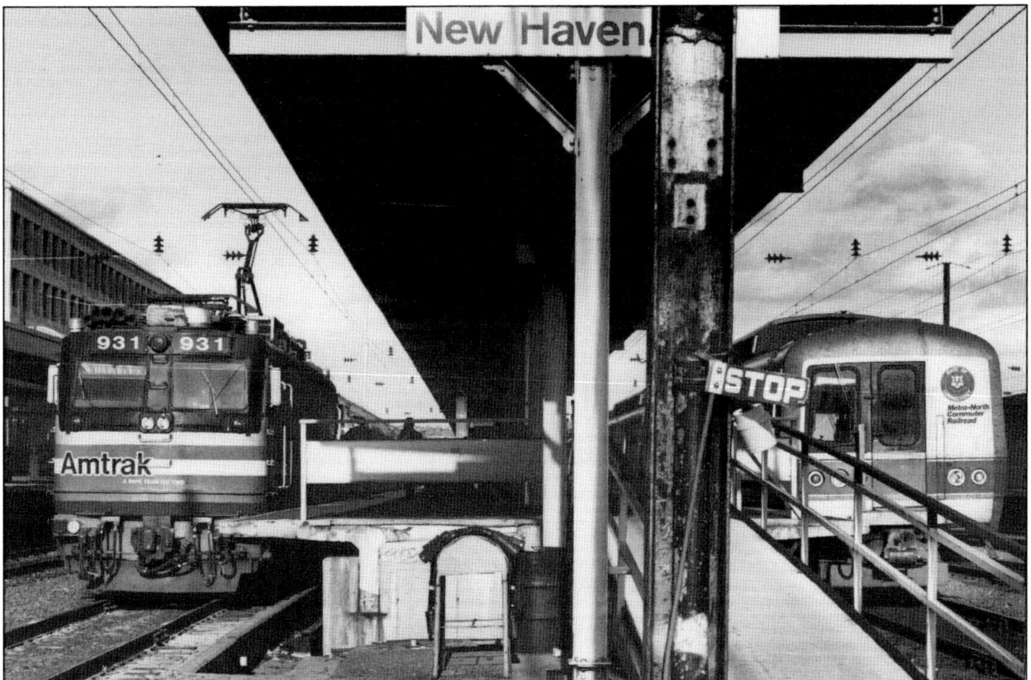

On December 7, 1992, a little Amtrak and Metro-North operation is going on, as only Jack Swanberg can capture it, at New Haven Station. The Amtrak passenger train is at the left, and the Metro-North commuter train is at the right. (Courtesy J.W. Swanberg collection.)

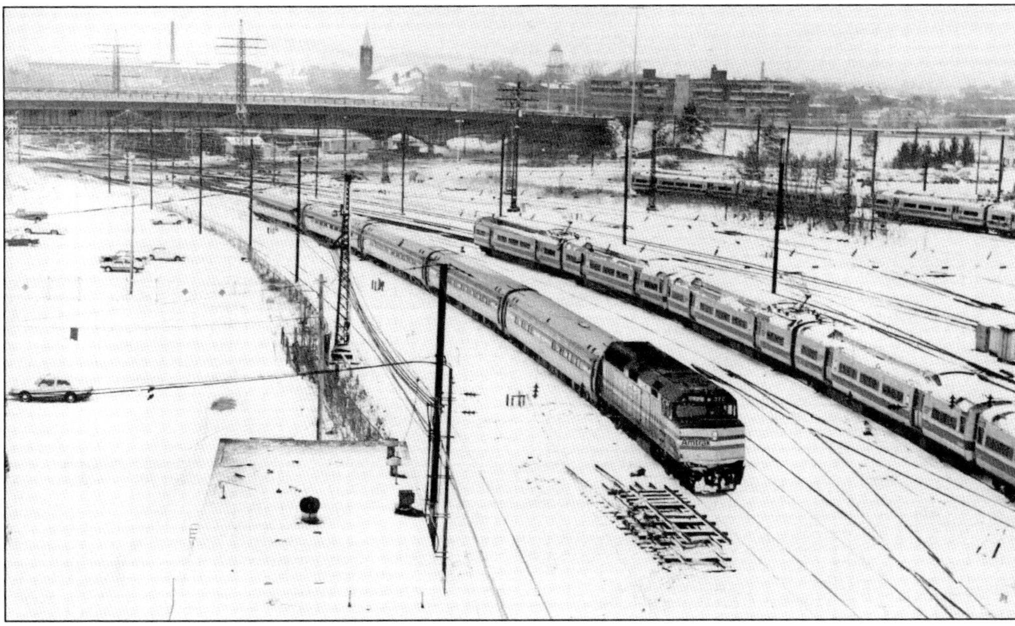

Day and night photographs by Jack Swanberg include two more views of Amtrak and Metro-North trains. Above, an Amtrak pulls into New Haven from Boston with a Metro-North train at the right. Below, an Amtrak leaves New Haven for Washington, D.C., with a Metro-North commuter train at the left. (Courtesy J.W. Swanberg collection.)

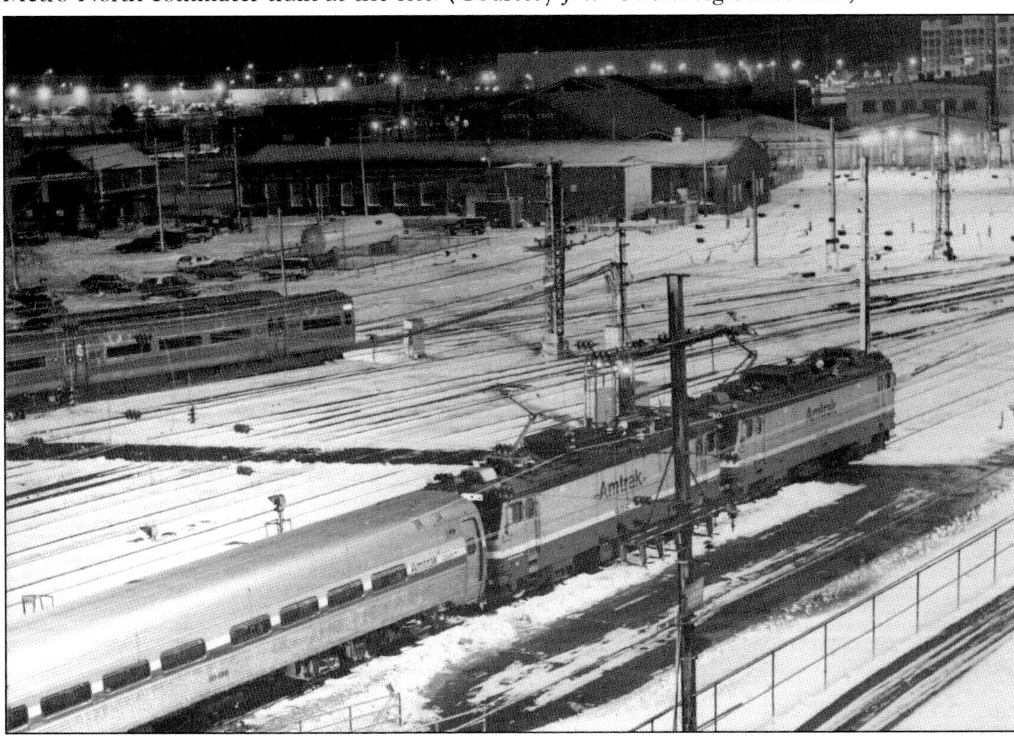